Plays by Women from the Contemporary American Theater Festival

Gidion's Knot
The Niceties
Memoirs of a Forgotten Man
Dead and Breathing
20th Century Blues

Edited by PEGGY MCKOWEN *and* ED HERENDEEN
With an introduction by LYNN NOTTAGE

methuen | drama
LONDON • NEW YORK • OXFORD • NEW DELHI • SYDNEY

METHUEN DRAMA
Bloomsbury Publishing Plc
50 Bedford Square, London, WC1B 3DP, UK
1385 Broadway, New York, NY 10018, USA

BLOOMSBURY, METHUEN DRAMA and the Methuen Drama logo are trademarks of Bloomsbury Publishing Plc

First published in Great Britain 2019

Gidion's Knot copyright © Johnna Adams, 2019
The Niceties copyright © Eleanor Burgess, 2019
Memoirs of a Forgotten Man copyright © D.W. Gregory, 2019
Dead and Breathing copyright © Chisa Hutchinson, 2019
20th Century Blues copyright © Susan Miller, 2019
Introduction © Lynn Nottage, 2019

The authors have asserted their right under the Copyright, Designs and Patents Act, 1988,
to be identified as authors of this work.

Cover design: Toby Way
Cover image: Robin Walsh and Joey Parsons in *Gidion's Knot* by Johnna Adams. Photography by Seth Freeman

All rights reserved. No part of this publication may be reproduced or transmitted
in any form or by any means, electronic or mechanical, including photocopying,
recording, or any information storage or retrieval system, without prior permission
in writing from the publishers.

Bloomsbury Publishing Plc does not have any control over, or responsibility for, any
third-party websites referred to or in this book. All internet addresses given in this
book were correct at the time of going to press. The author and publisher regret
any inconvenience caused if addresses have changed or sites have ceased to exist,
but can accept no responsibility for any such changes.

No rights in incidental music or songs contained in the work are hereby granted
and performance rights for any performance/presentation whatsoever must be
obtained from the respective copyright owners.

All rights whatsoever in these play are strictly reserved and application for performance etc. should be made
before rehearsals by professionals and by amateurs to the following agents:

Gidion's Knot: Dramatists Play Service, Inc. 440 Park Avenue South, New York, NY, 10010 www.dramatist.com
The Niceties: Chris Till, Creative Artists Agency, 405 Lexington Ave. New York, NY 10174
Memoirs of a Forgotten Man: Elaine Devlin Literary, Inc, 411 Lafayette Street, 6th Floor, New York, NY, 10003, USA
Dead and Breathing: ICM Partner, 65 E. 55th Street, New York, NY, 10022
20th Century Blues: General Inquiries to The Gersh Agency, Joyce Ketay, 41 Madison Ave., 33rd Fl. New York, NY 10010
For performance rights: Dramatists Play Service, Inc. 440 Park Avenue South, New York, NY, 10010 www.dramatist.com

No performance may be given unless a licence has been obtained.

A catalogue record for this book is available from the British Library.

Library of Congress Cataloging-in-Publication Data
Names: McKowen, Margaret, 1965- editor. | Herendeen, Ed, editor. | Nottage, Lynn, writer of introduction.
Title: Plays by women from the Contemporary American Theatre Festival: Gidion's knot; The niceties; Memoirs of a forgotten man;
Dead and breathing ; 20th-century blues / edited by Margaret McKowen and Ed Herendeen; with an introduction by Lynn Nottage.
Description: London, UK; New York, NY: Methuen Drama, 2019. | Includes bibliographical references and index.
Identifiers: LCCN 2018035521 (print) | LCCN 2018054147 (ebook) | ISBN 9781350084827 (ePDF) | ISBN 9781350084834 (ePUB) |
ISBN 9781350084810 Subjects: LCSH: American drama—Women authors. | American drama—21st century. |
Women—United States—Drama.
Classification: LCC PS628.W6 (ebook) | LCC PS628.W6 P597 2019 (print) | DDC 812/.60809287—dc23
LC record available at https://lccn.loc.gov/2018035521

ISBN: PB: 978-1-3500-8481-0
ePDF: 978-1-3500-8482-7
eBook: 978-1-3500-8483-4

Typeset by RefineCatch Limited, Bungay, Suffolk

To find out more about our authors and books visit www.bloomsbury.com and sign up for our newsletters

Plays by Women from the Contemporary American Theater Festival

Ed Herendeen founded the Contemporary American Theater Festival (CATF) in Shepherdstown, West Virginia in 1991 with the mission to produce and develop new American theater. Through his leadership, the theater festival has produced 127 new plays—including 52 world premieres and ten commissions—and has gained a reputation as one of America's most important curators of new work.

Ed has also worked at the Walnut Street Theater in Philadelphia, The Milwaukee Repertory Theatre, The Missouri Repertory Theatre, The Old Globe in San Diego, and the Williamstown Theatre Festival. In 1999, CATF was presented with the West Viriginia Governor's Award for Excellence in the Arts and, in 2012, the Governor's Award for Leadership in the Arts. Other honors include the College of Fine Arts Distinguished Alumni Award in Theater from Ohio University, and serving on the Admissions Committee for New Dramatists and as a panelist for the National Endowment for the Arts. Since 2011, he has served on the board of the Theatre Communications Group, the national service organization for American theaters.

Peggy McKowen began her association with the theater festival in 2006, when she designed the costumes for *Mr. Marmalade* and *Jazzland*. She joined the full-time staff the following year. As designer, her work at CATF includes costumes for *The Wedding Gift, Not Medea, Everything You Touch, 1001, H2O*, and *Scott and Hem in the Garden of Allah*; and scenery for *From Prague, Wrecks,* and *Gidion's Knot*. Previously, Peggy was the resident designer for the Obie-award-winning Jean Cocteau Repertory in New York. International theater work includes the B.A.T. Studio Theatre (Berlin), the Teatro Alfa Real (Sao Paulo, Brazil), and for the E.T.A. Hoffmann Theatre in Bamberg (Germany). She designed the first full-length English-speaking production of *The Tempest* performed in Beijing, China and the first Mandarin translation of *How To Succeed In Business Without Really Trying,* also in Beijing. She is a member of United Scenic Artists 829 and was the featured artist in the exhibition, "HIGH DRAMA: Costumes from the Contemporary American Theater Festival" at the Museum of Fine Arts, Washington County, Maryland. In 2018, Peggy was named West Virginia Artist of the Year at the Governor's Awards for the Arts.

Interviews were conducted by Sharon J. Anderson. Sharon, a writer and creative director in the Washington, D.C. area, is also a trustee of the Contemporary American Theater Festival.

Contents

Acknowledgments vi
Introduction *Lynn Nottage* viii
Production History x

Gidion's Knot Johnna Adams 1
The Niceties Eleanor Burgess 65
Memoirs of a Forgotten Man D.W. Gregory 131
Dead and Breathing Chisa Hutchinson 209
20th Century Blues Susan Miller 261

Acknowledgments

Contemporary American Theater Festival:
Ed Herendeen, Founder and Producing Director
Peggy McKowen, Associate Producing Director
Joshua Midgett, General Manager
Vicki Willman, Director of Development
Gaby Tokach, Public Relations Manager
Nicole M. Smith, Company Manager
Trent Kugler, Production Manager
Chase Molden, Properties Manager
Jen Rolston, Eden Design, Graphic Designer
Jared Sheerer, Season Image Designer
Pat McCorkle, CSA
Katja Zarolinski, CSA
Seth Freeman Photography
CATF Board of Trustees
Shepherd University

Special Thanks:
Casey Hayes-Deats
Lindsey Long

Creative Teams:
Gidion's Knot—Director, Ed Herendeen; Production Stage Manager, Catherine Fay Wallis; Stage Manager, Lindsey Eberly; Set Designer, Peggy McKowen; Costume Designer, Danae McQueen; Lighting Designer, William C. Kirkham; Sound Designer, Jamie Whoolery; Fight Director, Aaron Anderson
Cast: Joey Parsons and Robin Walsh

The Niceties—Director, Kimberly Senior; Stage Manager, Lindsay Eberly; Set and Costume Designer, Jesse Dreikosen; Lighting Designer, John Ambrosone; Sound Designer, David Remedios; Technical Director, Kassidy Coburn
Cast: Robin Walsh and Margaret Ivey

Memoirs of a Forgotten Man—Director, Ed Herendeen; Production Stage Manager, Debra A. Acquavella; Stage Manager, Lindsey Eberly; Set and Projection Designer, David M. Barber; Costume Designer, Therese Bruck; Lighting Designer, D.M. Wood; Sound Designer, Victoria Deiorio; Technical Director, Clifford Glowacki
Cast: David McElwee, Lee Sellars, Joey Parsons, Erika Rolfsrud

Dead and Breathing—Director, Kristin Horton; Stage Manager, Lori M. Doyle; Set Designer, Luciana Stecconi; Costume Designer, Trevor Bowen; Lighting Designer, Tony Galaska; Sound Designer, Eric Shimelonis; Dramturg, Theresa M. Davis; Technical Director, Joel Schiebout
Cast: Lizan Mitchell and Nathan L. Graham

20th Century Blues—Director, Ed Herendeen; Stage Manager, Debra A. Acquavella; Set Designer, David M. Barber; Costume Designer, Therese Bruck; Lighting Designer, D.M. Wood; Original Music Composer and Sound Designer, Nathan A. Roberts and Charles Coes; Projection Designer, Hannah Marsh; Technical Director, Zack Hiatt
Cast: Betsy Aidem, Alexandra Neil, Franchelle Steward Dorn, Mary Suib, Kathryn Grody, and Jason Babinsky

Introduction

Lynn Nottage

Why theater? Why write plays? What is the role of a playwright in our culture today? Indeed, these are questions that I grapple with when I am struggling to put down words on the page and find greater meaning between punctuation. We are living in a culture that has become more distracted and fragmented by the noise generated by digital media, and as such there is something refreshing and quite beautiful about inviting people into a space where they are asked to sit quietly and listen to a story together.

So, why write plays? We can lyrically explore our relationship to our past and present, look inward . . . and then outward to find ways to better understand ourselves. We are protectors of past traditions and shapers of new ones. We are asked to recycle and refashion ideas, while meeting the demands of an audience who want us to innovate, titillate, and entertain. Theater explores life through metaphor, using poetry and dramatic action to help us understand our existence. Like religion, the theater helps us to navigate the unknown. Theater helps us explore questions such as: How do we love? Why do we go to war? How do we move through pain? How do we find happiness? How do we mourn? How do we heal? It allows us to look at lofty themes, like spirituality, politics, sexuality, friendship, death, and the nature of humanity. Theater is a place where catharsis can occur and demons can be exorcised. We can collectively share our laughter, shed tears and demonstrate our joy or frustration.

Ultimately, theater is a conversation between audience and artist; artist and culture. It is a collaborative and communal art form, a dynamic animal that is dependent on the mood of its participants. It is completed in the moment and as a result allows for the possibility of uncensored dialog at any given performance. It is that very dialog that I believe makes the medium unique. It has the element of surprise that forces the audience to engage and be alert . . . they must be observer, witness, participant, spectator, and respondent all in one.

This anthology of plays produced by the Contemporary American Theater Festival (CATF) represents some of the best new writing by women for the American stage. Each year the Festival is committed to presenting a diversity of voices, as such the playwrights in this smart and illuminating collection of plays, and invite the reader to traverse multiple emotional landscapes, answering the question of why theater is a vital and necessary part of our cultural discourse. The plays hold a magnifying glass to our culture, asking difficult questions about race, friendship, death, and the truth. Their stories poke holes in our social narrative, which has become bloated and distorted, filled to the brim with the kind of pabulum distributed by marketers, advertisers, pundits, and politicians. It is so hard to find humanity in the midst of the cultural pollution, and yet the writers in this anthology—Susan Miller, Johnna Adams, Chisa Hutchinson, Eleanor Burgess, and D.W. Gregory—all offer a multitude of compassionate and fresh perspectives.

contemporaryamericantheaterfestival
AT SHEPHERD UNIVERSITY

Production History

2018 Festival
The Cake by Bekah Brunstetter
Berta, Berta by Angelica Chéri *
Memoirs of a Forgotten Man by D.W. Gregory ^
Thirst by C.A. Johnson *
A Late Morning (in America) with Ronald Reagan by Michael Weller *
The House on the Hill by Amy E. Witting *

2017 Festival
The Niceties by Eleanor Burgess (developmental production)
Welcome to Fear City by Kara Lee Corthron *
Wild Horses by Allison Gregory ^
Everything is Wonderful by Chelsea Marcantel *
Byhalia, Mississippi by Evan Linder
We Will Not Be Silent by David Meyers *

2016 Festival
pen/man/ship by Christina Anderson
Not Medea by Allison Gregory ^
The Wedding Gift by Chisa Hutchinson *
20th Century Blues by Susan Miller *
The Second Girl by Ronan Noone

2015 Festival
World Builders by Johnna Adams *
Everything You Touch by Sheila Callaghan
On Clover Road by Steven Dietz ^
WE ARE PUSSY RIOT by Barbara Hammond **
The Full Catastrophe by Michael Weller *

2014 Festival
The Ashes Under Gait City by Christina Anderson *
One Night by Charles Fuller
Uncanny Valley by Thomas Gibbons ^
North of the Boulevard by Bruce Graham
Dead and Breathing by Chisa Hutchinson *

2013 Festival
A Discourse on the Wonders of the Invisible World by Liz Duffy Adams *
Modern Terrorism, or They Who Want to Kill Us and How We Learn to Love Them by Jon Kern
H2O by Jane Martin **
Heartless by Sam Shepard
Scott and Hem in the Garden of Allah by Mark St. Germain **

2012 Festival
Gidion's Knot by Johnna Adams *
The Exceptionals by Bob Clyman
In A Forest, Dark and Deep by Neil LaBute
Captors by Evan M. Wiener
Barcelona by Bess Wohl *

2011 Festival
From Prague by Kyle Bradstreet *
Race by David Mamet
Ages of the Moon by Sam Shepard
We Are Here by Tracy Thorne
The Insurgents by Lucy Thurber **

2010 Festival
The Eelwax Jesus 3-D Pop Music Show by Max Baker & Lee Sellars *
Lidless by Frances Ya-Chu Cowhig
Breadcrumbs by Jennifer Haley *
Inana by Michele Lowe
White People by J.T. Rogers

2009 Festival
The History of Light by Eisa Davis *
Yankee Tavern by Steven Dietz
Dear Sara Jane by Victor Lodato
Farragut North by Beau Willimon
Fifty Words by Michael Weller

xii   Production History

2008 Festival
Stick Fly by Lydia R. Diamond
A View of the Harbor by Richard Dresser *
Pig Farm by Greg Kotis
WRECKS by Neil LaBute
The Overwhelming by J.T. Rogers

2007 Festival
Lonesome Hollow by Lee Blessing *
The Pursuit of Happiness by Richard Dresser
My Name is Rachel Corrie from the writings of Rachel Corrie edited by Alan Rickman and Katharine Viner
1001 by Jason Grote

2006 Festival
Augusta by Richard Dresser *
Jazzland by Keith Glover **
Mr. Marmalade by Noah Haidle
Sex, Death, and the Beach Baby by Kim Merrill *

2005 Festival
Augusta by Richard Dresser +
Jazzland by Keith Glover ++
Sonia Flew by Melinda Lopez
On the Verge or the Geography of Yearning by Eric Overmyer ~
The God of Hell by Sam Shepard
American Tet by Lydia Stryk *
Father Joy by Sheri Wilner *

2004 Festival
Amazing by Brooke Berman ~
Flag Day by Lee Blessing *
Rounding Third by Richard Dresser
Homeland Security by Stuart Flack
The Rose of Corazon: A Texas Songplay by Keith Glover **
Father Joy by Sheri Wilner +

2003 Festival
Whores by Lee Blessing *
Flag Day by Lee Blessing +
Bright Ideas by Eric Coble
The Clandestine Crossing by Keith Glover +

Production History   xiii

The Last Schwartz by Deborah Zoe Laufer
Wilder by Erin Cressida Wilson

2002 Festival
Thief River by Lee Blessing
Rounding Third by Richard Dresser +
Silence of God by Catherine Filloux **
The Late Henry Moss by Sam Shepard
Orange Flower Water by Craig Wright *
Melissa Arctic by Craig Wright +

2001 Festival
Tape by Stephen Belber
Carol Mulroney by Stephen Belber +
Silence of God by Catherine Filloux ++
The Ecstasy of Saint Theresa by John Olive *
The Occupation by Harry Newman *
The Pavilion by Craig Wright
Orange Flower Water by Craig Wright +

2000 Festival
Something in the Air by Richard Dresser
Mary & Myra by Catherine Filloux *
Miss Golden Dreams, A Play Cycle by Joyce Carol Oates *
Hunger by Sheri Wilner *

1999 Festival
Coyote on a Fence by Bruce Graham
Compleat Female Stage Beauty by Jeffrey Hatcher **
Tatjana in Color by Julia Jordan *
Flo's Ho's by Julia Jordan ++
The Water Children by Wendy MacLeod

1998 Festival
Gun-Shy by Richard Dresser
Interesting Times by Preston Foerder **
Carry the Tiger to the Mountain by Cherylene Lee **
BAFO by Tom Strelich

1997 Festival
Lighting Up the Two Year Old by Benjie Aerenson
Below the Belt by Richard Dresser

Demonology by Kelly Stuart
CATF Dance Ensemble

1996 Festival
Tough Choices for the New Century by Jane Anderson
The Nina Variations by Steven Dietz
The Nose by Elizabeth Egloff
Octopus by Jon Klein *
Bad Girls by Joyce Carol Oates *

1995 Festival
Betty the Yeti by Jon Klein
Maggie's Riff by Jon Lipsky
Psyche Was Here by Lynne Martin *
Voir Dire by Joe Sutton

1994 Festival
What are Tuesdays Like? by Victor Bumbalo *
Shooting Simone by Lynne Kaufman
Spike Heels by Teresa Rebeck
Forgiving Typhoid Mary by Mark St. Germain

1993 Festival
A Contemporary Masque by Stephen Bennet
Dream House by Darrah Cloud
Alabama Rain by Heather McCutchen
Black by Joyce Carol Oates

1992 Festival
The Baby Dance by Jane Anderson
The Swan by Elizabeth Egloff
Still Waters by Lynn Martin *
Static by Ben Siegler

1991 Festival
Accelerando by Lisa Loomer
Welcome to the Moon by John Patrick Shanley

** world premiere; commissioned by CATF
* world premiere
^ NNPN rolling world premier
⁺⁺ staged reading; commissioned by CATF
⁺ staged reading
~ CATF Actors' Lab Workshop

Gidion's Knot

Johnna Adams

Cast of Characters

Heather Clark, *40s–50s*
Corryn Fell, *40s–50s*

Setting

A fifth grade classroom in a public school in the Lake Forest suburb of Chicago.

Time

Early April. The present year. Monday. 2:45 p.m. to 4:15 p.m.

Playwright's Note

When a character name is followed by an ellipsis, as such:

Heather . . .

This indicates a non-verbal response to the previous line.

The ellipsis line may be played in many ways: as a pause, a beat, a look, a movement, a silence, a smile, a sudden thought, or it can just be used to give the scene some air, some room, some tension, etc.

A slash (/) in the middle of a character's line indicates an interruption. The next speaking character should begin her line where the slash appears.

A fifth grade classroom.

Twenty desks are arranged facing a blackboard. Each desk has a cubby hole filled with books, pencils and other detritus of childhood.

To the side there is a teacher's desk where **Heather Clark** *sits grading papers.*

The walls are filled with bright and cheerful posters of Greek and Hindu gods (Zeus, Aphrodite, Hera, Vishnu, Ganesh, Shiva, Buddha, Kwan Yin, etc.)

Children's writing assignments (poems, stories, reports, etc.) fill every part of the walls not covered with gods or lesson notes. There are probably 50 posted assignments.

Five or six decorated foam core boards on one wall, featuring reports on Greek mythology and Alexander the Great.

It is 2:45 p.m. Classes end at 3:00 p.m.

Heather *grades her papers and from time to time sips from a cup of tea on the desk in front of her. Her cellphone is on the desk beside her.*

She looks at the phone. She picks it up and checks to see if she has a message.

Nothing. She puts the phone down and leaves her hand on it for a long time, staring at it.

She goes back to grading.

There is a knock at the door. She is surprised. No one knocks. People just walk in. She stands, a little uncertain.

Heather   Yes?

Another knock. The knocker can't hear her through the door.

She goes to the door and looks out a moment through a small window.

She opens the door.

Heather   Yes?

Corryn Fell *enters hesitantly.*

Heather   Are you looking / for . . . ?

Corryn   I have a parent teacher conference. Is / this—. . . ?

Heather   Do you know the room?

Corryn   I thought . . .—

Heather   If you go to the office and speak to the office manager she can tell you which room you're looking for. Just give her the teacher's name.

Corryn   The office manager?

Heather   Carole. She's at the desk.

Corryn   Thank you.

Heather   All right.

Corryn *goes out.*

Heather *returns to her desk. She stares at her phone.*

Another knock, then **Corryn** *pokes her head back in cautiously.*

Corryn   I'm sorry. The office?

Heather   It's down the hall and to your left—at the end of the hall there.

Corryn   Oh. Okay. Thank you.

Corryn *leaves.*

Heather *stands for a long moment in the middle of the room.*

She goes back to grading papers.

Something breaks inside her.

She stops and puts her head in her hands, taking deep breaths almost hyperventilating, trying not to sob.

She shakes her head, and under her breath—

Heather   God . . . oh God . . . God . . .

She gets up and walks around the room.

She picks up her cellphone and puts it down.

She almost has herself under control.

A knock at the door.

Heather   Oh God.

She crosses to the door as **Corryn** *comes back in.*

Corryn   I'm / sorry—

Heather   Down the hall and to your left—

Corryn   I found it. I found Carole.

Heather   You need directions to the room?

Corryn   You're very helpful, aren't you? I mean you're irritated and not very good at hiding it, but still . . .

Heather   . . .

Corryn   I'm sorry. That came out—. . .

Heather   Yes. It did.

Corryn   . . .

Heather   Do you need help finding the room?

Corryn   No, I found the room.

Heather   No one was there? If you ask Carole—

Corryn   This is the room.

Heather   No. No, I don't—

Corryn   418.

Heather   No, I don't have anything.

Corryn   Two thirty. I'm a little late.

Heather   I don't have anything scheduled.

Corryn   Yes. I wrote it down.

Corryn *pulls a rumpled piece of paper out of her purse.*

Corryn   Two thirty. April 5th. Room 418. Ms. Clark.

Heather   . . .

Corryn   You're Ms. Clark.

Heather   Yes.

Corryn   I set it up. Here—

Corryn *gives* **Heather** *the paper.*

Heather   That's strange, I—I'm sorry.

Corryn   That's all right. You forgot, I guess.

Heather   . . .

Corryn I can come back. You're unprepared, I can see that.

Heather No, it's fine. Come in.

Corryn Thank you very much. And thank you for making time.

Heather I don't think you were at open house.

Corryn No.

Heather . . .

Corryn I set it up with Carole, I guess. I called her. Friday afternoon.

Heather About?

Corryn About my son.

Heather Who is your son?

Corryn Gidion.

Heather . . .

Corryn . . .

Heather . . .

Corryn . . .

Heather . . . oh God . . .

Corryn We set up a parent teacher conference. The principal was supposed to come, too.

Heather . . .

Corryn I guess she forgot.

Heather No. Of course not. It's just—. . .

Corryn . . .

Heather . . .

Corryn I missed open house. So we never got to meet.

Heather You're Gidion's mother. Mrs. Gibson.

Corryn No. That was his father's name. Ms. Fell.

Heather Mrs. Fell.

Corryn You can call me Corryn.

Heather . . .

Corryn You sent a note home with my son. Asking to meet with me.

Heather Mrs. Fell.

Corryn Telling me he was suspended.

Heather . . .

Corryn There was a voicemail message, too . . . Saying to call.

Heather . . .

Corryn And I called and set something up. I guess with Carole maybe. Someone in the office. She didn't tell you?

Heather No, she did.

Corryn You forgot.

Heather . . .

Corryn Well. We set this up.

Heather Yes.

Corryn So here I am.

Heather . . .

Corryn . . .

Heather Mrs. Fell—

Corryn No, it's Ms.

Heather Ms. Fell.

Corryn You can call me Corryn. If you'd like.

Heather I'm so sorry. I'm so sorry. I'm so very, very sorry.

Corryn Thank you.

Heather I didn't forget. I just . . . I didn't think you'd—

Corryn You sent a note home with my son. And left a message. Asking to meet with me. How could I not come?

Heather . . .

Corryn He's my son.

Heather . . .

Corryn You look pale. Have I given you a shock?

Heather Oh God.

Corryn I didn't mean to.

Heather . . .

Corryn We did have an appointment.

Heather . . .

Corryn . . .

Heather . . .

Corryn What did you want to talk about?

Heather . . .

Corryn About my son?

Heather . . .

Corryn Was it his grades?

Heather . . .

Corryn Attendance? Excessive tardiness? Running in the halls?

Heather I don't . . .

Corryn The reason you suspended him?

Heather . . .

Corryn I'd really like to know. I've been wondering. Your note was vague. The voicemail was cryptic. I've been up for about 72 hours. I can't sleep. I can't sleep because I've been playing this conversation out over and over again in my mind, wondering how it will go. You were more vocal in these little fantasies. You contributed. You explained . . . I don't know why you . . . did this to him. I don't know what happened.

Heather . . .

Corryn He looked devastated. When he handed me the note. He was shaking. He—

Heather God! . . . oh God . . .

Corryn . . .

Heather . . . God

Corryn I'm sorry.

Heather   I don't know / what—

Corryn   I didn't mean—

Heather   God. / I just—

Corryn   Would you like me to get you some water?

Heather   I didn't think—. . .

Corryn   You look bloodless.

Heather   I didn't think you'd keep the appointment. It never occurred to me that you would keep the appointment.

Corryn   He's my son.

Heather   I took it out of my calendar.

Corryn   I see.

Heather   I didn't think you'd—

Corryn   Well, I did.

Heather   I didn't think you'd still want to talk about—

Corryn   About my son?

Heather   That it might be painful to . . .

Corryn   Yes?

Heather   To talk about him so soon after his death.

Corryn   . . .

Heather   . . .

Corryn   . . .

Heather   . . .

Corryn   Well.

Heather   . . .

Corryn   We had an appointment.

Heather   . . .

Corryn   . . .

Heather   Yes. Okay.

Corryn   Good.

Heather I'm really very sorry—

Corryn You've said so.

Heather . . .

Corryn Thank you . . . I'm sorry I missed open house. Gidion's father is dead. I'm a single mother. Getting a babysitter on a school night is like squeezing milk from stones. Do you have children?

Heather No.

Corryn Oh . . . I never thought I would either. Pets?

Heather What?

Corryn Do you have pets?

Heather I'm not sure how I can help you, Ms. Fell.

Corryn Corryn, please. This doesn't have to be adversarial. Does it?

Heather . . .

Corryn How long have you been teaching?

Heather Two years.

Corryn Really? You don't look young enough to be right out of school. You must have had a career before this, am I right?

Heather Yes.

Corryn What was it?

Heather I was in advertising.

Corryn And you got sick of making all that money and wanted to make a difference.

Heather . . .

Corryn Good for you.

Heather Maybe we should reschedule. Find a time when the principal can join us.

Corryn Maybe she's just running late.

Heather You should be with family now.

Corryn I'm exactly where I should be.

Heather . . .

Corryn . . .

Heather Okay.

Corryn You sent a note home with my son.

Heather Yes.

Corryn You suspended him. Five days.

Heather Yes.

Corryn He was fighting with another boy.

Heather No.

Corryn He came home bruised. With dried blood on his mouth.

Heather I don't know anything about that. That must have happened after he left school.

Corryn Was he beat up a lot? Picked on?

Heather I never saw that happen.

Corryn But the day he was suspended he was beaten up. You didn't know?

Heather I'm not surprised.

Corryn You're not?

Heather . . .

Corryn I was.

Heather . . .

Corryn . . . ?

Heather He made some of the children angry.

Corryn And you. He made you angry.

Heather Yes.

Corryn . . .

Heather . . .

Corryn This isn't what I expected.

Heather . . .

Corryn That was very honest.

Heather ...

Corryn He made you angry.

Heather ...

Corryn Okay.

Heather ...

Corryn This is nice. Your room. Colorful.

Heather Thank you.

Corryn It's warm.

Heather Thank you.

Corryn I envisioned a barren tomb. Painted prison green. Desks in depressing rows. Hard tile flooring that your heels made ominous clicking noises against as you paced up and down the rows, stroking the black chins hairs and warts covering your thick, bovine neck. A lovingly framed portrait of Stalin at the front of the room for the children to genuflect before as they file in.

Heather I sent it out to be cleaned.

Corryn That's funny. You surprise me, too.

Heather ...

Corryn What did you imagine I was like?

Heather ...

Corryn You must have little mental images of all the parents. What they're like.

Heather ...

Corryn Do I surprise you?

Heather I knew you were a single mother.

Corryn How?

Heather A writing project I gave. I asked them to describe their father.

Corryn He had nothing to write about.

Heather He wrote about his grandfather instead.

Corryn He never met either grandfather. He made it up.

Heather No. He wrote about what he imagined his grandfather's corpse was like. In the earth.

Corryn Well, that's original. I bet you never had a paper like it in all your two years of teaching.

Heather No.

Corryn Is that when you began to hate him?

Heather . . .

Corryn Come on.

Heather I didn't hate him.

Corryn Come on.

Heather I didn't hate him.

Corryn Honestly?

Heather I did not hate him.

Corryn Liar.

Heather Ms. Fell. I think you should leave.

Corryn It's all right. I'm not angry about it. For Christ's sake. I don't like everyone I meet or everyone I know. I freely hate some of them. It isn't their fault. It just happens that way. I'm sure Gidion was the same. I'm sure you're the same.

Heather I don't think this is accomplishing anything.

Corryn And in return, I don't expect everyone I meet to like me. I hated some of my teachers. My fifth grade teacher, in fact.

Heather It's too soon for this.

Corryn I feel certain she hated me too.

Heather Let's reschedule for a time when the principal and the school counsellor can join us.

Corryn I don't expect you to like each and every one of your students, that would be inhuman.

Heather I'll walk you to your car.

Corryn He hated you. It just happens sometimes.

Heather . . .

Corryn   . . .

Heather   You should take some time to grieve before . . . this. We all should take some time—

Corryn   What did you mean when you said we should reschedule for a time when the principal can join us? Is the principal not able to join us?

Heather   I'm sure she thought that you wouldn't feel up to this discussion at this time.

Corryn   Or that it no longer mattered.

Heather   That it might be in poor taste.

Corryn   That this conversation no longer mattered.

Heather   That it wasn't the priority at the moment. Your grief is the priority.

Corryn   We had an appointment.

Heather   . . .

Corryn   And no one canceled it. You didn't cancel it.

Heather   . . .

Corryn   I would appreciate it if the principal would join us.

Heather   . . .

Corryn   Please.

Heather   She's taking a personal day.

Corryn   Excuse me?

Heather   She's taking a personal day today.

Corryn   That's what I thought you said.

Heather   She took the news about your son very hard.

Corryn   . . .

Heather   . . .

Corryn   Okay.

Heather   . . .

Corryn   Get her in here. Call her at home.

Heather ...

Corryn ...

Heather   I'll talk to Carole.

Heather *goes out.*

Corryn *walks around the room. She reads some of the children's reports posted on the walls.*

She looks for Gidion's name on one and does not find it.

She looks inside a desk.

She looks at one of the foam core board presentations on Alexander the Great. It is titled: "The Gordian Knot." There is a large, complicated knot fastened to the center of the foam core board with a tin foil-covered cardboard sword hovering above it.

She touches the knot and reads some of the text on the report board.

The school bell rings.

Children pour out into the hallways, calling to one another and banging lockers open and shut.

Corryn *is startled.*

Slowly, she works up her courage to approach the door and stare through the window into the hall.

She watches the children closely as the sounds die away.

She stands not moving.

She sits at a desk and waits.

Heather *reenters.*

Heather   Carole spoke with her. She says she's on her way here.

Corryn   Where does she live?

Heather   Not far. Fifteen minutes.

Corryn   Good. I'll wait.

Heather ...

Corryn ...

Heather ...

Corryn Do you have that paper?

Heather . . . ?

Corryn The one Gidion wrote about his grandfather? I saw some of them posted on the wall but not his.

Heather I gave them back their papers. Except for the ones I posted.

Corryn Oh.

Heather He didn't bring it home?

Corryn I don't know if he did.

Heather You could check his book bag.

Corryn I'll do that.

Heather Or his locker.

Corryn Where is it?

Heather We'll call the facilities manager and he can take you to Gidion's locker and cut off the lock.

Corryn Thank you.

Heather . . .

Corryn . . .

Heather Or it might be here. In his desk. If he didn't take it home.

Corryn Which is his desk?

Heather You're sitting at it.

Corryn Oh—. . . This? This is . . . ?

Heather I assign them the seat they sit in on the first day of class. And you see it a lot during open house. The parents come in and choose the same seat.

Corryn Oh.

Heather . . .

Corryn How strange.

Corryn *stands up and stares at the desk.*

Heather *comes over and begins to take things out of the desk and lay them on the desktop when it is clear that* **Corryn** *can't do it.*

Corryn *watches the items as they are revealed: two textbooks (math and social studies); a box of pencils and map pencils; a compass; a protractor; three folders with comic book superheroes on the covers; a spiral notebook; two stapled class assignments with A+ written on them in red ink; and a folded note.*

Corryn *takes the note as* **Heather** *looks at the two writing assignments.*

Heather *puts one of the papers in front of* **Corryn**.

Heather   It's this one.

Corryn *opens and reads the note.*

Corryn   Who is Seneca?

Heather   She's a girl in my class. She sits behind Gidion.

Corryn   She passes him notes.

Heather   Sometimes. She uses her phone and texts people the rest of the time.

Corryn   Gidion doesn't have a phone, so I guess she had to do it old school. She did this.

Corryn *goes to the Gordian Knot presentation and points to it. Seneca's name is written on it.*

Heather   . . .

Corryn   This is nice. I like this.

Heather   I did too.

Corryn   Good topic.

Heather   Yes.

Corryn   . . .

Heather   . . .

Corryn   Who names their daughter Seneca? That's as bad as Gidion. No wonder she liked him. She did like him?

Heather   Yes.

Corryn   Did she have a crush on him?

Heather   I think she did.

Corryn   A girl named Seneca sat behind Gidion and had a crush on him! She passed him notes because she couldn't text him! How wonderful. This says "Jake's a peehole. He's LYING like a peehole." Lying, all caps. "Don't get mad. That's what he wants. I believe you that he did it. I always believe YOU not that dicksnot." You, all caps.

Heather   . . .

Corryn   She expresses herself well. Very clearly.

Heather   . . .

Corryn   I like her. She reminds me of me. They say boys always look for their mother in a mate. What does she look like?

Heather   She dyes her hair platinum blonde and wears false eyelashes and a stuffed bra. She has a nose ring.

Corryn   She's eleven?

Heather   Yes.

Corryn   Wow . . . *Wow.*

Heather   . . .

Corryn   Did her parents have a parent teacher conference with you at some point, too?

Heather   No.

Corryn   Really?

Heather   . . .

Corryn   Okay. Lucky me then. Who's Jake?

Heather   He's a boy in the sixth grade.

Corryn   Is he one of the children that Gidion made angry? On Friday? The day he died?

Heather   . . .

Corryn   There's a Jake on Facebook who left comments on Gidion's Facebook page over the weekend saying "You're a faggot" and "You're a lying faggot." After Gidion was dead, in fact, so—. . . untimely.

Heather   He couldn't have known Gidion was dead. The kids didn't know until this morning.

Corryn   Oh, well, then.

Heather	It's not an excuse.
Corryn	No, it's not.
Heather	...
Corryn	...
Heather	Jake's been troubled lately. It's out of character if he did that.
Corryn	You like Jake. He's one that you like.
Heather	He's a good boy who has had a difficult year.
Corryn	What did he think Gidion was lying about?
Heather	...
Corryn	... ?
Heather	We should wait for the principal.
Corryn	... All right.
Heather	...
Corryn	...

Corryn *picks up the paper about Gidion's grandfather and skims it.*

Heather	...
Corryn	...

She reads part of it out.

"My grandfather's hands are brown apple cores. Buried in dirt like seeds. He used to take me hunting for ravens on a lake and put handfuls of candy corn in my pockets when I wasn't looking. His teeth twisted in his mouth when he smiled and now they have fallen out and his jawbone smiles empty. We miss the smell of his cigars around the house sometimes."

...

He never met his grandfather.

Heather	...
Corryn	... A+?
Heather	Yes.
Corryn	Good grade. But you didn't post it? On the wall?

Heather   No.

Corryn   Too depressing?

Heather   I can't post everything that's good.

Corryn   Oh.

Heather   ...

Corryn   It has a hole in the corner.

Heather   ...

Corryn   From a thumbtack. A hole here in the corner. Like the papers that are posted.

Heather   ...

Corryn   It was posted once. You took it down.

Heather   I rotate the papers posted on the walls. Take some down on Fridays. Put more up.

Corryn   When did you take it down?

Heather   I don't remember.

Corryn   Okay.

Heather   ...

Corryn   ...

Heather   Can I get you something to drink? The faculty lounge is just / down the hall.

Corryn   No thank you. I'm fine.

Heather   ...

Corryn   ...

Heather   Just let me / know.

Corryn   Yes. I will.

Heather   ...

Corryn *stares at her.*

Corryn   Oral hygienist?

Heather   I'm sorry?

Corryn Truck stop waitress?

Heather ... ?

Corryn I'm trying to guess what you imagined I was like.

Heather I didn't really.

Corryn After I didn't come to open house.

Heather There are lots of parents who can't make it.

Corryn Tattoo artist? ... Horse wrangler?

Heather No.

Corryn What did you think?

Heather I had no idea.

Corryn You must have formed an idea. From Gidion. An impression of what his mother was like.

Heather You can't ever predict.

Corryn Stripper?

Heather ...

Corryn Oh, come on. You thought about it.

Heather ...

Corryn If you didn't think about before, you did after you heard what happened.

Heather ...

Corryn ...

Heather I thought you might have a job that required overtime, I guess.

Corryn Okay.

Heather Or that made a lot of demands on your time.

Corryn Oh. Doctor. Lawyer. Something important.

Heather I suppose.

Corryn Rocket scientist. Maybe a labor organizer trying to unionize Walmart.

Heather I didn't have anything to form an impression around.

Corryn Do you want to know what I do?

Heather Of course.

Corryn Yes, I can see you're eaten alive with curiosity.

Heather I don't think your personal life or your son's is any of my business.

Corryn Why should you care?

Heather I just don't want to be intrusive.

Corryn . . .

Heather . . .

Corryn . . .

Heather What do you do for a living?

Corryn You'll laugh.

Heather I doubt it.

Corryn No you will. You won't see this coming. Any guesses?

Heather No.

Corryn Oh, guess. Guess. One guess.

Heather Accounting?

Corryn Accounting? God, no. Accounting?? Why on earth . . . ?

Heather I don't know. It came to mind.

Corryn I don't know why.

Heather I'm sorry.

Corryn Gidion wasn't good at math. What gave you the idea?

Heather I'm not good at guessing games.

Corryn Accounting.

Heather What do you do, then?

Corryn You won't see this coming.

Heather All right.

Corryn Wait for it—. . . Wait for it—. . .

Heather . . . ?

Corryn I'm a teacher.

Heather ...

Corryn ...

Heather Oh.

Corryn I told you. You didn't see that coming.

Heather That's terrific.

Corryn What's terrific about it?

Heather ...

Corryn ...?

Heather What do you teach?

Corryn Literature.

Heather Where?

Corryn At Northwestern. In the graduate program.

Heather You're a professor.

Corryn That's different from a teacher?

Heather That's a different kind of teacher.

Corryn All right.

Heather What sort of literature?

Corryn Poetry. Medieval and earlier forms.

Go, thou first of my bards!
Take the spear of Fingal.
Fix a flame on its point.
Shake it to the winds of heaven.
Bid him in songs, to advance,
And leave the rolling of his wave.
Tell to Caros that I long for battle;
That my bow is weary of the chase of Cona.
Tell him the mighty are not here;
And that my arm is young.

Heather ...

Corryn ...

Heather That's very . . . martial.

Corryn They all are. Fighting and fucking. That's all anybody really writes about.

Heather . . .

Corryn . . .

Heather . . .

Corryn That was part of an Ossian poem. "The War of Caros." Probably not authentic. In the eighteenth and nineteenth centuries it was fashionable for a while to write poetry in the style of ancient Scots Gaelic and pass it off as a genuine work of antiquity. Makes the job for modern scholars a real bitch. A lot of what we do is to search for something authentic in a field of bullshit.

Heather . . .

Corryn Lonely search.

Heather Sounds like a very specialized discipline.

Corryn Yes.

Heather And very fascinating.

Corryn Really?

Heather You're an archeologist as much as literary critic.

Corryn Perhaps.

Heather That must be a whole world unto itself.

Corryn Oh, yes.

Heather A place you could get lost in.

Corryn . . .

Heather Disappear into.

Corryn . . .

Heather . . .

Corryn What was your major in college?

Heather Marketing.

Corryn Did you get a master's degree?

Heather I have an MBA and I went back and got my master's in education.

Corryn Two years ago? Wow. Something must really have gone wrong at that advertising job to prompt that.

Heather . . .

Corryn All that time and money spent on the marketing degree and the MBA! Just to throw it all away for this.

Heather Okay.

Corryn Did you turn forty and have a mid-life crisis?

Heather . . .

Corryn Men get hair implants, sports cars and new twenty-year-old girlfriends. We just make bad choices.

Heather . . .

Corryn . . . Fifteen minutes?

Heather About that.

Corryn Well, if she hits all green lights, she should be here to rescue you soon.

Heather I wouldn't put it that way.

Corryn No. You seem very careful.

Heather (*sighs*) . . .

Corryn I would really hate to start without her. I know you would really hate to start without her, too. I guess you feel you need backup.

Heather No. I think she wants very much to be here with us.

Corryn We're interrupting her personal day.

Heather I'd like to give her that opportunity.

Corryn She might be out golfing or something. Does she golf?

Heather If the situation were reversed, and I wasn't here, I hope she would give me a chance to get here before she discussed this with you.

Corryn You want to get your stories straight?

Heather No. To give you a complete picture.

Corryn At this point a fragment of a picture would be fine, Ms. Clark.

Heather . . .

Corryn Do you have a first name?

Heather Heather.

Corryn That's pretty.

Heather Thank you.

Corryn Is she coming?

Heather Carole called her.

Corryn . . .

Heather I'm sure she's coming.

Corryn . . .

Heather You could wait in her office if you'd prefer.

Corryn Nice try.

Heather . . .

Corryn . . .

Heather . . . (*Sighs.*)

Corryn Could something be delaying her?

Heather I'm sure she's on her way.

Corryn All right.

Heather . . .

Corryn . . . We're being watched by the Gods.

Heather . . . ?

Corryn Aren't we?

Heather . . . ?

Corryn *points to the deities in the posters on the walls.*

Corryn Zeus. Siva. Vishnu. Ganesh. Hermes. I thought our forefathers died for separation of church and state in this country.

You've let the gods into your classroom.

Heather We're learning about mythology.

Corryn Do your Hindu students think of this as mythology?

Heather We don't have any. We do have a Greek boy. But he's Greek Orthodox.

Corryn Oh, that's funny.

Heather . . .

Corryn Do you personally believe in any of them?

Heather . . .

Corryn . . . ?

Heather No.

Corryn I believe in Siva.

Heather . . .

Corryn I don't think I could have the eyes of the Gods on me all day.

Heather . . .

Corryn . . .

Heather . . .

Corryn . . .

Heather Have you planned the memorial?

Corryn No.

Heather . . .

Corryn . . .

Heather We want to make it a half day at school. That day. Give the children and their parents the opportunity to attend.

Corryn All right.

Heather We had an assembly this morning. A crisis management counsellor spoke to the children.

Corryn . . .

Heather And we've told them to speak to someone if they think they need private counseling.

Corryn Was Seneca upset?

Heather Yes.

Corryn Did she ask for private counseling?

Heather No.

Corryn Well. Dyed hair, nose ring, stuffed bra. She wouldn't. She's tough. Probably has an image to maintain.

Heather I spoke to her.

Corryn Individually? That was nice of you.

Heather We are going to send a note to all the parents on warning signs to watch out for.

Corryn Maybe her parents will get her counseling.

Heather . . .

Corryn What did she say when you spoke to her?

Heather That she missed him.

Corryn Was Jake upset?

Heather All of the children are upset.

Corryn . . .

Heather They're making you cards.

Corryn . . . ?

Heather The children. Sympathy cards.

Corryn All of them?

Heather We wanted to help them express their feelings.

Corryn What is that? 180 cards? Is that how many—?

Heather 220.

Corryn 220 sympathy cards?

Heather Yes.

Corryn My, my, where will I put them all?

Heather . . .

Corryn Thanks.

Heather The principal will be collecting them and—

Corryn No, you collect them, Heather. You collect them for me.

Heather . . .

Corryn . . .

Heather All right.

Corryn Good.

Heather I can bring them to the memorial—

Corryn I don't want you at the memorial.

Heather . . .

Corryn But go ahead and collect the cards. Do that. Collect them and then take them home and burn them. In a trash can. Outside if you think that would drive your smoke detector crazy.

Heather . . .

Corryn I don't want them.

Heather . . .

Corryn I don't want to even see them.

Heather . . .

Corryn Jesus Christ.

Heather . . .

Corryn . . .

Heather . . .

Corryn You don't have to tell the children that you burned them. Tell the children I loved them. I wallpapered Gidion's empty room with them. They've really eased my burden and brought me closer to the god Siva. Or something. Ask the crisis management counselor what to say.

Heather . . .

Corryn . . .

Heather . . .

Corryn Except Seneca's card. You can mail me that one.

Heather Okay.

Corryn I don't want to see the others.

Heather Okay.

Corryn   Thanks.

Corryn *reads Seneca's note again.*

Corryn   Seneca seems all right. She seems perceptive. Is she?

Heather   She's sensitive.

Corryn   Not perceptive?

Heather   . . .

Corryn   What side did she come down on? In her Gordian Knot report?

Heather   . . .

Corryn *points to the Gordian Knot presentation.*

Corryn   Cut it? Or figure it out?

Heather   . . .

Corryn   Figure it out? Right?

Heather   . . .

Corryn   . . .

Heather   . . .

Corryn   . . .

Heather   It wasn't part of the assignment to take a side.

Corryn   Oh.

Heather   . . .

Corryn   Okay.

Corryn *reads Seneca's note again.*

Corryn   "Jake's a peehole. He's LYING like a peehole."

Heather   Jake's become an easy target lately.

Corryn   What was he lying about?

Heather   I'm not sure.

Corryn   . . .

Heather   I can't make that note fit with anything I know of.

Corryn   Why not?

Heather   It's the reverse of what I would have expected.

Corryn   You think Gidion was lying like a peehole?

Heather   I would have expected Gidion to be accused of lying. Or spreading rumors.

Corryn   And that's what this is about? Something he said about this Jake?

Heather   It's not that simple.

Corryn   But there's some sort of fight between them. That's what this is about?

Heather   When the principal gets here, Ms. Fell, I promise / you, I will answer—

Corryn   Gidion started it?

Heather   But until she gets here, / I don't feel that I have the—

Corryn   What did Gidion say about Jake, the peehole, that got him suspended?

Heather   . . . (*Sighs.*)

Corryn   . . . ?

Heather   . . .

Corryn   We're waiting for the principal.

Heather   I'd prefer / that—

Corryn   Okay.

Heather   I'm trying to balance Jake's right to privacy / with—

Corryn   I think I've almost been here half an hour. Have I? My perception of time is shot to hell. I lose several hours in what feels like minutes and I get lost in minutes for what feels like hours. Have I been here for half an hour?

I came in here with a simple question. What the hell happened?

I thought this would be largely a transactional exchange. I ask, you give. Even—well, correct me if I'm wrong—you have two years of professional experience, but, even if the circumstances around my son's suspension weren't . . .

charged, let's say, by the fact of his death, I would expect the reasons for his suspension to have at least come up in the first half hour of conversation.

I don't know what happened.

I've been sitting here playing guessing games with you.

Has it been half an hour? You'd know. You've been looking at your cellphone when you think I'm not looking at you.

Am I interrupting something? You're waiting for a call? If it's something important, by all means—

Heather I'm sorry.

Corryn I don't want to wait for the principal.

Heather ...

Corryn I don't believe she's coming.

Heather ...

Heather *pulls out a key ring. She finds a key and unlocks a drawer.*

She takes out a folder covered in comic book superheroes and sets it on her desk.

Heather ...

Corryn ...

Heather ...

Corryn What is it?

Heather What got Gidion suspended.

She offers the folder to **Corryn**.

Corryn *doesn't take it.*

Corryn It's—?

Heather Something Gidion wrote.

Corryn About Jake?

Heather It doesn't matter who it's about.

Corryn *stares at the folder.*

Heather *walks over and puts it in front of* **Corryn** *then sits near her.*

Corryn *stares at the folder.*

She picks it up.

She sets it back down and goes back to Seneca's note.

Corryn   Okay. Wait.

"Don't get mad. That's what he wants. I believe you that he did it. I always believe YOU not that dicksnot." . . .

"I believe you that he did it." Wait.

Heather   . . .

Corryn   Gidion said that Jake wrote this and Seneca believes him.

Heather   No.

Corryn   Seneca thinks Jake wrote this.

Heather   No. She doesn't.

Corryn   How do you know—

Heather   It's in his handwriting.

Corryn   . . .

Heather   . . .

Corryn   His handwriting.

Heather   He admitted that he wrote it.

Corryn   His handwriting.

Heather   He wrote this.

Corryn   He typed his schoolwork. He had a computer.

Heather   He wrote this.

Corryn   . . .

Heather   . . .

Corryn   . . .

Heather   I don't know what Seneca is talking about in her note. Not this.

Corryn   What is it?

Heather   A story.

Corryn   . . . ?

Heather   . . .

Corryn   A story??

Heather   Yes.

Corryn   You have got to be kidding me.

Heather   . . .

Corryn   A story??

Heather   . . .

Corryn   You suspended my son over a story?

Heather   I'm going to leave this with you. I'm going to step outside and let you read it in private.

Heather *starts to leave.*

Corryn   No, you will not.

Heather   I think I should.

Corryn   No.

Heather   I think you'll want to process things without me here.

Corryn   . . .

Heather   It's disturbing.

Corryn   I have a feeling there are miles between what you and I find disturbing.

Heather   Read it and we'll see.

Corryn   . . .

Heather *starts to leave.*

Corryn   Don't.

Heather   . . .

Corryn   I want you to explain things to me. I don't want to sit alone here. I didn't come here for that. I don't want to figure things out. I want them explained!

Heather   . . .

Corryn *holds the folder out to her.*

Corryn   I want you to read it to me.

Heather I'm not going to do that.

Corryn Yes.

Heather I don't intend to read it again.

Corryn You will. With me.

Heather It's not the way you want your son remembered.

Corryn You don't know what I want.

Heather Trust me.

Corryn Read it.

Heather You can read it yourself.

Corryn ...

Heather I'm sorry. I honestly can't read that again. And certainly not out loud.

Corryn As bad as all that?

Heather Yes.

Corryn As bad as facing what you did?

Heather That's not fair.

Corryn ...

Heather That is not fair.

Corryn Read it to me.

Heather I can't do that.

Corryn Please read it to me.

Heather I know you're angry with me. I can't imagine how angry you must be with me. And you want to punish me.

Corryn *gets up and puts the folder in front of* **Heather**.

Corryn ...

Heather I'm not going to.

Corryn ...

Heather I'm very sorry. I don't think I could form the words. It / offends me.

Corryn I want you / to.

Heather My whole heart goes out to you. But you don't have the right. To make me do something / like that—

Corryn Do something unpleasant? I need you to.

Heather You don't have the high ground here!

Corryn I need you to.

Heather I don't know what went on in your house.

Corryn Okay.

Heather Once he left this classroom my responsibility ended.

Corryn . . .

Heather This—*this* is not a product of my classroom.

Corryn I can't read it.

Heather He learned this in your house.

Corryn I can't read it.

Heather Oh? As bad as that? As facing what you did?

Corryn . . .

Heather . . .

Corryn I need you to do this . . .

Heather . . .

Corryn Because it's in his handwriting . . .

Heather . . .

Corryn And I can't read his handwriting without seeing his suicide note in my hands.

Heather . . .

Corryn . . .

Heather . . .

Corryn Please?

Corryn *holds the folder out to* **Heather**.

Heather . . .

Corryn . . .

Heather *takes it and opens it.*

Heather . . .

Corryn . . .

Heather It began during a war, as things do. We all formed tribes and began killing the teachers. I cut Mr. Shawn apart myself with a hunting knife my grandfather gave me the last time he took me hunting ravens. We needed his entrails for our weavers and our poets.

I think Mr. Shawn was grateful.

A group of sixth graders had caught him in the cafeteria earlier, by the vending machines, and cut out his eyes, flayed him and raped him with the clubs they had fashioned by cutting the dicks off of their fathers and stretching the skin over thick poles. He was spitting blood up because of something they'd broken in him and I think he loved me for cutting him open.

I took a broomstick out of the janitor's closet and nailed one end of his intestines to it and then rolled the rest of his intestines out of his stomach, twisting them around the broomstick—they stretched more than 25 feet when I was done. Mr. Shawn had told me that intestines were that long in science class a month ago, but I didn't believe him until we started collecting them for the weavers and the poets. He was lucky. Most kids wouldn't have killed him first.

I put the thick roll of Mr. Shawn's intestines over my shoulder and started walking to the gym, which is the room where we kept the weavers.

Outside of Ms. Harris' room, a tribe of fifth graders were raping Ms. Clark, Ms. Tologos and Ms. Harris. The boys were raping them, the girls were slowly slicing away their nipples with vegetable peelers they'd won in the great cafeteria war against the lunch ladies. These kids didn't want anything more than this. They didn't care about the weavers or poets. So they left the teachers raped and scarred and blind, but didn't take their entrails. So I killed Ms. Tologos and Ms. Harris and rolled their entrails onto the brookstick with Mr. Shawn's.

It was harder with Ms. Clark. They'd left her one eye and she was watching me. She was naked and they'd taken her nipples, her tongue and she was so ripped apart down there, it looked like dogs had been at her and not just kids. But, I really needed her entrails. More than she did at this point.

So I put my knife in her remaining eye and twisted it into her brain. And I rolled her entrails up with the rest.

Around the corner in the hall outside the nurse's office, the nurse, Carole from the office and the fat principal were hanging from the walls by nails punched through their wrists and ankles and knees and shoulders. Their bodies were just gaping, empty bags. No entrails to salvage.

And then I saw Jake Powell. Jake's tribe and their first grade slaves. That was the truly sick thing. Jake was raping the same first grade kid he had been raping even before the war began. You all already knew about that. This dumb little kid with glasses. Jake used to have to sneak around about it, but with the teachers dead or dying, he could do what he pleased.

I watched him torture his first grade slaves for a while—he maimed and raped and bled and squeezed and screamed and sucked and chewed and twisted. Even before the war Jake was wrong.

When the weavers give me my cloak, maybe I can do something about him.

The broomstick was heavy and I had enough guts, so I made my way to the gym, where the weavers worked.

Since the weavers started working, the gym stopped smelling like a gym and started smelling like a butchers' shop and a toilet. All those entrails being braided and woven. You wondered how the weavers could stand it, but when they changed into weavers, maybe they lost their sense of smell. We had been in home period, in Ms. Clark's room when the first weaver was chosen.

We don't know by who, some think there are aliens on earth like the body snatchers and some think God did it.

But whoever did it, in the middle of class this girl suddenly screamed and her eyes turned into balls of blue glass and her arms stretched out like poles and her hands grew new fingers and grew big. This was happening in other classes, but we didn't know that. And she started asking for entrails. Not to eat, but to make things with.

So we put her and the others in the gym and they started making looms out of the janitor's supplies. And we started killing for them. We had to give the weavers what they needed.

Some of us sort of hung back to see what the weavers were making from the teachers' entrails before we started killing and gutting. But when the first cloak was made and the first poet climbed the hill, I knew I had to kill however many teachers I needed to so that I could have one.

I gave a weaver my last pile of entrails and she tied them onto the ends of the other entrails I had brought her and started weaving. The cloth the weavers make from the teachers' entrails is like nothing you've ever seen. It's like a river and a taste of salt. It's like an ocean with fish moving through black water.

When the weaver finished my gut-cloak she put it around my shoulders and I felt the pull. And I walked out of the building to the soccer field where the tribes who kept the first through third grade kids as slaves had made them build a mountain. And I climbed the mountain and joined the poets there.

We watch the war and we write about the great deeds done or the horrors done. And that is how God remembers you—the way we write you. And no other way.

Corryn   . . .

Heather   . . .

Corryn   . . .

Heather   . . .

Heather *shuts the folder and puts it in front of* **Corryn** *on a desk.*

Corryn   . . .

Heather   . . .

Corryn   . . .

Heather   He was passing it around. To the other students.

Corryn   . . .

Heather   . . .

Corryn   . . .

Heather   It's my responsibility to—. . .

Corryn   . . .

Heather   I'm sure you understand.

Corryn   . . .

Heather   I'm sure you understand now.

Corryn ...?

Heather ...

Corryn ...

Heather I don't know what it must be like to listen to this. I can't imagine what it—... I don't think, at heart, that he—... Well ...

Corryn This—

Heather Hard to stomach. I know. Believe me.

Corryn No. This is— / it's—

Heather I know this isn't all there was to him.

Corryn No. This is—

Heather I know he / was—

Corryn This is magnificent!

Heather ...

Corryn ...

This is wonderful writing.

Heather ...

Corryn Strong. Fearless. Fierce. Brave. Cruel.

Heather ...

Corryn Remarkable.

Heather ...

Corryn This is a wonderful story. About art and its purpose. About man and divine judgment. Oh God.

Heather ...

Corryn God, it's beautiful.

Heather ...

Corryn Oh, God ... It's the most beautiful thing I've ever heard. How can you—?

Heather ...

Corryn How could you?

Heather   ...

Corryn   It's beautiful.

Heather   ...

Corryn   ...

Heather   I disagree.

Corryn   Why?

Heather   I have a responsibility to my students. To protect them.

Corryn   From what?

Heather   From things like this. Damaging things.

Corryn   Poetry?

Heather   Hate-filled, poisonous attacks.

Corryn   Oh, God!

Heather   He passed this around to a room full of children.

Corryn   What do you think children are?

Heather   I know what they are. I work with them. For them. Every day.

Corryn   All right, what are they?

Heather   Fragile.

Corryn   Fragile! Bullshit! Children are not fragile. They're stronger than any of us.

Heather   That's not true.

Corryn   Yes, it is true. You want children to be something they aren't.

Heather   Protected.

Corryn   Innocent. That is some ridiculous Victorian-era idea that we've inherited about childhood. That it's sacred, that children are innocent and pure. And that they want to be that way. / To stay that way.

Heather   I don't think it's / ridiculous.

Corryn   Childhood is not a suspended state of innocence—it is the condition of rapidly losing / innocence.

Heather   You asked what I expected you'd be like—

Corryn You can't stop that from happening.

Heather This.

Corryn You shouldn't want to.

Heather This.

Corryn Am I wrong?

Heather Yes.

Corryn Oh, God. I put him here. Into a pit. Full of the unenlightened. Into the hands of / the conventional.

Heather An inability to accept responsibility

Corryn . . .

Heather is what I expected.

Corryn . . .

Heather . . .

Corryn Have you ever heard of the Marquis de Sade?

Heather I don't see the relevance.

Corryn Have you heard of him?

Heather We don't teach him here.

Corryn Yes, but surely you've heard—

Heather I've heard of him.

Corryn Was he a genius?

Heather I don't think your son was a tortured genius, Ms. Fell.

Corryn He's been studied for hundreds of years.

Heather I think something was wrong. In his life.

Corryn He's in libraries, except where they are censored by people with limited imaginations.

Heather Maybe he had been hurt.

Corryn Who the hell are you to tell my son what not to write about?

Heather His teacher.

Corryn What were you teaching him? How to disappear into some mold you wanted to pour him into?

Heather This decision wasn't about him. It was about the other children. Their well-being.

Corryn Have you read the Marquis de Sade?

Heather Why?

Corryn That's probably a yes.

Heather God.

Corryn Did you enjoy it?

Heather This is a fifth grade classroom.

Corryn This is a small box. Full of smaller boxes. One of which you tried to keep my son in. And when he couldn't fit inside it, he shot himself in the head.

Heather . . .

Corryn Over not fitting in a box cut to your dimensions.

Heather . . .

Corryn . . .

Heather . . .

Corryn The Marquis de Sade is going to be in libraries and studied and marveled over for centuries after you are a dead, forgotten fifth-grade teacher who failed to make a go at advertising.

Heather . . .

Corryn . . .

Heather . . .

Corryn . . .

Heather . . .

Corryn He was a beautiful writer.

Heather I don't share your appreciation for the Marquis de Sade.

Corryn No . . . My son.

Heather . . .

Corryn   Gidion was a beautiful writer.

Heather   . . .

Corryn   He wanted to be a writer. He was going to be one.

Heather   . . .

Corryn   . . .

Heather   . . .

Corryn   Jake raped a first grader.

Heather   No.

Corryn   Gidion thought Jake raped a first grader.

Heather   He did not.

Corryn   That's what he / wrote—

Heather   No. He did not. That's / absolutely—

Corryn   Was Jake accused / of—

Heather   That's not the point.

Corryn   Not the point?

Heather   This—

She gestures toward the folder.

Heather   No matter what this was about, it was—in itself—enough to / justify a suspension—

Corryn   But, is it true?

Heather   No.

Corryn   Jake was never accused / of anything like—

Heather   Jake is the victim here. What your son / did to Jake—

Corryn   Raping a first grader?

Heather   Don't. Just don't. I can't / discuss it—

Corryn   It's a simple / question.

Heather   With you.

Corryn   . . .

Heather   . . .

Corryn   Jake's just an easy target lately.

Heather   . . .

Corryn (*from Seneca's note*)   "Don't get mad. That's what he wants. I believe you that he did it. I always believe YOU not that dicksnot."

Heather   . . .

Corryn   "Don't get mad. That's what he wants."

Heather   . . .

Corryn   Jake wanted to make Gidion mad. Faggot. Revenge. He read this. He beat Gidion up.

Heather   This isn't his fault.

Corryn   I know that.

Heather   . . .

Corryn   But was Gidion right?

Heather   If he left those messages on Gidion's Facebook page—it had to be the first time he has ever done anything / like that—

Corryn   I don't care if he and Gidion fought. I don't care if he raped the entire first grade class. I just want to know if my son was right. If this—

The folder.

Corryn   —is what I think it is.

Heather   . . .

Corryn   I don't care about Jake. You think that I think like you. That I have a cause. That this is an opportunity for me to demonstrate my essential human goodness. By putting together a PR campaign at my kitchen table to raise awareness about cyber-bullying. Going on talk shows and bragging about how I'm turning lemons to lemonade by lobbying for legislation to prevent eleven-year-olds from typing the word faggot on Facebook.

You know all about PR campaigns, Heather, being an advertiser—you could help me with my cause. Get someone to write a movie of the week about our selfless campaign. How we quit our teaching jobs to devote ourselves full-time to lobbying congress to pass "Gidion's Law" which is the name we will give our new legislation to make it sound touching and socially necessary. Instead of fascist and inhumanly invasive. And they will create keyboards intelligent enough to detect when a child is typing the word faggot on the Facebook wall of another child, and then the keyboard will deliver a paralyzing electric shock to the child's fingers while simultaneously erasing every word the child has ever written.

God, we'll be famous, Heather. Warmly praised, too.

If you want to violate human rights in this country. All you really have to do is slap a dead child on the issue. You want every person who has ever looked cross-eyed at a child put on a registry and denied basic civic rights? Point out a dead child. You want a camera on every street corner? Find one corner where a child died. You want tougher seat belt laws, massive product recalls—dead, dead, dead child.

He didn't die because of what Jake did. Or what Jake wrote on his Facebook page. He didn't die because of what he wrote, or because you suspended him. He died because he couldn't face telling me about it—

. . . God damn it . . .

He could have told me this. God. I'm not a good mother. There are a million things he could have done and not wanted to tell me. A million things I would have been unequipped to hear. I lived in fear of those things. I'm not a good mother. There are so many things that could go wrong—so many ways I could ruin things—but this? This?

This was my good mother moment.

What happened?

He could have told me this. I would have told him: "This is magnificent. You *are* a poet. You're perfect. They're wrong."

My good mother moment. The one time—the one time I would have been the mother he needed and not just the one he got.

Heather . . .

Corryn . . .

Heather . . .

Corryn . . .

Heather . . .

Corryn   I don't know what I did to make him think he couldn't tell me. And I'm honest with myself. If I knew I wouldn't be afraid to tell you I'm a failure—I just don't know at what.

Heather . . .

Corryn . . .

Heather . . .

Corryn . . .

Heather . . .

Corryn . . .

Heather We had a boy at the school this Fall. A first grader. He was troubled.

Corryn . . . ?

Heather There were things going on at home. Things with his older brother's soccer coach. Things happened to him. And Jake was his math tutor.

Corryn . . .

Heather And he accused Jake of touching him.

Corryn . . .

Heather We kept it quiet.

Corryn But the kids found out.   Gidion found out.

Heather The boy's parents apologized when he admitted to them that he was lying.

Corryn Was he lying?

Heather Yes.

Corryn Gidion believed Jake did it.

Heather No. He liked Jake.

Corryn They were friends?

Heather . . .

Corryn Gidion was standing up for this kid. This little kid.

Heather I don't think so.

Corryn He was. He believed that Jake did it. This was an accusation!

Heather Jake spent a lot of time with this younger boy.

Corryn Right or wrong—he thought it was the truth. That he had to tell the truth.

Heather   No.

Corryn   He wanted to tell the truth! *Yes!*

Heather   . . .

Corryn   Yes.

This.

It's based on a story I used to tell him when he was little. About the Great Poet's war.

Once upon a time in the green hills of ancient Gaul, two warring clans met on the battlefield of Ballycrief.

Each clan had a master poet and a poet's apprentice. And they sent their poets to the top of the hill. So they could see.

Because men aren't afraid of dying, but they are afraid of not being remembered.

Heather   . . .

Corryn   . . .

Heather   No.

Corryn   . . .

Heather   No. That's not what I meant.

Corryn   . . .

Heather   . . .

Corryn   He liked Jake?

Heather   Yes.

Corryn   Jake beat him up. Called him a faggot.

Heather   Before that.

Corryn   . . .

Heather   . . .

Corryn   . . .

Heather   . . .

Corryn   He liked him?

Heather   Yes.

Corryn ...

Heather ...

Corryn ...

Heather ...

Corryn Liked him?

Heather ...

Corryn ...?

Heather Yes.

Corryn *picks up the folder.*

Corryn You think ...

Heather ...

Corryn Angry?

Heather ...

Corryn Jealous? Of the first grader that he thought Jake had raped?

Heather ...

Corryn Jealous.

Heather ...

Corryn Oh.

Heather ...

Corryn Oh ... Ha! Poor Seneca.

Heather ...

Corryn ...

Heather ...

Corryn Okay.

Heather Sometimes there are situations in life where you want to do something very much, but you just can't.

Corryn No. There are situations where you don't do what you want. That's all.

Heather ...

Corryn   . . .

Heather   . . .

Corryn   Fifteen minutes.

Heather   . . .

Corryn   She said she was coming. She's a liar.

Heather   Yes.

Corryn   Why isn't she coming?

Heather   . . .

Corryn   . . . ?

Heather (*sighs*)   She talked to the school superintendent. He told her not to talk to you.

Corryn   . . . ?

Heather   Without the school board's attorneys present.

Corryn   . . .

Heather   They're worried about you suing the school district.

Corryn   Do I have a case?

Heather   . . .

Corryn   Are you supposed to be talking to me?

Heather   . . .

Corryn   . . . ?

Heather   . . .

Corryn   I see. She's a coward.

Heather   Yes.

Corryn   You're not. Whatever else you are, you're not a coward. Or a liar, which is surprising given your background in advertising.

Heather   . . .

Corryn   Are you married?

Heather   No.

Corryn   No kids. You live alone?

Heather   Yes.

Corryn   You have a cat. There's a photo on your desk.

Heather   . . .

Corryn   . . .

Heather   . . .

Corryn   . . .

Heather's *control slips, like at the start of the play.*

Her control dissolves.

She sobs. Painfully.

Corryn   Oh, God! . . . Oh, God! . . . hey . . . hey—. . . It's all right.

Corryn *goes to* **Heather** *and holds her awkwardly. She finds tissues and puts them in* **Heather**'s *hands.*

Corryn   It's—. . . It's all right. . . oh, God. Please don't. You'll make me, and I can't, I'll—. . . It'll be all right. It's all right. Just don't—. . . (*Sighs.*)

Heather   ! ! ! !

Corryn   . . .

Heather   ! ! !.

Corryn   It's okay.

Heather   ! ! . .

Corryn   It's okay.

Heather   ! . . .

Heather *has most of her control back.*

Corryn   There. Okay. There.

Heather   . . .

Corryn   . . .

Heather   . . .

Corryn   Okay.

Heather   I'm all right.

Corryn *moves away.*

Corryn   Okay.

Heather   . . .

Corryn   Okay.

Heather   . . .

Corryn   . . . ?

Heather   . . .

Corryn   . . .

Heather *touches her cellphone.*

Heather   The vet.

Corryn   . . . ?

Heather *holds up the cellphone.*

Heather   The vet.

Corryn   Oh, God. Your cat's sick? You're waiting for a call from the vet?

Heather *nods.*

Corryn   Is she going to be okay?

Heather *shakes her head.*

Corryn   . . .

Corryn *laughs.*

Corryn   I'm sorry! Oh, God. I'm sorry . . .

Laughs again.

Corryn   But, Jesus, really? How much more depressing is this conversation going to get?

Oh, God.

Heather   . . .

Corryn   . . .

Sorry.

Your cat is dying?

Heather *nods.*

Corryn I'm sorry. What's wrong with her?

Heather Diabetes.

Corryn Oh. She won't get better?

Heather . . .

Corryn Well . . .

Heather They're going to call me.

Corryn But she isn't going to get better.

Heather He.

Corryn He.

Heather They're going to call.

Corryn So, the vet's going to call you and—what? You're going to go down there?

Heather . . .

Corryn And put your cat to sleep?

Heather . . .

Corryn Well, this is bad timing. Huh?

Heather . . .

Corryn You've been through this before? With other pets?

Heather *shakes her head.*

Corryn Well. It's never easy. It won't be.

Heather I don't think I—. . .

Corryn . . .

Heather I don't think I—it's hard—

Corryn I've done it three times. Two dogs and a cat. Now—no more pets.

Heather . . .

Corryn How long did you have him?

Heather Fifteen years.

54   Johnna Adams

Corryn   He had a long life for a cat.

Heather   ...

Corryn   What happened?

Heather   ...

Corryn   Was he just prone to diabetes?

Heather   ...

Corryn   Or did you overfeed him?

Heather   ...

Corryn   ...

Heather   ...

Corryn   ...

Corryn *takes a paper out of her bag and puts it on* **Heather***'s desk.*

Heather   ...?

Corryn   Sign this.

Heather   ...

Corryn   You're supposed to sign it when we've had our parent teacher conference.

Heather   ...

Corryn   Part of the bureaucratic machinery of school suspension.

Heather   ...

Corryn   A form you need for his file, I guess.

Heather   ...

Corryn   The principal needs to sign it, too. To confirm that we chatted.

Heather   ...

Corryn   I don't know what we'll do about her signature. Write the word "coward" in the blank?

Heather   ...

Corryn   You sent this home with him. I'm supposed to meet with you and get it signed.

Heather . . .

Corryn Unless it is no longer important.

Heather *takes the form and finds a pen.*

Corryn I was grading papers when he gave it to me. I knew it was something big. He couldn't look at me.

He was shaking.

He gave it to me. I looked at it. I saw what it was and told him everything would be all right. Asked him if he wanted to talk about it.

He had blood on his nose. Someone had hit him in the nose. Jake, probably. Jake, who he liked at one time. I guess.

He shook his head no. He pulled away when I tried to wipe the blood away. He went up to his room.

I called after him telling him everything was all right and I would take care of this. I called the office. Carole. I made this appointment.

I didn't hear him go into the garage.

I called him to come down for dinner. He didn't answer so I started up the stairs to go get him and I heard the gun shot. I thought he was upstairs still and I couldn't imagine—

I called out again and told him to stay in his room and then I went into the garage.

He had taken garbage bags—the ones for gathering dead leaves, and taped them in a large rectangle on the floor. Like a tarp. But, he didn't understand. Because he put the gun under his chin. So, nothing . . . nothing landed on the tarp. So.

He didn't leave behind the tidy mess he thought he would.

Heather . . .

Corryn He left a note.

Heather . . .

Corryn "I've gone to stand with the poets."

Heather . . .

Corryn . . .

Heather ...

Corryn ...

Heather That's beautiful.

Corryn ...

Heather ...

Corryn Thank you.

Heather ...

Corryn ...

Heather ...

Corryn That was honest.

Heather ...

Corryn You don't say that to someone. When someone tells you what her child's suicide note says, you aren't supposed to say "that's beautiful." It really isn't appropriate. But you said it. Because you felt it.

Heather ...

Corryn Thank you.

Heather ...

Corryn ...

Heather ...

Heather *signs the paper.*

Corryn Do you have someone to go with you?

Heather ...?

Corryn The cat.

Heather ...

Corryn I'm not offering. Just asking.

Heather No.

Corryn Oh.

Heather ...

Corryn ...

Heather They said that I don't have to be there. If it turns out that nothing can be done, I can just give them permission to do it

Corryn . . .

Heather And they'll just

Corryn . . .

Heather And I don't have to

Corryn Yes you do.

Heather . . .

Corryn You have to. He was your cat.

Heather . . .

Corryn Come on. You're tough. Right?

Heather . . .

Corryn . . .

Heather *shakes her head.*

Corryn You have to! He's your cat! You do it!!!

Corryn *grabs her and shakes her.*

Heather *cries out, surprised, and tries to push her off.*

While **Corryn** *is talking, they end up on the floor.*

Corryn Do it! DO IT! He's your cat! You talk to him while they kill him. Talk to him and tell him you love him. Sing him his favorite songs. Put his favorite stuffed toy in his paws and then watch them do it to him! It's your job, damnit! Watch! You watch his eyes—that's how you'll know it's time—you won't be able to breathe for watching his eyes and waiting for them to turn glassy—and even if he doesn't know you're there with him—you'll know—you overfed him, damnit! It's your fault. Your fault! You be there! You put out the damned cat food. And now your cat's become an ocean and the vet can't catch it in the cup he's holding out. You have to be there to catch the rest of it. The whole ocean and the fish and cold and black and the way he's going to die and wave after wave of that ocean until he's gone! It all matters until he's gone—every second of it!

Corryn *lets her go. They are on the floor, staring at one another.*

Heather . . .

Corryn . . .

Heather . . .

Corryn Or you'll always regret it.

Heather . . .

Corryn . . .

Heather Okay.

Corryn . . .

Heather . . .

Corryn Okay. Good.

Corryn *gets up and goes to Gidion's desk. She gathers everything that was his together, putting some things in her purse and carrying others.*

Corryn . . .

Heather . . .

Corryn Tell the principal I was sorry I missed her. Give her that form. If you have someone cut the lock off of Gidion's locker have someone bring his things to my house and leave them on the porch.

Heather . . .

Corryn I blame you for this.

Heather . . .

Corryn . . .

Heather . . .

Corryn I'm sorry.

Heather . . .

Corryn *leaves.*

Heather *gets up and straightens the desks and chairs that were moved around during her struggle with* **Corryn**.

She goes to the door, which **Corryn** *has left partly open, and pulls it shut.*

She sits at her desk and picks up her mug. She stares at it as if it were unfamiliar.

Her cellphone rings. It rings again.

It rings.

It rings.

End of play.

Johnna Adams received a Steinberg/American Theatre Critics Association citation in 2013 for her play *Gidion's Knot*. She is the 2011 recipient of the Princess Grace award and a 2012 finalist for the Susan Smith Blackburn award. *Gidion's Knot* was published in the December 2012 edition of *American Theatre* magazine. The Contemporary American Theater Festival premiered *Gidion's Knot* in 2012 and twelve regional productions were planned around the country in the following 2013–14 season. Flux Theatre Ensemble (New York) produced her play *Sans Merci* in 2013 and was nominated for a New York Innovative Theatre award for best play. *Gidion's Knot* and *Sans Merci* are published by Dramatists Play Service, Inc. Johnna received a 2012 MFA in playwriting from Hunter College with Tina Howe.

Grief Encounter: An Interview with Johnna Adams[1]

Tina Howe

My first and most essential question is this: How did you come to write this extraordinary play?

Well, I wrote it in class (*laughter*)—at Hunter, which you'll remember, of course. You had to sit through all the scenes I brought in. It was a longer process than that, though. I carried the idea around for several years and couldn't find the right play for it. I tried a three-man version of the same idea—a son and a father, and the principal and the teacher—and all I was able to write was this terrible, extensive backstory to the scene I actually wanted to write, which was the parent-teacher conference. Eventually I became fascinated with how much stronger the story would be if it were about women—how that would change the dynamics. And what great roles these would be for actresses! I always write for actors.

Have you, or anyone you know, ever had an experience like this as a student, parent or teacher?

As a student, I was constantly writing stuff that—had I been caught—would have triggered something similar to events in the play, I'm sure. That's part of the reason this was a fascinating idea to me. As a younger playwright, I wrote *The Sacred Geometry of S&M Porn*. My dad came to see it in California, and it was just what it sounds like: dirty, lots of nudity, lots of crazy things happening. There's a group marriage scene involving members of the audience. My dad went through this, got flirted with by the actors, had his beard pulled on, had this whole crazy experience, and I said, "What'd you think, Dad?" and he said, "It was very interesting, honey." But every time I've talked to him since, the play's gotten better—now he thinks it was amazing, wonderful, he loved it. The fact is, we had lots of walkouts from *The Sacred Geometry of S&M Porn*—which is a legitimate reaction. But it's the type of relationship that I have with my dad, I think, that really inspired *Gidion's Knot*—the idea that if the world were to condemn me for some piece of writing

---

[1] "Grief Encounter" by Tina Howe. Originally published in *American Theatre* magazine, vol. 29, no. 10 (December 2012). Used with permission from Theatre Communications Group.

(which the world does often to writers), he would stand against the crowd and shout them down.

Can you talk a bit about your process of writing it? You'd bring in these heart-stopping, beautifully crafted scenes week after week that would leave us speechless, and there was hardly any rewriting, so I had this feeling that it was being dictated to you by the gods.

It just emerged, for the most part. Now the child's story, you may recall, was completely different when we read it in class. I could not write the child's story in the first go-through at all—that proved very difficult. My process tends to be improvising at the keyboard more than really laboring through scene-by-scene. I got my undergraduate degree as an actor. I don't act much anymore—but the way I write is to put myself in both characters' roles and do an improvisation to write through the scene. I tend to write very fast, and I'm lazy, so I don't like rewriting. I've trained my subconscious to get it right the first time, or else the pages are going to be thrown away. I can't write every day for that reason—I kind of have to wait for the fairies to come and abduct me and take me to the fairy ring, which can be very frustrating because you don't know when.

You talk about the difficulty in nailing the horrifying but beautifully written story that got Gidion suspended, which is clearly the heart of the play. Can you describe the balancing act that writing it entailed? You had to keep it in the voice of an 11-year-old boy, but it also had to reflect the size and horror of the medieval battle poems he grew up with at his mother's knee.

You have to give yourself permission to write in a way that would horrify the people you love, in some ways. I had to justify the mother saying, "That's magnificent"—there had to be a reason she would be able to stand up for it—so it couldn't be just offensive. It had to be something bigger. I don't like to see audiences get so offended that they can't engage with a play. In almost every production, I have to stop myself from taking out the one or two sentences that cross *way* over the line for the audience, because that's the point—the boy didn't know those boundaries existed, and crashed into them.

Talk about your uncanny approach to dialogue in this play—when the characters reach an impasse, rather than toss in that good old stage direction "Silence," you give them line after line of agonizing ellipses, so that sometimes there are only a handful of words on a page. Why all the blank space?

Well, to me, that's tied in with the transformation from male characters to female ones. Women will take to these kinds of social confrontations that may involve life-and-death-level emotions, but you're within the constraint of a parent-teacher conference, thus constrained by certain social norms of politeness. The ellipses, I think, are trying to make that part of the scene. They kind of show the structure of social conversation—even if I think you've killed my child, if we're sitting here having a polite conversation as two adult, well-socialized women, we're not going to leap across the table—at least not immediately—and strangle one another. So the awkwardness of fitting those huge emotions into this encounter results in these hard-to-avoid silences that are structuring the whole conversation.

Are these silences also a nod to the actors?

That's part of it. I will say, having had it done at Contemporary American Theater Festival in West Virginia, working on these pauses with Ed Herendeen and the actresses there, I realized that, for me, it's musical underscoring, in some ways. It's a rhythmic pacing. You can hear musically when those pauses go on too long, or when they're too short. The whole play has an aria feel, in some ways. It also is—I hope—freeing for the actors to own and endow the moments as they want to. Really, as I said, the piece was written for actresses more than audiences, in some ways.

This may be an unfair question, but do you think there's a villain in the play? If so, who is it? Or is it the system?

Um . . . the system. That's good—you supplied a good villain! Thank you. That's a nice answer.

My idea was that both the play's characters are trying their best to do the right thing in a situation where there really isn't a right thing that can be done. That both the teacher and the mother would go into this encounter to face the person they least wanted to be in the same room with in the world—who was, at the same time, the person they most *needed* to be in the room with. I specifically tried to undercut the sympathy the mother might have garnered had she been really virtuous, by making her rather arrogant, a strong and abrasive personality, in some ways, and opinionated to the point of inflexibility. Although the teacher also has her strong opinions.

Early on, regarding the teacher, you have the stage direction "Something breaks inside of her." We feel that the teacher is in some kind of extreme pain.

Yeah, I hope that moment helps any actress doing the role, that it will give her something underneath, because being the teacher in the room with the grieving mother, you don't have permission to indulge in your own long, revealing monologues about yourself or your life. The teacher has to live in those ellipses, you know, and that's a real challenge, I think, for the actress.

What do you want the audience to come away with?

I want the audience to have had an experience in the theater that's memorable. This can be a very difficult play to sit through. It's not a feel-good play. When I listen to it, I usually put my head in my hands and close my eyes while it's going on, and I'm not the only one! In West Virginia, at least three-quarters of the audience did the same thing. But there's a tremendous release, I think, at some point after that—the play gives you permission to think and talk about things that we don't think and talk about normally that are very important.

Tina Howe also writes plays and is the playwright-in-residence for the Rita and Burton Goldberg MFA in playwriting at Hunter College.

The Niceties

Eleanor Burgess

Characters

Janine Bosko, *female, white, early 60s. A college professor.*
Zoe Reed, *female, black, 19. A college student.*

Setting

An elite university in the Northeast.

Act One—late March, 2016

Act Two—three weeks later

Notes

Both of these women can be noble. Both of them can be charming. Both of them can be petulant, snotty, arrogant, overwhelmed and immature. Let them be both people. And resist the temptation to think of only one of them as a mouthpiece for the truth. When it comes to the facts of history, almost everything that both of the women in this play say is right.

The events and discussions in this play are deeply felt and emotionally difficult for both characters—but there is no crying in this play.

A line break within a character's dialogue indicates a new thought or a beat.

A slash within a line signifies interrupted dialogue.

I should like to have that written over the portals of every church, every school, every courthouse, and every legislative body in the United States: "I beseech you, in the bowels of Christ, believe that you may be mistaken."
— Learned Hand

Act One

An office at an elite Northeastern college. There's a stately, antique mahogany desk. There's a high wall of bookcases, filled with an overwhelming number of books.

There are a few framed images from revolutionary movements: a Lech Walesa/ Solidarity poster; a painting of the tennis court oath; a photo of Emiliano Zapata; a photo of Nelson Mandela in Springbok uniform; and a portrait of George Washington.

Janine, *early 60s, white, is behind the desk in an ergonomic chair.* **Zoe**, *19, black, sits in a folding chair across from her.*

They are looking over a paper. **Zoe** *sips from a venti Starbucks cup.*

Janine   You're missing a comma here.

She holds the paper out to **Zoe**. **Zoe** *looks.*

Zoe   Oof. Yeah. I definitely am.

Janine Always proofread in hard copy. Proofreading on a computer *does not work./* Excellent word choices by the way. I don't think I've ever had a student use "bedeviled" in a paper before. I love that word. All the "be" words, bemuse, beguile.	**Zoe** *(agreeing)* Mmm.

Zoe   Bedazzle. Beseech.

Janine   Beget.

Zoe   Classic. Betoken.

Janine   Bemoan. Oh, I could do this all day. Focus Janine. Next comment. Ah, here, you have—

"Washington succeeded owing to his presenting himself as a leader, elite status as a plantation owner, and his ability to establish commonality."

Zoe   Yes . . .

Janine Have you heard of the idea of parallelism? / Of— matching grammatical structure—Because you have "presenting himself as a leader"—gerund—"elite status"—noun—"his ability"— noun with possessive pronoun. Can you hear it? / Whereas if you imagine—"His ability to present himself as a leader, to project elite status, and / to establish commonality"

Zoe Oo—shoot, yeah.

Zoe Yeah, yeah—

Zoe "and to establish commonality."

Janine Yes—yes! There are a plethora of options, three gerunds, three nouns, but any one of them telegraphs to your reader—"you are in safe hands. This writer will not do anything truly horrible to you, like assaulting you with grammatically incompatible clauses."

Zoe No, totally. My English teacher had us do like 800 worksheets on it senior year I just—I wanted to get the draft in early so I could get your comments before the deadline, and to be honest I had kind of a tough weekend and I didn't get to proofread as much as I normally would.

Janine Oh. Well.

Zoe Okay. So I correct all of that, and then the writing's good?

Janine Well . . . It's a bit more complicated. I've written suggestions, but—

Do you have a little more time?

Zoe Yeah, I mean, I want to make it as strong as possible.

But I know office hours are almost over, if you—

Janine Oh, it's no problem. I just turned in a draft of my new book so there's *no* chance I'll be productive. I have absolutely nothing to do until dinner with my better half at 8:30.

Zoe Haha, well, hopefully it won't take that long!

Um, so what else is there to fix?

Janine Well . . . it could all use a bit more flair.

Zoe . . . flair?

Janine If you want to get through to a reader, you have to make the past feel human. And real. For instance!

Janine *gets up and goes to the bookcases to hunt for a book.* **Zoe** *checks her phone.*

Janine Have you ever been to India?

Zoe No. Never.

Janine It's really—it's quite spectacular. The spirituality is—jubilant. And who knew lentils could be delicious? You really must go sometime.

Zoe Well I do like lentils.

Janine You know this place has oodles of money for travel, if it's related to research. I had a student once who developed his entire senior thesis around getting funding to visit places where he wanted to bunjee jump. He's now a district attorney for a major American city. You're a history major?

Zoe Poly sci.

Janine Ah. Well. That's alright. And you're a—which year are you?

Zoe Junior.

Janine My son is a junior! Zachary Wheeler.

Zoe Oh! He's in my section for Modern Poetry. He's really smart.

Janine I like to think so. His being a student here . . . it's been interesting. It's forced me to see my students not just as walking thesis statements but as human beings. Which is of course very disorienting.

Here it is!

I'm really not as informed about South Asia as I ought to be, I'm trying to bone up, and I ran into this anecdote.

So, there is a province called Sindh, okay, in what is today Southern Pakistan.

In 1843, Charles James Napier was sent there by the East India Company to put down a rebellion. But at the Battle of Hyderabad he conquered the whole area, and he sent a telegram—now, keep in mind, these British men, they had all been at the same fancy private schools, or rather, public schools, as the Brits put it *quite* ridiculously, and they all had these absurd classical educations, and anyway Napier sends a telegram back to the Colonial Office containing one word. *Peccavi.*

As in "quoniam peccavi ignosce pater"—forgive me father for I have sinned. Get it! Sinned. Sindh. "I have Sindh." As in the province!

Zoe Ha, yeah. That's—pretty disturbing.

Janine Oh, *God* yes, I mean he's making a *joke* about decimating a civilization.

Zoe Like—we just killed people—hilarious!

Janine It's *awful.*

Only, it's also so revealing. Armies were raised, lands ravaged, all in an attempt to impress friends from prep school.

You learn a lot from a story like that.

Zoe Yeah. Yeah. I can see that.

Janine *(coming back with the book)* Do you like my chair?

It's supposed to help you stretch out your cervical disks, or something like that.

I have bad back pain. The result, I'm afraid, of a lifetime of scouring sources. It's like some ghastly metaphor about the price we pay for knowledge. Don't hunch, Zoe, when you are looking for your new, illuminating evidence, never hunch. Pull the evidence up to you. What my son would call a protip.

You see what I mean though?

Zoe Yeah, it looks like a really supportive chair.

Janine No, about—about evidence. Peccavi. *That's* the kind of story I want you to put in your paper.

Or or or—here's one of my favorites. So—1775, fighting has broken out near Boston, and the Continental Congress meets to appoint a general for their new army.

George Washington's a top contender - he's probably the person in the country most experienced with military command. But - colonial Americans—you'll remember from class, they were so worried about tyranny. There had never been a country before, in human history, that managed to sustain a system where the people chose their own government.

Zoe Right. They all ended in chaos or dictatorships.

Janine *Exactly.* They're terrified the new general will just seize power.

Zoe The Julius Caesar thing.

Janine Now, Washington wants the job very badly, but he's strategic. When he's asked about taking command, he tells congress: "Though I am sensible of the high Honour done me, yet I feel great distress, for fear that my abilities and my experience may not be equal to the task." But here's the best part - he showed up to give that speech in his military uniform. So he's basically saying, please don't give me this job, and the whole time, he's *wearing his resume.*

Can you hear it?

The, the detail—the/palpable—

Zoe Yeah. Definitely

Janine I think it's an absolutely wonderful story.

To imagine those men—not knowing they would pick Washington. Struggling to figure things out.

I would give anything to be in that room. Wouldn't you?

Zoe Um. Probably not. No.

Janine Hah, right, I'm probably a bit more obsessed than the average person.

Handing over the book.

You can borrow this, if you like.

Zoe Thank you.

She tucks it in her purse.

Janine Have to give it back! Though God knows why, I'll never reread it, but—

Zoe Of course. So—the parallelism, the footnotes, more flair in the evidence, and then I hand it back in?

Janine Actually, these comments were more about writing than argument.

I like to offer very thorough comments purely on writing, for three pages.

Most teachers in this gothic pile don't see that as part of their job—to teach any practical skills. I'm glad you brought this in early. I can see you've done an impressive amount of work on it.

Zoe Yeah, well. I tend to get a little intense about fulfilling requirements. Only child.

Or—it's weird that you never get to graduate from being an only child to being an only adult.

Janine True!

I wish you hadn't plowed ahead like this—written the full draft without getting comments on the thesis.

Zoe I was just excited to lay out the ideas.

Janine I'm afraid you're in for quite a substantial rewrite.

Your argument is . . . fundamentally unsound.

Zoe Unsound?

Janine flips to the front of the paper.

Janine "The successful American Revolution was only possible because of the existence of slavery."

Zoe Yes.

Janine Yes?

Zoe Yes.

The whole idea came out of your lecture on how most revolutions have two phases. There's the initial, moderate revolution, led by the upper middle class people. And they make moderate, constitutional changes. But they don't help the people who are *really* suffering—they don't do anything about . . . economic inequality . . . *real* injustices.

Janine Yes. That's—mostly—yes.

Zoe And so new leaders with broader popular support take over in a second, radical revolution. The moderates and the radicals can't agree. And so revolutions usually turn into violent, drawn-out conflicts. Basically civil wars.

That's what happened in France, in Russia. In Mexico. In China with Mao overthrowing the Nationalists.

That's what you talked about in class.

Janine   . . . Yes.

Zoe   Is any part of that wrong?

Janine   No.

Zoe   But in the U.S., the people who were *really* suffering, who *would* have become radicals, were the slaves. And everybody else, upper middle class white people and poor white people, were pretty happy with the way things were. That's why the U.S. never had a radical revolution. It stopped in the moderate phase and had one of the most unified, non-destructive revolutions of all time.

Janine   Is this a theory that you read somewhere? Is there a book that—

Zoe   No. It's my theory.

Janine   Because—there are a lot of prevalent theories about why the American revolution was so moderate.

Do you remember the ones we discussed in class?

Zoe   Yes.

Janine   We can review them, if you like.

Zoe   I don't need to review them.

Janine   There were a lot of factors—

Zoe   Revolutions tend to stay moderate when people are fighting an outside enemy, like the British. Pre-industrial revolutions were more moderate because radicals couldn't get their message out.

Janine Good. Very good! There's also my own theory, that diverse economies lead to more gradual change. /	**Zoe**
	Right
Admittedly that was my first book, I'm not very proud of the execution—	

Zoe   Yeah, I understand that, I mean I get that all of that definitely played a role.

Janine   I should have started by saying—it's a very interesting idea.

It's one of the more imaginative arguments I've seen—

Zoe   You don't have to start with a compliment if you don't respect my work.

Janine   I *do* respect it. Don't get me wrong—it is bold, original thinking.

Reading it made me wish you'd speak up in class. But—your thesis is not an explanation that any scholars who really know the period could agree with.

Zoe   Wow. Um. You're saying you think that *universally*, everyone who's studied the American Revolution would disagree with me.

Janine   Well. Yes.

She waves at the bookcases.

I've read what they think.

They're my colleagues. I edited their work together for your Comparative Revolutions textbook.

None of them have reached the conclusion you did.

Zoe   Like you said, it's original.

Janine   It's also not a good fit for the available evidence.

Zoe   Yeah, I'm sure that's the reason none of them thought of it.

Janine   How do you mean?

Zoe   Never mind.

She decides she does want to say it.

I just think it's—I think it's *funny*—that a lot of smart, educated people don't think that an institution affecting millions of people/ a role

Janine   It wasn't millions. Technically. In this era it was more like 500,000.

Zoe   —that an institution affecting 500,000 slaves played a role in the revolution. Except it's also maybe not surprising given who those historians are.

Short beat as **Janine** *figures out what this means.*

Janine   It's not about who the historians are.

A *lot* of historians have written about the role race has played in American history.

There's clear evidence that during the *Civil* War, wealthy Confederates used racism to get poor white support. Our modern electoral map is a drawing of who liked and who hated the Civil Rights Act.

No one is questioning the role of race in American politics—

One need only turn on the TV and watch these stupid Republican primary debates. I'm sorry—if you're a Republican, of course I respect that—

Zoe I'm not a Republican.

Janine Oh good. Well, *right?* Am I right?

Zoe I actually haven't been watching much? I can't really handle the fact that this is our last year with Obama.

Janine I know. Well thank God they're hopelessly divided because otherwise the situation would be dire.

What I'm trying to say is that the evidence from *this* period doesn't fit.

You're saying that if there hadn't been slavery, poor whites would have pushed for radical economic change. But that doesn't hold up. Even in colonies like New Hampshire and Massachusetts, where slaves made up less than 2 percent of the population, there was no serious discussion of economic reform. Unlike France, there was no famine, no crisis. Read the letters, the diary entries. This was long before Karl Marx. The idea of democracy already felt huge and exciting and terrifying to these people. More radical change just wasn't on the table, with or without slavery.

Zoe Well I found sources that said different.

Janine *looks over the paper, thoughtful.*

Janine (*reading*) "Wealthy and poor whites were unified by their interest in preserving slavery."

Where did you read that?

Zoe It's in my footnotes.

Janine *flips to the footnotes.*

Janine www.revolutionarywar.net

You know what they're calling your generation? I think this term is much better than "millenials," millenials makes it sound like you're all hopeful religious fanatics. "Digital natives." Have you heard that?

Zoe Yeah, somewhere. I think I saw it online.

Janine I think it's *wonderful*. I heard it at a modern pedagogy workshop, and another professor there, for the rest of the day he kept deliberately confusing it and saying "technological savages."

She finds this funny, **Zoe** *does not.*

Janine Well the trouble that I have with this info from www.revolutionarywar.net is that it's wrong. Five states abolished slavery during the war. Northern delegates to the constitutional convention fought tooth and nail to try to end the international slave trade. Far from being *unified* by slavery, whites were actively fighting over it.

Zoe Okay. Maybe. But—

But you can't say they weren't unified—Even if they didn't all *like* slavery—They were unified by *not caring* much about it.

You said they were willing to fight over slavery at the constitutional convention but *how much* were they willing to fight? Not enough. They compromised over it.

If there had been a slave revolt, they wouldn't have supported it. They wouldn't have risked division to support it.

Janine That's almost certainly true.

Zoe Having the biggest injustice in a society all concentrated on just 20 percent of the population made it easier for the rest of the population to agree. Why did the American revolution go so much better than any other revolution in any other country ever? It's easier to be pro-equality when there's a subjugated minority in your midst.

Janine Well that's a horrifying possibility.

I like that you stick by your opinions.

You know so many of your classmates—and, I hate to say it, but the women especially—they come in here. In their cute outfits and their faces full of makeup. And I try to push them on their thinking and they nod, and tell me that's so interesting, or they'll do that right away, they're so eager to do what I tell them. When what I *want*, of course, is a debate.

Zoe Of course.

Janine And then when I get it, it's always from the men—and who wants them to sharpen their debating skills?

Zoe Ha. Right.

There's actually—there's this joke—

Where did the male debater get his water?

From a well, actually . . .

Janine Oh. Ha. That's funny.

 . . . You know I was in the third class of women here.

And the men couldn't decide whether they were *allowed* to argue with us. Or whether it was unchivalrous. And then if you argued with them they thought that meant you wanted to go out.

Zoe *laughs a little, thinks about this.*

Zoe That must have been pretty crazy.

Janine	**Zoe**
Oh it was.	
You know when I found out I was having a boy I thought oh no. I was sincerely worried that I would impair my son in some way. / Hold him back. Because I don't want him to be president, or head of the history department, or CEO. I want that to be—well, you. I wanted a daughter. I could have made her unstoppable.	Oh—no . . .

I change my mind. I want you to keep your thesis.

But you'll need better research.

Zoe What exactly does that mean, better research?

Janine The section on the white standard of living was great, it's very compelling.

But many of the paragraphs are—conjectures. You make huge claims about what *might* have motivated people.

You cite—psychologists. *Bloggers.* But you offer no primary documents. No perspectives from people who were there about what they saw going on. You need to hit the library.

Zoe   The library?

Janine   Yes. The *library*. Go find some *books*. Big heavy books made of paper. / It's not always that easy, you can't always type a couple words in a box and know everything there is to know, sometimes you really have to work to get at the truth.

Zoe   That's not what I—

John Adams hated Paris. You know how I know that?

Zoe   . . . From a book?

Janine *goes to the bookcases, looks for a book.*

Zoe   I *believe* you—

Janine   Hmmm, I thought it was here. . .

She looks in the wrong place at first, it takes a while for her to find it.

Zoe *checks her phone.*

Janine   I can never tell, whether my memory is going or whether I've lived through so many things that it all blurs together. I've lent so many—aha!

Janine *comes back with a heavy book. She sees* **Zoe** *on her phone.*

Janine   Well please, if I'm *boring* you—

Zoe   No, you're not.

Zoe *sets her phone down.*

Janine (*colder now, more irritated*)   Look. Adams says it right here. In a letter to Abigail. And there's a footnote, where Hollings tells me, in case I don't believe him, I can go find the letter, at the Massachusetts Historical Archives, and I can hold it in my own two hands, and see where Adams signed it. *That*'s how I know it's true.

Zoe   But there won't be proof like that for a thesis like this.

Janine Not proof you can *google*, no.

Zoe There won't be proof I can hold in my hand either.

No one writes down what they're actually feeling.

Like if someone emails you tonight and says how were office hours, you're not gonna write back, actually, this one student had some ideas about American history that made me uncomfortable—

Janine You haven't made me uncomfortable—

Zoe You're gonna write "pretty good. Think I gave some good advice." And if someone wrote a paper a hundred years from now on these office hours they'd think they were "pretty good." That maybe you gave some good advice.

I'm not gonna to find a diary entry where someone says, "June tenth. Today I used racism to bond with the other delegates!" That piece of paper doesn't exist. But I know that's what happened.

Janine No—no / you can't—

Zoe You can say what you want, but I know, I *know*, because I know how race affects people, I understand / how people work. I mean we don't have a bunch of letters by a bunch of slave women saying, "hey, I hate being raped—/ sometimes I think about killing myself, or him," but I *know* that's how they felt—	**Janine** You can't just invent— Actually we have those letters. Read Harriet Jacobs.

Janine Wait a minute, were you—have you been raped?

Zoe NO! I'm saying, I am a human being, I have *empathy*, and *experiences*, and I can tell how they must have felt.

Janine You may be right.

You're probably right.

About the feelings that were there. It's possible you're right about the effects those feelings had.

But that isn't history.

Zoe Yes it is history. It's a part of American history.

Janine I don't mean it's not important or it's not part of the American story. I mean, you're using your personal experiences to embellish on the past. That's historical fiction. It's not what historians do. Historians sift through *evidence*—documents, objects, recordings—to draw informed conclusions about the past. That is our trade.

Ordinary people guess. They tell themselves stories that seem to make sense and then because they seem to make sense they believe them.

"Women are naturally less intelligent than men."

"The sun goes around the earth."

"There are weapons of mass destruction in Iraq."

Those ideas *sound* convincing to some people, some people may "just know" they're true, but when you look at the *evidence*, they're false.

The entire point of a university is the idea of *expertise*.

We are people who refuse to go with our feelings, our guts. We look at the evidence. And by doing that, we drive back ignorance.

Zoe But if you say you need evidence . . .

You're excluding the people who couldn't leave evidence behind.

People who couldn't write. Anyone without money, or an education.

Anyone with no possessions for historians to dig up.

Janine Not *excluding*, no. There's archaeology. Court testimonies. The occasional stray magic letter. But some stories are easier to tell than others. It's an unfortunate consequence of sound methodology.

Zoe "An unfortunate consequence."

Janine Yes. A very unfortunate consequence.

It's still better than making things up.

Beat.

Zoe You know I remember going on field trips. When I was little.

My school was very into like, *fancy* activities, we went to a lot of museums. And I remember these . . . ten foot high paintings in gold frames with—Kings. And Gods. And Soldiers. And beautiful women in big shiny dresses. I loved the dresses, I used to say I wanted to be a duchess when I grew up. And it took until I was maybe eight, or nine? To realize none of the women in the paintings looked like me. And there were like, ships. Churches. Fruit—a lot of fruit. But never the people who *sewed* the dresses. Or *picked* the fruit.

Janine I know.

Zoe It's messed up!

Janine Yes, it is.

Zoe But then—the textbook? The book you edited?

It's the exact same thing.

Soldiers, statesmen, women in big shiny dresses, and like bunches and bunches and bunches of white men. As if that's all there was in this country.

Janine It's a book about inner political workings, not a general history. But it stinks, I get it. Believe me, I hate it.

Zoe Okay, well then change it. Hello, you have power!! Let me do the kind of history I want to do.

Janine I'm afraid that I can't simply do that. Let's say you decide to apply to graduate schools—

Zoe I'm not going to apply to graduate schools.

Janine But if you did—a good grade from me is a signal to my colleagues, this young woman has all the skills you're looking for in a historian. But by the standards of academia, your current work is immature, and unsophisticated.

Zoe Unsophisticated?

Janine You have potential. A great deal of it.

Maybe you should think about graduate school.

The field could use people like you. People pushing, demanding modernization.

But if you want to change how people do things—it helps if you're the best.

I have gotten to do what I want in my career, because I have worked to be twice as good as anybody else.

Find the sources. Get the rock-solid evidence. Check every comma. *Prove me wrong.*

Zoe   So . . . But—it will always be harder to write a really excellent paper about black history than about white history.

Janine   From this time period? Yes. That's the way things are. I can't fix that.

Zoe *takes her paper back.*

Zoe   . . . If I made just the writing changes you suggested. Polished sentences, added footnotes. What grade would I get?

Janine   I can't tell you that. It's against university policy, and even if it weren't . . .

Zoe! You are a bright young woman. I don't want you to ask, am I meeting the bare requirements? I want you to pursue excellence. I want you to ask yourself, am I doing the absolute best I could possibly do?

Zoe   I can't rewrite my paper.

That much. I can't—get twenty pages of all new, very-difficult-to-find evidence in a week!

Janine   I'll help you, there's no need to worry.

Zoe   No I don't need help.

I mean I don't have time.

My schedule is already crazy.

I used Spring break to do this paper, I thought I'd already *done* this essay. More than / done it.

Janine   You know, you would be amazed what you can accomplish in six good hours of distraction-free time. What are you doing this weekend? I have a friend, who teaches African American history at Duke, I can ask her to recommend some resources.

Zoe   This weekend Sandra Day O'Connor's speaking on campus.

Janine   Yes I know, it's very exciting but it should only take about two hours.

Zoe   Well I'm part of the cross-cultural alliance and we're organizing a protest.

Beat.

Janine   You're protesting the first female supreme court justice.

Zoe Yeah. It's a ton of work. We're writing up leaflets on the real effects of her work. We're going to be live-tweeting rebuttals to her speech and staging a walkout. It's a lot to organize.

Janine Are you *opposed* to there being female supreme court justices?

Zoe In 41 decisions involving racial minorities, O'Connor voted against the minority all but two times.

Janine That can't be right.

Zoe You're forgetting that I know how to use Google.

She voted against extra funding for minority school districts.

Janine Well she didn't *vote against* it. She felt that it was unconstitutional.

Zoe She voted against redistricting to get black representatives elected.

Janine Well there are a *lot* of good reasons to oppose gerrymandering.

She supported affirmative action! I remember this, I lived through this, she was a supporter of affirmative action.

Zoe She supported the *idea* of affirmative action over and over again, but every time an actual plan came in front of her she struck it down.

Janine It does sound like she had a troubling record on racial issues. She had a troubling record in general. I mean Bush v. Gore. Bush v. Gore—I ask you! God, were you even alive for Bush's election?

Zoe Yes—

Janine Oh, thank God. But the thing is—the thing is, Zoe—

Zoe I don't need you to tell me the thing—

Janine A dark spot in her record—a *very* dark spot—does not negate everything she accomplished. Do you truly believe that a woman who was privy to 20 years of supreme court cases has nothing to teach you?

Zoe Thank you I know the facts about her and I will make up my own mind. Just like you've done.

I mean do you need to listen to a speech by everyone you disapprove of? Should I pull up a Dick Cheney video?

Janine So you're going to be so busy protesting against female supreme court justices that you can't rewrite your paper.

Zoe That's basically right, although it's a deliberate mischaracterization of what I said.

Janine Spoken like a historian.

You know I never do this.

But I can offer you a one week extension.

Zoe Thank you. But. . .

There's a rally next week in Bridgeport for police reform.

Janine You don't *live* in Bridgeport.

Zoe That's why it's going to take so long, we have to get there. And we're doing a recruitment event the day before.

And then Howard Stern is visiting campus.

Janine And you're . . . going to see him or protesting him?

Zoe Protesting him obviously.

Janine Ah—his jokes are offensive.

Zoe No, he supports Israel.

Janine Okay. Well I'm going to sidestep that—whole—thing.

Look—I have to break it to you—you're overcommitted to your extracurriculars.

Zoe It's not an *extracurricular.* It's not, like, *marching band.*

I don't do this for *fun.*

Janine Well if you don't want the extension then turn in what you have, and get the grade you get.

Zoe I need at least a B+.

Janine Well I need a new lumbar region, and yet I do not have one.

You have agency, Zoe.

You're making a choice about how to spend your time.

Can I tell you a story?

Zoe Look I understand your point but if you could try to understand mine—

Janine The summer between my freshman and sophomore year, a girlfriend and I made plans to bicycle from Paris to Amsterdam. Then I was offered an internship with the Smithsonian. A big opportunity, okay? But I had a feeling—*now* was my time. If I was ever going to be young, ridiculously young, and spontaneous, now was my time. I chose the trip.

Have you ever been to Amsterdam?

Zoe No.

Janine I had one of the best months of my life there. *But I paid a price for that.*

The point is choices have consequences/ You are choosing to spend your weekends organizing protests, instead of doing your homework. That's fine, that's even laudable. But the consequence is, your work does not merit a good grade.	**Zoe** I obviously understand that—

Zoe Well I need one.

Janine I did not take you for a grade grubber.

Zoe I'm *not*. I have a 3.84. I'm on track to be Phi Beta Kappa.

Janine Good for you. I made Phi Beta Kappa. I had to make certain sacrifices to achieve it.

Zoe The Carson Fellowship for Social Justice is my dream job for after graduation.

They train you in community organizing, lobbying, communications. It's perfect for me, and for what I want to do.

And I'd be perfect for it. But I've heard that they weigh transcripts heavily in the evaluation process. Campus activism has taught me all the *real* skills I would actually need for the fellowship. But because our society buys into bullshit credentialism and signs of elitism more than actual skill, I need a high GPA to get started on my life's work.

Janine Zoe—it's not bullshit credentialism. I am telling you that you are lacking some of the real skills that go into top-quality historical work.

Zoe Those skills are useless.

Janine *Useless*?

Strangely I have found them to be of enormous use.

Zoe But you don't have a normal adult human job. I mean - what do you think your students are going to become?

Janine Any number of wonderful things.

Zoe Would you admit that you're not training dozens of future historians? Everyone at this school is going into investment banking. Like, literally, everyone.

They're here for four years of parties, one semester of microeconomics and their on campus Goldman Sachs interview.

Janine Well we needn't concern ourselves with the lacrosse players.

Zoe Come on. You have to have some thoughts about the bullshit that is a liberal arts education. A bunch of rich kids spending literally half a million dollars to get bits of random knowledge and a piece of paper they can show lazy employers who can't spot skill, or work ethic, and just want to know, are you a half million dollar kid?

Janine It's easy, at your age, to be cynical about education. It is.

My son calls this place charm school.

Zoe That's actually pretty good. I might use that.

Janine But I think you will find as you grow older an ineffable—

Zoe *is about to interrupt.*

Janine —*but very real* difference between you and your less elitely educated peers. An ability to see nuance. An ability to serve the world in a way others can't. The state department calls me for advice about mass protests in foreign countries. I have been able to give sound, well-supported advice, because of my supposedly useless knowledge.

You want skills that translate directly to a job? Go to vocational school.

What we as an institution have on offer are 44 million manuscripts and some of the best minds in the world, available to you for picking.

Take advantage of that. There are others to take your place who would really welcome this opportunity.

Zoe I earned this spot. Some people might want to use that spot to party, some people might use it to get ready for a PhD. I want to study ideas that I find interesting, do some good, and qualify for the job I want. And for $64,000 a year, that's not a lot to ask. 64,000 a year that pays for your health insurance and your travel and your son's fully-funded tuition—

Janine You know women *fought* to go here? We petitioned, we held a sit-in. We knew this place was valuable, and we fought to be a part of it, and here you are taking it for granted.

Zoe Only it's not valuable, because you don't understand my work.

Janine I understand your work perfectly, it's just flawed work and it doesn't deserve an A, and it won't get one.

Beat.

Zoe What grade do you think you deserve?

Janine Excuse me?

Zoe Well it's a little bizarre, isn't it? You do something for me, I do something for you, but you get to tell me when my work isn't good enough and I don't get to tell you when your work isn't good enough?

Janine I'm afraid you're not yet educated enough to tell me when my work isn't good enough. But don't worry, there are plenty of mechanisms for that. Tenure committees, peer reviewed journals. Peers in general.

Zoe Don't you want to try to do the absolute best you could possibly do?

Janine Is there something you feel you're not getting from class?

Zoe Do you know that you consistently mispronounce several students' names?

Janine I'm mispronouncing *Zoe*?

Zoe Not *my* name. Other students' names. Ana Maria.

Janine Yes. Ana Maria.

Zoe No. It's *Ana Maria*. And NAHsir, not NaZEER.

Janine Neither of those students has ever corrected me. You know many people chose to anglicize their names.

Zoe *snorts.*

Janine It's true. My birth name was Yanina. I changed it to Janine in the third grade. It made me feel at home.

Zoe That's nice, I'm happy that that worked for you. You should offer your students a choice about what works for them.

Janine I do, they are welcome to come *talk* to me about their preferences. Like adults.

Zoe You could ask students about their pronouns.

Janine I don't think it's respectful to pry. I go by whatever pronouns a student indicates that they want to use—

Zoe Based on what?

Janine Their name, their general appearance.

Zoe But those things don't always align. A person could wear dresses and want to be called a he.

Janine Well in that case it seems to me like that person *wants* to confuse people and will enjoy watching me get it wrong.

Zoe *Are you being sarcastic about your students lives?*

Janine No, I'm not, but I mean *come on.*

Zoe *You come on.* You have students who are vulnerable, who may not feel as comfortable as you do in this elite environment, who are just trying to survive through their days without / reminders of discomfort.

Janine Trying to *survive*? They're trying to *survive* on the mean streets of this ivory playground? Is a thousand year old manuscript going to fall on their head?

Zoe They are trying to avoid emotional trauma—

Janine Trauma? I am not torturing anyone, I am not a war zone. Your whole generation, you have this cult of fragility, with your—your trigger warnings and your / safe spaces—

Zoe It's not being fragile it's being like—/ *aware*—

Janine I may be behaving *sub-optimally.* But when you throw around words like survive and trauma you invite people to belittle your cause.

Zoe Only if you are *looking* for ways to belittle your students. Which I think makes you unfit to be a teacher.

Beat.

Janine   That's preposterous. I am teaching you.

I'm trying to advise you about your use of language.

Zoe   People don't teach through mockery.

Janine   Well now you're undermining the entire British system of pedagogy.

Zoe   Please. Stop. Joking.

Janine   Look, yes, alright, humor can be difficult, but my point was—

Zoe   Could you not say *but* for once, could you listen? Could you try to hear, please?

Janine   I'm listening. It's inevitable that I'm going to have / *opinions*.

Zoe   That is a but—

Janine   —but I am listening.

What other suggestions do you have for me?

I'm listening.

Beat.

Zoe   Don't make jokes about savages.

Janine   No but / —*metaphorical*   **Zoe**   But?
savages, I wasn't referring to any
of the cultures historically referred
to as savages, I would never do
that. It was *ironic*, because I was
talking technologically advanced /
people—

Zoe   Maybe it would be.

If you hadn't told a *delightful* little story about the invasion of India.

The forcible colonization of millions of people, it's *funny* to you.

Janine   No it isn't—

Zoe   And those little snide remarks, like, "you're protesting the first female supreme court justice?"—as if I'm stupid as if you know so much more than me—

Janine   I do know more than you!!

Zoe   *Can you hear it?*

You have a contempt for your students. Particularly your students who think different from you.

Janine Different*ly*.

Zoe *takes a moment.*

Zoe You use your intelligence to critique and belittle people who have less power than you. Like your comments on my paper.

You think that's helpful? To take a person who's trying to put forward an underrepresented point of view, and to criticize them until they feel like they might as well just give up because you'll never understand?

Janine I didn't tell you to give up. I specifically told you that I thought you had a lot of potential.

Zoe If I work harder than anyone else to please you.

Janine To suit what good methodol—

Zoe *Listen.*

There is *one* appropriate way of responding to a woman of color who says, I have an idea to assert, and that is to shut up and listen.

Because she has experiences you cannot possibly know, and insight you can learn from.

Beat.

Janine To shut up and listen, as you so rudely put it, would be doing you a disservice.

I have been to you *exactly* the teacher I would have wanted.

Zoe But I'm not you. That's the thing—you like white ideas, you get white ideas, so you are not qualified to critique my thinking, and in lieu of that I would like for you to hear and validate what I have to say.

Janine I'm not going to *validate* you. You're not a *parking ticket*.

You are a very young person with a lot to learn, including that you will *never* get ahead in life if you are rude and confrontational with powerful people when they're trying to help you.

Beat. **Zoe** *gets out her phone. Seems to be engrossed by it.*

Janine What are you doing?

Zoe I'm canceling plans with a friend for tonight. I'm not going to be in any mood to go out.

Janine Look, I think we should call it a day, actually. I have some work to get done.

Zoe You said you were free until 8:30.

She sets her phone down on the desk.

Janine Zoe. Greatness does not come from a supportive environment.

I have a friend, she's one of the top cardiothoracic surgeons in the country. Do you think she got there because a doctor stood next to her during her first 100 surgeries, and said—you're doing great? Your approach is really valid?

No. He—and it was a he—said, that's not perfect. That's not nearly good enough. That's how she got better.

Zoe How did you raise your son? Did you correct him all the time? Say that's not perfect? That's not nearly good enough. Or did you *love* to listen to him express every little opinion. I want to be treated however you treated him. I want the white boy treatment.

Janine I certainly told him when I thought he was being petulant and disrespectful.

Zoe You haven't earned my respect.

You've earned my frustration.

Janine Because of a few jokes? Believe me I make jokes at home too.

Zoe *pulls out a spiral ring notebook with dozens of post-its sticking out from its pages. She flips to the first post-it.*

Zoe "America was beyond lucky to have Washington and Jefferson as two of its first three leaders."

Janine Yes . . .

We could have had Robespierre. We could have had Lenin. Purges. Beheadings.

Zoe You know you said that in a room that included at least five African-Americans.

Janine Yes, I—yes, I see that that is unpleasant. But you know—you must know, there's no evidence that any other leader would have succeeded in stopping slavery.

Zoe You love them. You *love* them.

"I would give anything just to be in that room."

That's what you said. To *me*.

And you know all I could think when you said that, was that if I'd been in that room it would have been as a slave.

Janine You know if I had been in that room I would have been a wife, or a servant, not a politician—

Zoe Oh that is not the same shut up that is not the same.

Janine No. It's not the same. I can see that that remark was not tactful. And I apologize.

Zoe So what are you going to do about it?

Janine Do?

Zoe Yes.

Janine I mean, I misspoke. I misspoke. But what you people have to understand is—

Zoe Us people?

Janine No, no, I did *not* mean that as a race thing. You *millenials*. You people who have not been out in the world.

What you never understand is that it is *easy* to pick apart all the ways in which a person didn't say things quite right, and what is *hard*, okay, is to put something out there in the world. To pass a law, or teach a class, even to be Howard Stern and tell a dick joke, it's challenging, you don't do it perfectly, but at least you're *adding* something to the world. Instead of complaining about it like a teenager.

Zoe Are you going to add more black history to your curriculum?

Janine Well if you wait a week we're about to start talking about Haiti.

Zoe Are you going to talk about the lives of Washington and Jefferson's slaves?

Janine It's a course on *revolutions*.

Zoe So no. You're going to ignore a fifth of Americans' experiences with the "revolution." You're going to ignore the bad bits.

I mean your whole generation. You say *we're* fragile.

And you've kept reading the children's book version of American history your whole adult lives. Well—trigger warning—

America was a land of equality and opportunity for white Americans because they stole their land. And then they didn't pay their workers. When 20 percent of the population has literally nothing, the other 80 percent gets more. That's your land of opportunity.

And that's why that 80 percent was so unified and so happy with their moderate democratic government and so able to have the most successful, prosperous un-radical revolution of all time.

Teach that. Spend your last 10 lectures on that.

Beat.

Janine It's horrible. So much of history is horrible. "Nasty, poor, brutish and short." Tainted with racism, sexism, classism, cruelty, exploitation, religious persecution, casual disregard for our mutual humanity. But we can't spend all of our time focusing on that. There are other important things to say.

Zoe For millions of Americans, slavery is the most important thing about American history.

Janine	**Zoe**
But . . . it isn't. It isn't! Democracy is the most important thing about American history./ If only because—slavery is a thing that has happened throughout human history, while the birth of constitutional democracy—that's us. We changed the world. "All men are created equal." Even if Jefferson didn't think that included women, or slaves, or white men without property, still *he wrote it down.* And as a result, it's something we keep, keep, keep striving towards. It's our North Star. America is a painstaking, lengthy, but ultimately revolutionary quest for freedom.	*Please.*

Beat. **Janine** *believes she's gotten through.*

Zoe America is an engine of racial oppression.

Janine I feel—sad. For you. That you can't see any of the beauty. I understand it. But you're missing something really wonderful.

Zoe You know when you were dicking around backpacking in Holland, or whatever? You know what I was doing the summer between my freshman and sophomore year? That was the summer Mike Brown was shot.

I was marching.

Have you ever been to Ferguson? You really *must* go to Ferguson.

Janine That's very impressive.

Look but you'd be surprised—the year when you are born makes an enormous difference in the ways you do or don't help the world.

By the time I got out of college, the Vietnam War was over.

The Civil Rights marches were over.

We didn't have the internet to tell us what was happening in St. Louis.

My activism has been in the workplace.

Zoe flips to another marked page in her notebook. **Janine** *gets irritated.*

Zoe "In an embarrassment of riches, America was blessed with not only Washington and Hamilton, but *James Madison* as well."

Janine Oh, you wish we didn't have the Bill of Rights? That's a novel opinion.

Zoe flips through the notebook.

Janine Did you prepare that notebook for this meeting?

Zoe In all my classes, I mark the things that I shouldn't have to hear. It's a little way to process it so I can move on. I was going to send you a note, at the end of the semester. A really nice note. Saying, excuse me Professor Bosko, I really enjoyed your class, but you said a couple things that I found problematic, and you might want to be more thoughtful next time around.

Janine Well it's not too many things.

Zoe *(flipping to another post-it)* "While the slave ownership and the hypocrisy of men like Jefferson is galling to us, we do have to understand them as men of their time."

Janine That's not dismissive, that is trying to understand the past, it's like the anecdotes—we have to understand that justice is not obvious, history is carried out by flawed, imperfect humans beings—

Zoe But *who* are you humanizing?

Janine Everyone!

Zoe (*flipping to another post-it*) "Washington commanded admiration, even *adoration*, from the people who knew him."

Janine He did. What? He *did!*

Zoe *Not all the people who knew him.*

Janine Oh yes, asterisk asterisk asterisk. You can't make an assertion today without adding four or five asterisks—you say "manual laborers had it rough in the nineteenth century" and you have to add, asterisk, but not all laborers had the same experience, because of race, asterisk, and of course within each race people were treated differently based on gender, asterisk, none of which is meant to suggest any sort of endorsement of the gender binary, asterisk, meanwhile let's not forget that any discussion of manual labor is inherently ableist, asterisk asterisk asterisk. I mean none of it's wrong, but it's a *seriously* inefficient way to discuss the working conditions of nineteenth-century laborers.

Zoe *You have a picture of George Washington on your walls.* You have a picture of a *racist criminal* on your walls / looming over me as I sit here, like this—like this constant reminder, that I *do not need*.

Janine I also have a picture of Zapata - he wasn't perfect. I have a picture of Lech Walesa, he was a / Catholic stooge—

Zoe You bought that, and had it framed, and hung it up / because you have *no* ability to understand the perspectives of your students of color—because you have never even *tried* to imagine our perspectives—and that is *traumatic*, yes, traumatic, the constant dismissal of slavery is traumatic, the fact that you don't care is traumatic—

Janine Of course if you refuse to listen to my explanation—

Janine Oh my god *get over it!!!* It didn't happen to you! Be angry at what's going on now, be angry about Ferguson, but don't / be angry about slavery.

Zoe Don't tell me what to be angry about.

The Niceties 97

Janine My family is Polish, okay?

Zoe Good for you!

Janine You know what was going on in Poland in the 1770s, the country was being partitioned, it was being carved up like a prize hog between Prussia, Russia and Austria, it was being wiped off the map, and I read books about Catherine the Great, and I do not start *weeping*.

Zoe Because everything turned out fine for your people.

Janine You're a student *here*, okay? You have one of the best lives of anybody in history ever. *Ever*.

Zoe I need you to say it. I need you to say out loud, that first came 250 years of slavery, and then came a hundred years of segregation, and then came a deliberate and systematic attempt to exclude black people from good school districts and good jobs and to lock them up or hunt them down for doing things white people do every day. I need you to say that whatever else it stands for, America has systematically persecuted one part of its population, in a way that has benefited you.

Janine You are oversimplifying.

Zoe I'm so tired of remembering for both of us. This should be a pain that we share. I have been carrying all of this around on my own. I have been carrying your share of history, as well as mine, and I need you to take your half. I can't carry it all anymore. I will get exhausted and go crazy, I will have no joy—

Janine *You are making yourself crazy.*

With your post-its, with your paper, with your refusal to see the good in anything, it is clearly more of a strain than you can bear.

Do you think you are the first person in history to get hurt?

The grand sweep of history is that some people hurt other people and they never really make amends and you have to move on and win the next round. But you will not win the next round if you keep thinking like this.

It will cost you a grade. It will cost you jobs. It will cost you political power. No one likes to feel pity. No one likes to feel guilt.

No one likes anything that sounds anything like whining.

No one wants to hear more about racism.

You are so relentlessly negative and you make everything seem uglier, why would anyone want to listen to that? I hate seeing the world through your eyes!

Zoe *picks up her phone.*

Janine   By all means, rather than engaging in a serious intellectual discussion, be on your phone instead. Be a *millenial*.

Zoe *turns her phone to face* **Janine**.

Janine   That's illegal . . .

Zoe   In the state of Connecticut only one of the parties participating in a conversation has to be aware that it's being recorded.

Google.

Janine   Look, you can't—I hope you're still recording—when people are speaking casually, they're not careful with every word.

Zoe *just keeps holding the phone in front of* **Janine**. **Janine** *thinks about trying to make a grab for it, but doesn't.*

Janine   God, I barely remember what I said.

I—I helped you with your paper.

I listened to your concerns about class.

I didn't say anything wrong.

I didn't say anything wrong!!

Zoe   Okay, then you won't mind if I share what you said.

Janine   With who?

Who are you planning on sending it to?

The provost? The dean?

Zoe   No. No. They'd just end up like, having a meeting with us to try to "mediate a better understanding" or whatever. I think no one does anything real unless there's public pressure.

Janine   I am *not* a racist. I'm not. Ask anyone who's ever known me, I'm not.

Zoe   You're more afraid of looking like a racist than you are of *being* a racist.

Don't you want to think about that?

Janine I care very, very deeply about equality. I care—

Zoe Okay. What are you doing to promote equality?

Are you using the money you saved on your son's tuition to fund a scholarship for a student of color?

Are you getting all your white friends together to call congressional representatives and demand criminal justice reform?

Or do you actually never bother to think about racial equality, and now you're just trying to claim that you do to save face when you know you've been behaving badly, because in that case you can go fuck yourself.

Janine What do you *want*?

Zoe I want this to be your problem. I have spent my *life* living with this problem. Why are my teachers talking to me the way they do? Why are my friends looking at me the way they do? Why is this boy interested in me? Why isn't this boy interested in me?

Janine I get it, I do—

Zoe No you *do not*. That is my whole *point*, you don't get to say, *enough*. It keeps coming. Was I just imagining it, or did my sociology professor jump when I jogged past him in the street after dark? And will I ever be safe if that's the kind of thing that happens *here*? *Here*.

Is there anything for me to love about my country, any way for me to look around this country with love when everything is tainted, *everything,* and no one else seems bothered by it, everyone else seems happy as a clam—and I have the burden of seeing it for what it really is, *I* have to educate people, and *I* have to decide when to stop educating people—

Zoe	**Janine**
—and just let it go in order to stay likable and employable and *I* have to try to focus on my dumb and problematic assignments with all this shit racing through my head, and it's all *my* problem, how is that fair?? So here I am. In your office. This is your problem.	Zoe I'm sorry—

Janine Look, Zoe. You have made your point.

We will start the conversation again and I will do better.

Just—delete the recording.

Zoe Don't tell me what to do.

Janine I'll make—I'll make any changes to the curriculum that you recommend. This week. I'll change my lectures.

Zoe That's not really enough anymore.

Janine So what is? What is?

Zoe Say, "I'm a racist."

Beat.

Janine The only assumptions I ever made about you were that you were capable of great work and able to handle honest conversation.

Zoe Your work favors one race more than another. That's racism. So say it.

Janine Perhaps my work has had unequal effects.

Zoe Say it.

Janine I'm racist.

Zoe Now say, I'm not fit to educate a diverse group of young people.

Janine No! I won't say it. I am fit!!

Zoe *waits.*

Janine I may not be the ideal teacher in some cases.

Zoe Now say, what was that thing? I have sinned.

Janine Peccavi.

Zoe A little louder.

Janine Peccavi.

Zoe Thank you.

Janine Are you satisfied now?

Do you want to hear that I've learned my lesson? I've learned my lesson.

Zoe I want everyone else to hear that lesson.

Janine What does that mean "everyone else"?

Zoe I'm going to release the whole thing.

Janine Fuck you.

Fuck you!!

Zoe I think I have enough.

Zoe starts typing on her phone, taunting.

Janine *lunges at her, trying to grab the phone from her hand. They grapple for it.*

Zoe *shakes* **Janine** *off, just as* **Janine** *manages to twist the phone away from her—* **Janine** *crashes to the floor with a CRY of pain.*

She thumbs through the phone, trying to find the recording.

Janine Where is it. Where is it?

Zoe It's too late. I hit send.

End of Act One.

Act Two

The office. Mid-morning. About a month later.

The portrait of Washington is no longer on display.

Janine *bustles around, tidying, making tea from a small hot water boiler. She wears a back brace. She does not walk or move quite as comfortably as she did before.*

Zoe *enters. She watches* **Janine** *for a moment, then clears her throat.*

Janine Hello! Welcome. Welcome.

It's possible that she initiates the world's most awkward hug.

Would you like to uh—to take a seat?

Zoe I'm good.

Janine Would you like any tea, by any chance? I was about to have tea.

Zoe No thank you.

Janine Oh—you know—I won't either.

She takes a seat.

Thank you. For coming in.

Zoe You're welcome.

Janine How are you?

Zoe Um . . .?

Janine I know, I know, that's a—what a ridiculous question.

Zoe A bit, yeah.

I am keeping it together.

Janine That's good.

Zoe Oh, yeah, real good.

How are you?

Janine I am trying to keep it together, as you say.

This whole thing has been—quite something.

If I had known how many people could be persuaded to care about a history course I would have—

I thought it would be good for us to meet.

Zoe I want to apologize.

I've gone back and listened to that recording of our conversation again and again. The things I said have haunted me.

I didn't understand your feelings. And instead of trying to understand them, I tried to talk you out of them.

Zoe Yes.

Janine And you tried to tell me that too, and I didn't listen.

And for all of that—I apologize. People may not always be able to agree. But we can believe that another person feels the way they say they do. And that they have reasons for feeling that way.

Beat. **Zoe** *takes a moment.*

Zoe You know— **Janine** I really—

Janine I'm sorry—you go.

Zoe My friends tried to tell me not to come today.

They said you'd disappoint me again. Upset me even more.

Janine Well I certainly hope to prove them wrong.

Zoe I thought they would probably be right.

I guess I'm just—

I've been feeling lost in all of this.

I mean my friends have been *so* supportive. Most of my friends.

My real friends.

They tell me that I am brave. And that I am beautiful. And strong.

But I am not feeling any of those things.

I mean it's insane! All of this has been *insane*.

Like, first came the nice articles. Saying it was high time we reexamine how we teach American history. Saying I called much needed attention to microaggressions in academia. Calling me a hero.

Janine Yes.

Zoe ... Did you read the one about how one of Washington's slaves ran away and tried to start a revolution in Sierra Leone?

Janine I did, yes. I thought it was a good article.

Zoe Lots of flair.

Then there were the articles I expected. Free speech yada yada. "Back in my day we weren't so sensitive."

That kind of thing.

Then came the pieces listing all of the points I forgot to make. The one about how I didn't mention that Latinx history is even more under-represented than black history.

Janine Well *that article* forgot Native Americans, who were much more involved in the Revolution.

Zoe And the one about how microaggressions have a disproportionate effect on poorer students and I couldn't possibly understand their feelings.

Janine I didn't think that was fair though—

Zoe No, they were right.

Janine I didn't know you were from Westchester, incidentally.

I'm from Tarrytown. My mother used to clean houses in your neighborhood.

Zoe You think that proves something?

Beat.

Then the marches.

Then the articles criticizing the marches for not having a clear enough platform.

Then the articles criticizing the criticisms of the marches.

Then the blog posts criticizing the articles for paying attention to an elite school when there are so many more serious problems.

And I just want to be like—I'm a *person*.

I am a *person*. I am not some sort of walking manifesto you can *grade*. I am a person you should seek to understand.

And then I thought—fuck.

I know who else probably feels that way.

Janine I've been reading everything. Absolutely everything.

I can't stop myself. Even the comment threads.

Zoe Yeah no don't read those.

Janine I must say, you come from a generation that doesn't know the difference between a hyperlink and a footnote. You're all convinced that if you can link to someone who agrees with you you've proven your point.

Zoe I saw your son's op-ed.

I didn't think he should have written that.

Janine I thought you would agree with him.

Zoe Oh I do. But I think family loyalty is important.

I was raised not to criticize my parents in public.

Janine He was raised to speak his mind.

Zoe I just—I wanted to say that I'm sorry if this has caused problems within your family.

Janine I appreciate your saying that.

But Zoe—I'm grateful that you did what you did.

You've made me look at my subject and see things I never saw before.

I'm planning a new chapter for my book. A comparative study of the role of minority populations in revolutions. Looking at the Kurds in Iran, Afro-Cubans under Castro. The Uighurs under Mao.

And of course, African Americans.

Zoe Okay I don't want to like that idea but that actually does sound like something I would read.

Janine I've especially been concentrating on tracking down more diverse primary sources.

We always—we speak about African American history in generalities. We say life tended to be like this, or roughly 60 percent of slaves experienced that, but the letters, the testimonies, so many are from white men—

Zoe Yes, I—I know.

Janine —and the result is a colossal failure of empathy. *All* the science indicates that people empathize more with individuals than with groups. And what we need is—

Zoe I really—I know all of this? I don't need you to explain this to me.

Janine I'm not explaining! I know that you know it.

I'm simply expressing what's on my mind.

And of course I'm not limiting my explorations to history. I've been reading about our contemporary situation too. Mass incarceration. Police brutality. Implicit bias.

I've been reading a lot of Ta Nehisi Coates.

Zoe You should get a hat that says that. So everybody knows. And they can give you credit.

I'm not an idiot.

Janine (*taken aback*) Of course not.

Zoe Your tenure's under review.

Because you verbally and physically assaulted a student.

The university put out a statement saying that they understood the protesters' concerns and that they would be examining whether your presence on campus was in the best interests of students' academic and personal well-being.

Janine That's true. I won't insult your intelligence by pretending that isn't part of why I wanted to speak with you.

Zoe I think you already did.

Janine I want to propose a joint statement.

I say I'm grateful that you've made me aware of certain issues in my teaching and in the field of American History.

Which is true.

Zoe And I say . . . what?

Janine Whatever you want.

Zoe *Whatever* I want?

Janine You could say you're proud that your work has given rise to a long-overdue conversation about race on this campus.

That you thank the protestors for their support, and that they should feel as if their efforts have been a huge success.

Zoe *just stares at her.*

Janine It's not as if I'm escaping without punishment.

I am suspended without pay.

Zoe You'll be fine. I'm sure your husband has a fancy job too.

Janine Wife, actually.

Surprised?

Zoe The articles just said spouse.

Janine Well my spouse is a wife.

So you see even though you think I do not understand—in some ways, I do.

I know what it's like to be missing from the history books.

I have had to fight for things too.

Zoe That makes me more mad.

You should be someone who *knows* how hard it can be. You should be someone who bothers to think about being inclusive.

Janine I failed you, maybe. I was not the right teacher for you.

But for many students, I have been exactly the teacher they needed.

And I have ideas the world needs.

Publication of my book has been postponed indefinitely.

I have no classes. No research assistants.

I've been gently shunted aside from my DC consulting work and replaced by a Republican *moron* from George Mason who wouldn't know a coup from a garden party, so at this point my reputation is actually an issue of national security. My son is barely speaking to me.

Zoe I've been getting death threats.

Like, a *lot* of death threats, actually.

Some were specific enough to make the police think they could be serious.

I took an incomplete for the semester.

Janine Zoe. I'm so sorry that's happening.

Zoe I wasn't actually at the protests.

My roommates went. But I—

Even before the threats, I stopped going to classes. My professors look at me like I'm a bomb that's about to go off.

I don't really go outside anymore. Except for—once a day I walk to Walgreens. And I buy like—anything I shouldn't. Like if they figured out a way to make chocolate flavored Cheetos I would buy those.

And I am someone who—I take *such* good care of myself. But now—*all* I want to do is sit in my room, and watch Netflix, and eat bags and bags of these disgusting things.

Not just because of you. Or this. Because of—the news. This country.

Janine Yes. Never in my life did I think that I would be pining for Jeb Bush. Yet here we are. The Republican nominee is a—well, you know.

Zoe Yeah.

So yeah. I sit around a lot.

And like, I've read enough blog posts, so I call it self care.

But then I ask myself what would Harriet do? What would Rosa do? What would Angela do. And I think—you were right.

I have one of the best lives of anybody in history ever. And then I feel like a real shit for being such a weakling. And that makes me want more Netflix.

Janine Zoe I don't mean to be insensitive—

Zoe That's like, an almost certain tipoff that you're going to be.

Janine Yes. But . . .

All of this—is another reason why this idea of a joint statement . . .

It's a good idea. It's a good idea for you too.

If everyone, all around the internet, heard that you and I were collaborating.

It could be safer, for you.

And if—

I'm sure you've thought about this but—

When you're done with school—because I know that you will finish school.

With flying colors.

When you're applying for jobs. Everyone is going to be able to Google you.

And see this.

That you recorded someone, without them knowing.

That you took that recording public.

And I know why you did it! I know it was the right thing to do.

But employers are scared of that sort of thing.

Zoe   If someone can't see the value in what I did, I don't want to work with them.

Janine   That's easy to say. But it could be a hard truth to live with. But—imagine—

If all the alumni, from fifty, or sixty years at this future leaders grooming ground, read about how you helped reunify a shaken institution.

How an esteemed professor thinks you did more to invigorate intellectual life on this campus than any student she's ever worked with.

Which is true.

Imagine the job offers you could get then. I still say what I always said—you're a person of enormous potential.

Position yourself to use it.

It is not too late for us to help each other.

Zoe   Could I get a cup of tea actually?

Janine   Um—yes. Yes of course.

Zoe *sits still while* **Janine** *waits on her.*

Zoe What you're offering—or, I mean, what you're suggesting, right, because it's not like a generous offer, it helps you too.

That would be my father's dream come true.

He's been furious at me. He says I've been careless with opportunities he fought to provide.

Janine He has a point.

Off **Zoe***'s annoyed look*:

Janine I'm not saying he has the only point!! Just, he has *a* point.

Zoe See I find myself with three possible paths.

Path 1 is my parents' path. The path you're describing. I get the best possible degree. I get the best possible job. I make the most possible money. I show my black excellence to the world and I hope, I hope, that the world sees it. I hope that they aren't too threatened by it, and I hope I don't get so tired of the everyday awful that I snap.

Again.

Snap again.

Path 2 is I could leave. I could say, I'm done with this country. I shouldn't have to sign a statement to not receive death threats. I could just make like Josephine Baker. Move to Paris, or Brazil, or Nigeria. Publish Nigericanah. Maybe there I'll be exotic—like, oo, that's the American black lady. Maybe there my feelings will seem new and interesting and no one will tell me to get over anything ever again.

Or Path 3, I could consecrate myself to the cause.

I could sign on for a lifetime of marches. And protests. And fighting. And threats. And taking it on my own shoulders to fix the world.

So I came here to choose. 1, 2, or 3.

Janine Well please. Anything I can do to help you figure it out.

Zoe Talk to me about this statement.

I mean—it can't just say, good job, you can all go home now, right?

Because nothing's really changed, right?

Janine No—of course not—

Zoe I mean—you were right.

I was worried about—such *stupid* things before.

My GPA. Protesting Howard Stern?

I want this pain to be worth it.

If I'm going to get—targeted, and blamed and threatened. I want it to be for real changes. Real, concrete changes that mean something.

Janine Yes—to move forward!

Beat.

What if it said—

We both agree—

We both agree that for this college to remain a leader in higher education—it needs to make certain changes.

It needs . . . It needs—

Zoe It needs a well-funded student resource center with people of color on its staff.

Janine Oh.

Okay.

Yes.

Zoe You sound like you don't really agree. I'd prefer for you to be / honest—

Janine No! No I'm just surprised.

I would have thought your concerns would be more academic.

Zoe I'm getting to those.

Janine Ah. Yes. Good.

Zoe Just—there should be a building on this campus where students can walk in and say, I have a problem, and someone actually qualified is there to help. There should be therapists of color, and queer therapists, and really good tutors. And better help with financial aid.

Janine Yes, yes, there should be.

God, is there still not? There certainly wasn't when I was here, but . . .

Yes. Good.

Pause.

. . . You know what we should really say.

That we call upon the university to invest its endowment more ethically.

We did this in the 90s, to try to stop apartheid.

We should divest from for-profit prisons.

Zoe Oil companies. Guns.

Janine Banks that engage in predatory lending. Which is all banks . . .

Zoe All of it. We demand that the university defund now from all of it.

And invest in minority-owned businesses instead.

Beat.

We demand a decolonized curriculum.

Janine A—*what?*

Zoe A curriculum that doesn't assume everybody needs to read *Beowulf*. And doesn't assume that the people who made the laws are more important than the people who suffered under them.

Janine What if we say, we urge the university to offer a curriculum that reflects the full breadth of human knowledge and experience?

Zoe That sounds vague.

Janine It's meant to sound inspiring.

Plus it gets you out of certain inevitable quibbles over the fact that the sort of soft-power cultural influence you're referring to is technically more imperialism than colonialism . . .

Technically.

Zoe Fine. Write it.

We demand that the school recruit a student body that matches the population of the United States—

Janine *Yes.*

Zoe Within five years.

Janine That—isn't realistic.

Zoe I don't see why not, I mean, the kids are out there, the school just literally has to admit them.

You don't think there are qualified people of color / out there?

Janine You're trying to fix problems at the university level that are better fixed in the public school system—

Zoe You can't just wait for everything to be perfect—

Janine It does more harm than good to admit someone to an education they aren't ready for / and can't handle.

Zoe Of course you're afraid of it—of course you keep trying to do less.

Janine Zoe, what do you think is the ideal outcome from this statement?

Zoe This campus becomes a positive place for students of color.

Janine Yes, and for that to happen—we need to get more people onboard.

Ideally, faculty read this statement and think *"yes*. I will fight for those changes. I will try to make that happen."

Zoe Oh, yeah, as long as the old white people like it.

Janine Ideally other *students* want to help.

Ideally it becomes a model for other schools.

Zoe . . . Sure. Yes.

Janine I am telling you—from research and experience—that if you want support, you need realistic goals.

Zoe Was this college totally, 100 percent ready to admit women? Was that an easy, popular, realistic goal? Did you want them to take their time?

Beat.

Janine You're right.

Within five years.

Zoe Then once those kids are here, we demand that the university support them. Financially, academically, emotionally.

Janine *Yes.*

Zoe We demand questions on student evaluations about whether professors are biased or problematic.

Janine Well . . . yes.

Zoe We demand clear and immediate consequences for biased or problematic behavior.

Janine Wait—

Beat.

You're describing punishments. For people who make other people feel uncomfortable.

Zoe Yes.

Janine That is—

Uncomfortable is a very broad—

There are important ideas that can make people uncomfortable.

Facts can make people uncomfortable.

Zoe Sometimes, yes.

Especially when they're incomplete.

Janine The idea of evolution once made people uncomfortable.

The idea of gay rights makes many, many people uncomfortable.

Zoe I'm talking about ideas that make vulnerable people uncomfortable.

Janine And who do you think is going to draw that line?

Zoe I can draw it.

I can draw it easily.

Janine	**Zoe**
Zoe—my parents, okay? They fled Poland, because of this sort of thing. Under the Communists./ You never knew when the person you were talking to might report you for—for "wrong"/ thinking, and it was *crippling*.	But I am not talking about Poland. This is not a negotiation.

Zoe   Stop trying to teach me, or correct me.

You are not in charge of this conversation!! You shouldn't be sitting there approving or disapproving or weighing in on what *students of color need*—

Janine   I am trying to help—

Zoe   You cannot help, you are not an expert, you don't know anything about this—

Janine   I am an expert in change, I am an expert in university power structures, I have watched people try to change this college before—and I am telling you that many people will not be able to get on board with what you are describing—

Zoe   Fuck them for not coming on board!!!

Fuck them for caring more about their own needs than they do about *people in pain*.

Janine   Is that what you want me to write, you want me to write "fuck all of you," you think that will be persuasive?

Zoe   Fuck them for needing to be persuaded.

Janine   Zoe when you yell at people you do not change their minds.

Zoe   You do not get to dictate how I express myself. You want to help, okay, hear me, even if you don't like my tone, even if you *think*, based on your limited perspective, that I am getting something wrong, do the right thing anyways, help anyways, *that* is what helping looks like.

Beat.

Janine   Look Zoe, my movement—my people's movement.

In my own lifetime, I have seen it succeed.

Do you know how I found out that lesbians existed? How I found out there was a word for what I was?

I found out from a nun who was in the process of telling my class that it was something that got you sent to hell. The birth of my own identity came in the very moment when someone called my identity vile. I didn't have a chance to take one second of happiness from the fact that there was a word for it! Which also meant there were more of us!

That happened to me when I was fourteen years old.

And this year, the supreme court upheld my marriage.

Zoe Good for you.

Janine But if I had given up on everyone who hurt me.
I would not currently have a single friend, or family member, or colleague.

And if we had all done that, if we'd said, fuck you for not already caring, *you need to be punished for what you think*—We would never have gotten 60 percent of the country to agree with us. It's the reality of being gay in America. Or black in America. It's the pain of being 10 percent. You need other people on your side.

Zoe Some people aren't trying to win over friends. And family members.

Some of us have *enemies* who hate us on sight.

Some people don't get to stay in a closet and come out when it looks safe.

Janine That only makes it more important that you be careful, and that you be strategic.

Is it fair? No, no part of it's fair, it's not fair that you have to win over people who have hurt you, it's not fair that you have to prove your *humanity* to people who get to withhold their help, and quibble, and disagree, and offend, while you're fighting for your dignity, for your *life* it's not fair. It's infuriating.

But it *works*. It works it works it works it works.

It works to find language that appeals to people, it works to compromise, it works to play nice.

Zoe I should not have to try to appeal to people who have made themselves comfortable in a white supremacist world.

Janine No. You shouldn't have to.

But you are, in the end, stuck sharing the world with them.

That's how democracy works. You need a majority on your side.

Zoe Then maybe democracy doesn't work.

Janine Zoe—

Zoe I mean, "be nice?" That's your advice for me—*be nice*?

Janine Not "be nice," no, but there is a role for patience, for tolerance. For staying in a conversation with people you disagree with.

Zoe This is not the first time I have been asked to be nice. Or patient. This is the 500th time.

I was nice the first time I walked into your office. You did not show a lot of tolerance for my disagreements.

Janine I know. It's true. I didn't.

Zoe / I mean—all that I wanted was to like your class. I wanted to have the experience here that you had. I wanted to have the experience with this country that your family had. I wanted to thrive here. / That's all I wanted. My parents were asked to be patient. Their parents were asked to be patient.	**Janine** You still can.

Black Americans have tried *being nice*.

We have been so god damned fucking nice and patient—

Janine And it's *working. Things are getting better.*

Our parents had better lives than our grandparents. We have better lives than our parents. The moral arc of the universe is long, but it bends towards justice.

Zoe Uh uh. Don't quote Martin Luther King while you try to get a black woman to shut up and be patient with the problems in her world. Don't do that.

Janine Actually Theodore Parker said that. Technically. King was quoting him. Parker was a nineteenth-century abolitionist.

America is—it's taken too long yes, it's taken far too long, far far too long, but *America is working.*

We just had our first black president.

We're about to have our first female president.

Things are getting better. Now's a terrible time to give up.

Beat.

Zoe Yeah. We have our first black president.

And we're still getting lynched. We've been nice and patient for 400 years, and I'm not happy with the results. You are, clearly. You think things are good enough. Or nearly good enough. Getting there.

But I'm telling you they aren't.

And I'm tired of you not seeing that.

I'm tired of you trying to slow me down.

Beat.

Janine You know what.

Maybe it should read—

Zoe Maybe it should read, we demand that within five years, the faculty of this university match the population of the United States. And in furtherance of that goal, I, Yanina Bosko, am stepping down. Because I believe that it would be to the benefit of this college and this country if American history were taught by a person of color.

Janine Excuse me?

Zoe The thing is—I think someone else could do more with this platform?

I think someone else could do more to support students of color.

Janine That actually isn't most of what this job is.

Zoe I mean—let's say I sign your statement.

Let's say you go back to teaching. And then—what?

Maybe you give an extra handout on the the black experience during the Revolution. Maybe, before you discuss our miraculous democracy, you talk just a little about how American opportunity was fertilized by oppression. If I'm really optimistic, maybe you even remember to give me credit for those ideas. Maybe you show up for a couple protests. I mean I don't feel like I can count on that. But maybe you do.

Even if you do all the right things.

What are you really teaching?

You're teaching 100 future leaders a year, to say "yes, there are some *horrible* elements of the American past," asterisk, "there are still things to fix," and as long as they do that, they can go off into the world and become guilt free corporate lawyers, or investment bankers, or senators, or artists, and send their kids guilt free to great schools, and help them get good jobs, they don't actually have to give up a single bit of their money or their power. Because they're the *good* white people.

I don't think I can be complicit in one more generation of American leaders learning that if they get 5 percent better than their parents, then they can keep running the world.

I can't sign that piece of paper.

Because I think you should be fired. I think you should be done.

Beat. **Janine** *starts laughing.*

Janine Why me? Why couldn't you have wanted to study microeconomics. Or cognitive psychology. Or art history—oh, you would have loved them.

Them and their Dutch Masters. I mean have you met the other people on this faculty?

There are multiple people in this department who told me to quit when I had a kid. There is a person in the math department who voted for George Wallace. And you go after me?

Zoe It takes work to not be a bad person.

You know that right?

You can't just be the least bad person in a lineup and call yourself good.

Janine I did everything that was ever asked of me. I did the best that I possibly could. If you had been born who I was, when I was, you would have the same opinions, you would have made all of the same mistakes. You cannot say I am a bad person if there was no way for me to be better.

Zoe Someone else can be better. That's why I want you out / of the way.

Janine I have won teaching awards. I have mentored accomplished people who have done wonderful things.

Zoe You are an inherently oppressive and uninspiring figure for the students who matter most.

Janine That's unfair.

Zoe *laughs.*

Janine Don't laugh—that's not—that's not funny. You are describing a world where I am not right for a job because of my age and my skin color that's not funny that's—that's awful.

Zoe Good. *Good.*

I want you to feel awful,
because that is what's fair.

You know I am actually enjoying the opiate crisis. I *like* it that white people are having trouble with drug addiction. I want them to know how it feels. I want a white student to walk into this college and have only black professors. I want an all-black supreme court. / And all-black juries. I want you to sit in front of an all-black tenure committee. I want you all to work for four hundred years and not be paid a dime.

Janine You're describing a fantasy—just—numerically—

Janine That's not justice. You are not describing justice, you are describing revenge.

Zoe I am describing the world as I see it.

Janine To want another human being to be "done"?

What a terrible sentiment.

You can't imagine what it is, to make it through sixty years doing your absolute best, and then one day you find out you've made a mistake, and that's all anyone can see.

Someday you will make a mistake Zoe.

And when you do, I hope you are up against a person as merciless and as bereft of empathy as yourself.

Beat.

Zoe Look it's—it's really simple.

It's not enough for you to be right. Or even for you to be good.

You have to give up some of your power. Because you have too much.

You have more than your fair share.

Beat.

Janine I do not think a renewal of this fight between us is what this campus needs.

We both know that there are very serious, very urgent problems / out there in the world right now. And I think good people should not be fighting amongst themselves.

Zoe I give up. I give up. I give up on you. You have wasted so, so much of my time, never hearing—

Janine Maybe above all—I don't think this is good for you.

More of these articles. More of these worries about your future.

Zoe Oh. Yeah. Very convincing.

Janine No, really.

I think given your history of mental illness it would be better for you if the news coverage stopped.

Zoe I don't have a history of mental illness.

Janine You took a month-long leave of absence your junior year of high school for mental health reasons.

Zoe No I didn't.

Janine I'm not going to say who, but someone from your high school faculty went to teachers' college with a college friend.

Zoe I didn't take a leave of absence, I completed an independent project instead of going to class. Because my classes were uninspiring and stupid.

Janine You wrote a piece in your creative nonfiction class here about your search for a perfect antidepressant.

Zoe A piece that ended with my decision to do without them.

Janine Only—it's easy to imagine the articles. "Behind public activism, a history of personal trouble."

It would be—more unpleasantness. More division.

Another friend, who went to Johns Hopkins with my wife, said that the recording of our conversation included many classic symptoms of people who've suffered repeated mental trauma, and who've become a bit paranoid and hysterical as a result.

Zoe I'm not paranoid. Or hysterical.

Janine You did say, "I will go crazy, I will have no joy."

"Everything is tainted," you did say that.

Zoe Anyone can listen to that recording. Anyone can hear what you did.

Janine And do you think they will hear it? The general public in this country? The members of the tenure committee?

Do you trust my colleagues to agree with you instead of me?
The same ones who you say look at you like a bomb that's about
to go off?

Beat.

Zoe What would your son think of you now?

Janine All I want is what I had before.

The thing is, Zoe. If you make it too difficult to be a good person, you all of a sudden make people strangely comfortable with being a bad person.

Beat.

Zoe Do you know what made me decide to turn on my recorder?

Janine I haven't the faintest clue. I've wondered about that. I'd assumed when you showed me the phone that you must have been recording from the beginning but you weren't.

Zoe No. I wasn't.

Janine So? What was it?

Zoe You said I wouldn't get ahead if I alienated powerful people like you.

Janine That?

That's all?

That's all I did? I told you the truth?

Zoe That's exactly how power works. You get to say that people have to make you happy.

They have to talk just so. Act really perfect. If they ever challenge you, they have to do it in just the right way, very respectfully—and never too much. Or you'll hurt them.

With a grade. With an article. With a taser. With a bullet.

Do things my way or I will hurt you.

That's the opposite of whatever America's supposed to be.

I'm not playing along.

I do—I have enough privilege to say, "uh uh." Publish whatever you want. Do. Your. Worst.

Because the minute you do not hold anything over me.

I think that's the minute I will finally be free.

The thing is—I'm done with this place.

I am tired of trying to work with these compromised, rotten things.

My whole generation's done with it.

The past can go fuck itself.

America's still waiting for its real, radical revolution.

I'm gonna help bring it about.

Janine You. Idiot.

You missed the whole point of class!

Radical revolutions don't work.

They turn out terribly for the countries they happen in. Do you want to know countries that had a radical revolution? Haiti. Russia. Iran. Do you seriously think you'd rather be living in one of those countries right now? Seriously? Do you think the cultural revolution made China better off?

Zoe I think people in those countries aren't still living under their old oppressors.

Janine Because a hundred million of them *died*.

Do you have no respect for that?

You little American baby. You have no idea how badly things can go.

You know how many people moved to the U.S. in the last century?

Zoe Well a lot of them are moving back since they were treated so terribly—

Janine You know how many people moved to Poland in that time? Nobody. Fucking. Nobody. Revolutions. Suck. They suck. Revolutions lead to death, and chaos, and scarcity, and then two years later a brand new oppressor. They are not. Worth it.

That was the whole point of class.

Thank God America didn't have a radical revolution.

Zoe Thank God those slaves never rose up.

Janine . . . Yes.

Zoe You know what you are?

Janine Let me guess. A racist.

Zoe You're a coward.

You could never have been Washington. You would have been tugging on his arm, saying "wait a minute George, someone might not like this, wait, there's tiny little things you're not getting right."

Janine You never listened.

You learned absolutely nothing.

And now whatever you set out to do is going to go wrong.

10 percent, Zoe.

You're in the minority.

How exactly do you think a war is going to go?

Zoe If you were so afraid of revolutions—you should have worked harder to make them unnecessary.

Oh, I brought this back.

She hands **Janine** *her book on South Asia.*

Zoe I don't want your books.

Janine No. Of course you don't. Of course you don't. You and your whole fucking generation. Of savages.

Zoe You know what I hear when I listen to you?

Janine Your own thoughts?

Zoe A death rattle.

Zoe *leaves.*

Janine *is alone with her stately office and her piles and piles of books.*

The lights brighten on the portraits of the revolutionaries all around her. Including—previously hidden—but now visible again—George Washington. A spotlight appears on **Zoe**'s *face, alone in the darkness— exhilarated and terrified.*

Maybe we hear something that sounds something like drums. Maybe we hear something that sounds something like Trump's inaugural address. Maybe we hear something that sounds something like gunshots.

Then the lights snap out.

End of play.

Eleanor Burgess's work has been produced at Manhattan Theatre Club, McCarter Theatre Center, Huntington Theatre Company, the Alliance Theatre, Merrimack Repertory Theatre, Portland Stage Company, and Centenary Stage, as well as at the Contemporary American Theater Festival, and developed at New York Theatre Workshop, The New Group, Ensemble Studio Theatre, Salt Lake Acting Company, the Lark Play Development Center, and the Kennedy Center/NNPN MFA Playwrights Workshop. She has been the recipient of a 2050 Fellowship from New York Theatre Workshop, the Alliance/Kendeda National Graduate Playwriting Fellowship, and an EST/Sloan Commission, and a member of Page 73's writers group and the Civilians' R&D Group. Originally from Brookline, Massachusetts, she studied history at Yale College and Dramatic Writing at NYU/Tisch.

Interview with Playwright Eleanor Burgess

Researched, interviewed and edited by Sharon J. Anderson, CATF Trustee

Why don't we listen to each other anymore?

At my age, it's hard to imagine the halcyon days of thoughtful political discourse. When we were able to listen, it was because some groups were dominating the conversation and other groups were staying quiet or talking amongst themselves. Now everyone is speaking up and advocating for themselves and creating conversational chaos.

The Internet is also a huge, huge factor, and that is why I love theater because theater is the anti-Internet. The Internet allows us to put anything out there without looking another person in the face and seeing its impact. Its incredibly fast pace of exchange, dialogue and interacting with semi-strangers diminishes the obligation to listen to another person. If you lived in a small village, you would have accountability because you would probably know that person.

Zoe claims to be vulnerable yet she is very aggressive and her aggression is shocking and powerful. Janine's flippant and heartless approach to Zoe is equally shocking. They are both insightful, but aren't both monsters in their own way?

It was fun to write about two women who are both so firmly tied to their convictions that they will go down with the ship and bring a lot of other people with them. There's a joy to watching that on stage because in our personal lives, we seldom follow a conversation all the way through. We either have conversations with people we agree with, or we back out of a conversation the second it gets uncomfortable. The cathartic release of *The Niceties* is that neither of these characters will give up, so they follow that conversation *all the way through* and the audience gets to follow through to the wreckage they create. We never would do this in a conversation because somebody would clam up.

You are a Yale graduate. Did you experience the kind of academic rigidity dramatized in The Niceties*?*

No, but I'm now realizing that I took a lot of academia for granted such as the way we talked about American history or British imperial history. The emphasis at the time was on the priorities of British government and not the wreckage the British government created in other places amongst other groups of people. Looking back, I realize no one was saying, "This whole conversation is missing a huge element—the perspective of people who aren't from the elite Western canon."

Can an academic anticipate and address all the varied "triggers" the broad spectrum of women and minorities experience? Is it enough to treat students, especially those from marginalized communities with a modicum of respect and humanity? Could it be that simple?

It's not that simple because there are so many different interlocking issues. A professorship that reflects the population of the United States would be a good start. In a climate where minority students can expect to encounter very few professors who have shared their life experiences, "triggers"— individual, verbal missteps—are much more painful because they are part of a much larger system of curricula that is not sensitive. Professors can do their best to anticipate and try to address how students are going to perceive what they are saying, but they also have to push for changes in leadership and in how we put together our curricula. How do you put together a sourcebook? How do you put together an important document? It's a bigger undertaking than just trying to be nice or sensitive. It involves asking yourself, "Is a lot of what I know somewhat wrong?"

Zoe refers to her "mental trauma" or how "emotionally difficult" it is to learn from Janine. In light of that, an article in the September 2015 Atlantic *entitled "The Coddling of the American Mind" argued that too many college students engage in "catastrophizing," which is to say, turning common events into nightmarish trials or claiming that easily bearable events are too awful to bear. The article concludes, "smart people do, in fact, overreact to innocuous speech, make mountains out of molehills, and seek punishment for anyone whose words make anyone else feel uncomfortable." What do you think of that?*

Multiple things can be true at the same time which is what *The Niceties* is about. It's easy for people who are older and not a part of the political conversation to look at what's happening on campuses and say, "Those are petulant children." And it's partly true. Of course, this is not a traumatic thing. But, in dismissing the small parts, it's important that people not let themselves off the hook to the point of not seeing the more serious issue.

Why are American history textbooks not also addressing the black experience in America?

Janine is fiddling while Rome burns. She's addressing all the ways Zoe is not getting things just right: Zoe's putting her point across in a messed-up way, she's not following the rules of academic procedure, she's using words like "trauma." However, Janine does not hear the basic fundamental point which is, "Why did your course ignore black experience in America?" If she could hear that point, Zoe would probably feel a lot less traumatized.

What is Zoe not hearing?

Zoe is hearing things, but not valuing them as much as Janine does because Zoe is younger. She is *hearing* that freedom of speech and rigorous intellectual methodology are important, but Zoe disagrees that it is as important because she's had a different life experience from Janine. Janine's experience is that you have to use these old-fashioned techniques to gain prestige. Zoe doesn't want to hear that.

How do you respond to this quote from Becoming Wise: An Inquiry into the Mystery of Art of Living *by Krista Tippett: "The conundrum of the twenty-first (century) is that with the best intentions of color blindness, and laws passed in this spirit, we still carry instincts and reactions inherited from our environments and embedded in our being below the level of conscious decision... What we're finding now in the last 30 years is that much of the work, in terms of our cognitive and emotional response to the world, happens at the unconscious level." If this is the case, can Janine and Zoe not help themselves?*

All of this is so complicated and a two-hour play can't begin to understand this. Janine and Zoe do see each other as individuals, and they do engage with each other's thought. We can declare ourselves color blind, racist and post-racist, but America is still very racist in terms of who gets a job and who goes to jail. As an individual, I am totally capable of treating a person of another race with dignity and respect, but that does not absolve my structural role. That, in many ways, is what *The Niceties* is about. In a different universe, Janine would be a very good teacher for Zoe. She is able to see Zoe's intelligence, promise and potential, and is smart enough to encourage it. In the old use of the term "racist," Janine doesn't have much bias against Zoe. But outside of the office where they are meeting, the world is messed up, the country is messed up and Janine and Zoe to different extents care about that. That's where they can't get along. Janine is offering what she thinks is equality. She's trying to be for Zoe the mentor she wishes she had had when she was an undergraduate. But because Zoe has lived in an America that has never listened to her, equality doesn't feel equal. That's the real dilemma of the twenty-first century.

You have said that your mantra is, "Theater as church."

As a society, we have lost places where we can go to and tackle and wrestle with difficult, ethical ideas. Fewer people are regularly attending a church, temple or synagogue, and there really isn't any other place where you go to wrestle with how to be a good person in the world.

How about Starbucks?

Yeah, corporations would love to be the place where by buying a tote bag you have done your ethical duty. Film and TV sometime wrestles with those things, but film and TV are caught up in a much larger international financial system where things can't be talked because an advertiser wouldn't like it. Also film and TV are not "in person," and you can change the channel or turn it off the second you're challenged or uncomfortable.

Theater is a place—kind of like church—where you go to be in person with other human beings and to watch a live human tell you about feelings and take you on a journey that may be very challenging or uncomfortable to you. Theater can challenge you to be better in ways that you don't want to be challenged. If you are willing to go on that journey, you come out on the other side perhaps ready to look at your life with fresh eyes.

Memoirs of a Forgotten Man

D.W. Gregory

Cast of Characters

Kreplev, *a government investigator, mid to late 50s*
Natalya Berezina, *psychologist, mid 40s*
Alexei S., *a man with an incredible memory, early 30s*
Vasily, *his brother, late 30s*
Sonia, *their mother, 40 at first, later about 60*
Markayevna, *Alexei's childhood teacher*
Utkin, *Alexei's editor*
Demidova, *a displaced aristocrat, nearly 60*
Azarov, *a carnival performer, about 50 years old*
An old peasant woman

The action moves between an office in Moscow, circa 1957, and various locations in Leningrad in 1937–8.

The play is written so that four actors can double into 10 parts, as follows:

Actor 1: Alexei/the Amazing Azarov
Actor 2: Kreplev/Vasily
Actor 3: Natalya/Madame Demidova
Actor 4: Peasant Woman/Miss Markayevna/Mother/Utkin

It is also possible for Actor 2 to double as Utkin.

The Playing Space

I envision a space that can stand in for various locations—the office of the investigator, Natalia's office at the psychological hospital, Mother's kitchen, a schoolroom and so forth. Through the use of lighting, projections and on-stage costume changes, the action is intended to move fluidly from place to place and back and forth through time.

Note on Production

Any production or presentation of the play must include this statement in program materials.

Memoirs of a Forgotten Man was first produced as a National New Play Network Rolling World Premiere by Contemporary American Theater Festival (WV), New Jersey Repertory Company (NJ), and Shadowland Stages (NY). For more information please visit www.nnpn.org.

Act One

The set is a stark, stylized playing space that doubles for various locations. It is furnished with a table and two or three chairs, as well as some form of storage for props and costumes. Upstage, a large window—or the representation of one—and beyond it, AT RISE, an enormous image of Stalin, smiling benignly through the window. All we see of Stalin is an eternally staring eye, the tip of a smiling mouth, but the face is unmistakable.

As the action begins, this image fades and **Azarov** *appears: Dressed in a tuxedo, like a magician, holding a blindfold in his hand. In the window we now see a display—about 30 random words in various hands, as if each word has been written on a blackboard by different individuals.* **An old peasant woman** *writes one final word as* **Azarov** *watches. She hands the chalk to* **Azarov** *and walks off.* **Azarov** *addresses an unseen audience with a showman's flair.*

Azarov Thank you. Thank you, ladies and gentlemen, for your help in creating this list. I've asked you for words and dates that mean something to you. And since we've created this list just now—you know that I've never seen it before.

Azarov *looks at the display for a brief moment, silently mouthing what he sees. He turns to the audience, smiles. A beat, then he repeats exactly the display behind him.*

Azarov Story, donut, Petrograd, apple, bottle, Palm Sunday, promotion, sunstroke, organ, June 16, jewelry, kiss, December, drama, railroad, meeting, lemons, handshake, pickles, orange grove, grandchildren, harvest, avenue, perfume, discharge, Feast of St. Stephen, dacha, May 1, tulip.

Applause. **Azarov** *bows.*

Azarov Now ladies and gentlemen, shall we try a much longer list?

Lights fade on **Azarov** *and rise full on* **Kreplev***, in a drab government office, with a manuscript in his hands.*

The image of Stalin returns to the window.

Kreplev Memory. Madness. How do these things work together? When nothing can be relied upon? Consider a man tormented by a memory he cannot shake. It tortures him. Because he cannot be sure whether he lived it. Or imagined it. On this point, perhaps we can all agree: He must be mad. But consider another man. One whose understanding of the world is shaped by memories of things he knows never happened. Is he mad? Or merely accommodating?

A beat as **Kreplev** *assesses his audience.*

Kreplev   Perhaps a metaphor will help. Suppose we are married, you and I. And we agree to a shared understanding of our history. We tell the story often. How we met at the ballet. You, descending the grand stair on your lover's arm. I, at the bottom, bored, waiting for the crowd to clear. Suddenly our eyes meet. And we know at once. Within minutes, we're in the cloakroom, where we devour each other with a passion that has not abated to this day! (*Beat.*) Even though, in fact, you were alone that night. And though I saw you on the stair, it wasn't until weeks later, in a long queue to buy new boots, that I dared speak to you at all. And even then you were rude. (*A smile.*) We like the other story so much better. So that's the one we tell. Many a marriage relies on such accommodations. Should it not be the same for a nation?

The image in the window is now a solid brick wall—the unhappy view from **Kreplev**'s *office.*

Kreplev   When survival requires that we pull together for the common good. Who would refuse to make accommodation?

Natalya Berezina *enters with a satchel. She locks eyes with* **Kreplev**.

Kreplev   But suppose you are a man with a peculiar kind of memory. One without limits.

Berezina *clutches the satchel to her chest protectively.*

Kreplev   Capable of recalling every detail of everything he ever saw or experienced.

Natalya   You ask his name. (*A weak smile.*) I'm afraid I cannot tell you that, Comrade Kreplev.

Kreplev (*to the audience*)   How does such a man make accommodation?

Natalya   His identity is . . . uh, confidential.

Kreplev (*to the audience*)   It's a question that eats at me. I cannot sleep for want of the answer. (*Crossing to* **Natalya**, *with great courtesy.*) I'm sorry, Comrade Doctor. What do you mean by "confidential?"

He smiles. A beat.

Natalya Uh. Well, for the purposes of my study—any scientific study—that is to say, no professional is authorized—

Kreplev Not authorized?

Natalya The . . . that is, any . . . in any *medical* study, Comrade Kreplev . . . In order to gain the cooperation of the subjects, you see—

Kreplev Ah! You must assure the patient of anonymity!

Natalya That's, yes. It's standard practice.

Kreplev I see. (*With a smile.*) That does present a difficulty, though. If I'm to conduct a *thorough* review of your paper.

A beat. He regards her pleasantly.

Natalya I do wish to cooperate, of course.

Kreplev Of course.

She digs into the satchel and produces a file thick with papers.

Natalya I brought my notes.

Kreplev (*with great warmth*) Dr. Berezina. You are a woman of true integrity. Of course you cannot disclose *unauthorized* information. Nor would I expect you to. (*Beat.*) We can work around it.

Her relief is palpable, but she dare not move. He returns to the manuscript.

Kreplev Let's see . . . Natalya Petrovna Berezina. You're a psychologist by training. A fellow at the Moscow Institute. (*Turning a page.*) It appears you were on a track towards a medical degree at one point?

Natalya Neurology.

Kreplev But you never completed that degree.

He smiles, waits for her explanation.

Natalya My health. (*Beat.*) I took a leave of absence.

Kreplev (*sincerely*) What a pity.

Natalya I was ill for some time.

Kreplev Yes, I see. There's quite a gap in your resume. All the more impressive, then, that the Institute took you on as a fellow.

Natalya There's a new director now.

Kreplev Yes. Quite a few new directors now.

He notices she is still standing, nervously.

Kreplev Oh, but where are my manners?

He retrieves a chair for her.

Kreplev (*gesturing*)   Please.

Natalya *sits.*

Kreplev Can I get you something, Comrade Doctor? Cup of tea, perhaps?

Natalya Thank you, no.

Kreplev I'd offer you something stronger, but it's a bit early for a nip. (*Inspired.*) You won't say 'no' to this, though.

He opens a small tin.

Almond cookie? My mother's recipe.

Natalya (*as she takes one*)   Lovely.

Kreplev *returns the tin to its resting place. Then he consults the manuscript:*

Kreplev Where was I? Oh yes. Your paper. What an honor, that it's been accepted for publication.

Natalya Thank you.

Kreplev This will surely open doors for you.

Natalya I do hope so.

Kreplev Don't be so modest, Comrade Doctor. It could be a complete turning point.

Natalya It's very difficult to find a permanent position, these days— even with publication.

Kreplev And impossible without it. (*Cheerfully.*) Or so I'm told.

Natalya Yes.

Kreplev Well! I'm delighted that it falls to me to review your work.

So many of these scientific writings—deadly dull business. But this! This is fascinating. Psychology is a personal interest of mine, and the workings of memory—I confess, it's almost an obsession. (*Pleasantly.*)

Which is why it pains me to say this, Comrade Doctor, but . . . I do find some troubling gaps in your narrative.

Natalya In *my* narrative?

Kreplev You never explain how you came to treat this man.

Natalya It wasn't treatment so much as research.

Kreplev He was a guinea pig, then?

Natalya Not at all. (*Beat.*) I made a study of him. Not as an experiment. To understand how his mind worked. How his memory worked.

Kreplev And I for one am very glad you did. (*Indicating the folder of notes.*) May I?

Natalya Of course.

He sifts through the file.

Natalaya It's all in there—any questions you might have. I'm sure you'll find the answers there.

A beat.

Kreplev You call him Mr. S. Why is that?

Natalya I had to call him something.

Kreplev (*with a laugh*) To be sure. And after your paper, what remains, Doctor? A book, perhaps?

Natalya (*a bit flattered*) Hard to say.

Kreplev It is much easier these days to get a book published. Fiction, non-fiction, poetry. Even Pasternak is back in style.

He waits for her response.

Kreplev Not a fan of Pasternak?

Natalya Most of my reading is technical.

Kreplev Naturally. You being a scientist. And Pasternak is a sentimentalist. I never cared for his stuff, myself. But there's no denying, it's much easier to publish now. With the new leadership in place.

Kreplev *offers a pleasant smile as he waits for her response.*

Kreplev We are free now to disagree with the old leadership.

He regards her with a steady but friendly gaze.

Natalya (*carefully*)   My paper has no political aspect.

Kreplev   You never know what might give comfort to our enemies, in these uncertain times. (*At the notes again.*) Which is why every publication must undergo the most intense scrutiny. It's a matter of national security, as I'm sure you understand.

Natalya   Of course; absolutely. I do understand.

A silence.

Natalya   It's just that. (*A deep breath, a forced smile.*) I was told the procedure for review would be much different. (*Off* **Kreplev**.) Done by post?

Kreplev   Ah. Yes, I see! You weren't expecting to be called in. (*Beat.*) You're correct, Doctor, this is not the usual procedure for review. (*Confidentially.*) I've taken a . . . personal interest, you see. In your topic. And I found it . . . quite truly, so exciting, that I felt I had to meet you. In order to do it justice.

Natalya   I see.

Kreplev   I hope you're not cold, Comrade Doctor? These drafty old buildings. They always turn the heat down on Sundays.

He bangs on a grate in the wall.

Kreplev   Between you and me? I suspect there's a few
(*stage whisper*) old Tsarists managing these properties. Thinking we're all off to St. Basil's for Sunday mass. Instead of putting the time to better use.

He tests the grate. A beat as he observes her.

Kreplev   I met Comrade Stalin once. Shook his hand in fact. I was a young man then. And he was a fantastic hero to me. At the time.

He waits for her response.

Kreplev   His passing. Came as quite a shock.

Natalya (*steadily*)   It was a shock to us all.

She holds his gaze. Then, abruptly:

Kreplev   May I confide in you, Doctor?

Natalya (*a bit thrown*)   If you wish.

Kreplev *pulls a chair close to* **Natalya**.

Kreplev (*urgently*)   What does it mean to be dogged by an unshakable memory?

Natalya   Depends on the memory.

Kreplev   Not a memory that you summon, but a memory that intrudes upon you. Like Proust and his madeleines. (*Off* **Natalya**.) You're surprised I've read Proust?

Natalya   Why should I be surprised? You've read Pasternak.

Kreplev *laughs.*

Kreplev   Yes, to be sure.

He leans in, as if in a confessional.

Kreplev   But to my point: When I was a child, Comrade Doctor, there was a boy in my neighborhood who had an annoying little dog. Yapped, yapped, yapped all day long. His father used to shout about it; the boy would cry; there was banging about. That sort of thing. Then one day the yapping stopped. No one said a word. But walking to school, I saw that boy sitting on his front stoop. With blood all over his hands. His face had an expression of absolute . . . what is the word? Resignation? Despair? After that, I never saw the dog again. But every time I hear a high-pitched little bark, the image of that boy's bloody hands comes roaring back at me. As if to grab me by the neck. (*Urgently*.) What do you make of that?

Natalya   Hard to say.

Kreplev (*pressing*)   Is it normal? To be tormented by such a memory?

A beat as he stares her down.

Natalya   We all have memories we can't shake. It seems to be a function of the times.

Kreplev   The times are changing. Khrushchev is going to China. Did you ever imagine such a thing? The old order is coming to an end.

Natalya   So I've read.

Kreplev   You don't believe it?

Natalya   Must I believe it? For my paper to be approved?

Kreplev (*amused*)   Good point, doctor. Very good point: I've gotten off track. (*Back to the file.*) Now then: How did you come to make a study of Mr. S?

Natalya   He was referred to me. I say so right at the beginning.

Kreplev   But you don't say *why* he was referred to you. And you don't say when.

Natalya   Does it matter when?

Kreplev   Of course it matters. These things don't happen in a vacuum.

Natalya   Our first meeting was early in 1937.

Kreplev (*genuinely surprised*)   1937? So long ago?

He looks to the notes.

Kreplev   Why did you wait until now to write about it?

Natalya   I didn't. (*Off* **Kreplev**.) I've waited until now to publish.

He regards her as the light shifts. The image in the window fades to a cityscape—the view from **Natalya**'s *old office.*

Natalya   Mr. S. came to me for an evaluation. Trouble on the job.

Kreplev *makes a note as* **Alexei** *enters, a bit breathless, in a rumpled suit, under an overcoat that is years out of fashion for the 1930s.* **Natalya** *regards him fondly.*

Alexei   My best memory, you say?

Natalya   Not what I expected at all.

Kreplev   What were you expecting?

Natalya   Memory is usually a problem for the elderly. Or the infirm. But this man was young and healthy.

Alexei   By best, I assume you mean . . . one that makes me feel good?

Natalya *shifts to a clinical mode; now she is in control.*

Alexei   Or do you mean the one that I am best at remembering?

Natalya   Your strongest, most vivid memory, Mr. S. (*To* **Kreplev**.) For the purpose of my story, we'll call him Alexei.

Kreplev   Alexei. (*Beat.*) Good.

Kreplev *steps away to observe as:*

Alexei   All my memories are vivid, Doctor.

Natalya   All right then: Your favorite.

Memoirs of a Forgotten Man   141

Alexei   Ah. That's easy. It's a warm morning in spring, before the troubles. (*Stops himself.*) I don't mean to say troubles, but . . . before things changed. The order of things. I'm walking to school with my brother, Vasily. I have to hurry to keep up.

Kreplev *joins the scene as* **Vasily**.

Vasily   Alexei! Come on!

Alexei   As usual, I am late. So many things to think about! The air is warming as the sun rises over the rye fields. My breath rings before me like a tin bell . . . and the air smells of cloves and peaches. Blackbirds wing across the sky as it shifts from purple to a milky pink . . . and the clouds are wispy and chirp like crickets.

He enjoys the sight of the sky.

Natalya   How's that again?

Alexei   The clouds. They sound like crickets. And the yellow clay road rolls ahead of us. Wet from the night's rain. So muddy our boots squeak as we walk: The squeak is the flavor of apricots! Vasily barks at me.

Vasily   Fool! Stop dawdling!

Alexei   Oh, it is true. I always dawdle.

The **Teacher** *enters.*

Teacher   Alexei S.!

Alexei   A new teacher.

Projection: A blackboard. With the inscription: "Poetry Competition." And the office becomes a school room.

Natalya *moves aside to observe.*

Teacher   Which one of you is Alexei S.?

Alexei   I can hardly make sense of what she says. Because the chalk on the blackboard is humming.

Vasily (*after a beat*)   You blockhead! Answer her.

Alexei *shyly raises his hand.*

Teacher   Come forward.

Alexei   Forward. That ought to be a happy word. But from her lips—

Teacher   FORWARD!!

Alexei It's dark and sour—like dung.

Teacher To the front of the room.

Alexei And her voice is the color of coal dust.

Teacher Are you listening?

Alexei Ma'am?

Teacher You are to recite your poem.

Alexei *My* poem?

Sound of children's laughter.

A beat, **Alexei** *recovers from his embarrasment, then recites as a child might:*

Alexei Forward.

All of Russia will move forward! Always forward!

Into the bright and certain future

Into the glory of a new day,

Mother Russia.

Father Tsar.

We march along together.

A beat; he waits, hopeful.

Teacher (*without conviction*)   Excellent.

Sound of students' applause.

Teacher A fine poem. This is for you.

She produces a blue ribbon.

Alexei First prize!

Teacher It is the decision of the committee.

Alexei And out of her mouth, her words fall like copper coins. Ping, ping, ping—

Sound of coins falling—only **Alexei** *hears it.*

Alexei You would think words of praise would be softer—like clouds. Or sugary, like fondant. And float away.

Natalya *walks into the memory.*

Natalya You have a strange way of describing things.

Alexei But she is harsh, is she not?

Natalya *regards the* **Teacher**. *She makes a notation.*

Teacher Write it on the board, boy. Write your poem. It will stay there through the week.

Teacher *hands a bit of chalk to* **Alexei** *and moves away.*

Natalya That must have been a proud moment.

Alexei And even better things to come. Because after school—

Vasily *moves to the table. The schoolroom becomes a parlor.* **Teacher** *transforms to* **Mother**.

Alexei After school, we join Mama in the parlor. We had a parlor then.

Mother (*embracing him*) Lyosha! My sweetest one!

Alexei (*aside*) Most everyone had a parlor then.

Mother What a day, what a blue ribbon day this has been!

Alexei Thank you, Mama. (*Aside.*) Even though we were in the provinces—our parlor was beautifully furnished—with lush red carpet and gold icons in the corner.

Mother I will put your blue ribbon right here, in the family album.

Alexei (*to* **Natalya**) Pressed between photographs of Papa and Vasily, in his school uniform.

A beat.

Mother And there sits your brother, saying nothing.

Vasily's *nose is in a communist newspaper.*

Vasily (*at the newspaper*) Ha! Look at this: a strike in St. Petersburg, the infantry is called in, but they defy orders to shoot! I tell you—the tide is turning.

Mother Will you stop reading such things at table? It's rude.

Vasily The future, Mama. This is the future of Russia, right here.

Mother Then the future is nonsense. And your manners are as well. (*Pulling his hat off his head.*) Say something nice to your brother.

Vasily You do know why they picked his poem, don't you?

Mother   Because it's beautiful.

Vasily   Because it praises the Tsar.

Mother   Stop trying to make everything political. (*Confidentially.*) Vasya. This is your brother's special day. Invite him to sit by the fire, won't you? Offer him a sweet?

Vasily   All right.

As she moves away:

Vasily   Come here, Lyosha. Come sit with me.

Alexei *does. He waits as* **Vasily** *rolls a cigarette.*

Vasily (*leaning in*)   You have to understand, Lyosha: The world is changing. The old order—the Tsar, the nobles, the landowners and capitalists—all of that is going away.

Alexei   Where's it going?

Vasily   Into dust! And in its place, a new world will rise. Where the poorest man is the equal of kings. No more hunger! No more greed! Only justice!

Alexei *turns to* **Natalya**.

Alexei   Vasily often spoke that way. I couldn't focus on his words, because they were such a circus—the verbs and nouns dancing around his head. Purple and red and orange. It was impossible to concentrate.

Vasily   You don't get it do you? How could you? You're just a kid. But one day, Lyosha. One day, you *will* understand. Mama never can.

Vasily *lights the cigarette.*

Vasily   It's not her fault, she's old school. Which is why, when the new world comes, we must look after her, you and I.

Alexei   Of course.

Vasily (*pleased*)   Have a fag.

Alexei   Ah.

He reaches for the cigarette as **Mother** *returns.*

Mother   Vasya! What are you doing?

Vasily   You said offer him a sweet.

Mother (*grabbing the cigarette*)   And so you'll corrupt him?

Vasily   It's time he grew up, Mama. Learned there are no fairy tales.

Mother   What fairy tales?

Vasily (*topping her*)   No saints in heaven!

Mother   Vasya!

Vasily (*blowing past her*)   No magic Father Tsar to save us from the Krauts.

Mother   You wouldn't talk that way. If you'd gone to the army, like your father.

Vasily   Pfah!

Mother   If you had to sacrifice, as he has done.

Vasily   Sacrifice! What do you call this—the third round for the same ball of tea?

Alexei   Please!

Vasily   Holes in my boots?

Alexei   Don't fight!

Vasily   We all sacrifice to that fool's bloody wars!

Alexei   Uncle Nikolai is coming.

Mother   No, you're right. We mustn't argue, not today. (*Apologetic.*) We have blinis.

Vasily   Blinis. That will fix it all. Three hundred years of waste and oppression, erased by a single blini!

Alexei   I was 11 years old. Vasily was 16. And I had no idea what he was talking about. But I soon learned. Because that night, when my uncle Nikolai came, he brought a telegram.

A light shift. Now **Mother** *has a telegram, folded and refolded. She clutches it to her breaking heart.*

Mother   Oh my dear. My dearest—

She sinks down at the table.

Alexei   I didn't understand much, but I understood this: I would never see my father again. And because of it, Vasily could not go back to school. Though he seemed not to mind. And in a strange way, it made my mother happy. With Father gone, it meant Vasily would not be conscripted.

A light shift. Outside, the sound of breaking glass. **Mother** *and* **Vasily** *move towards the window.*

Mother   Vasya—come away.

Vasily   It's begun. It has started, Mama—

Mother   Come away, Vasya. Please, sweetest—Vasya—please.

Vasily *pulls away from* **Mother**.

Vasily   The new world is coming!

Alexei   Vasily was not conscripted. Instead, he joined the Bolsheviks.

A beat. **Mother** *goes out, and* **Vasily** *transforms to* **Kreplev**.

Alexei   I suppose that's two memories—but they are both very vivid.

Alexei *sits, pleased with himself.*

Alexei   Is that what you wanted?

An excited **Kreplev** *moves into the scene to observe more closely.*

Kreplev   This is fantastic! The teacher whose words were the color of smoke . . .

Natalya   As he perceived // it, yes.

Kreplev (*over her on //*)   . . . the texture of copper coins—

Alexei   Your words are much sweeter, I must say. A bit like overripe strawberries.

Natalya *is charmed by this description.*

Natalya   Strawberries.

Kreplev   In all of Russia there can be only one man capable of such descriptions!

Natalya   I've never encountered another.

Kreplev   Apricot boots!

Natalya   The confusion of his senses was fascinating. (*Back to* **Alexei**.) You said something about apricot boots?

Alexei   Apricot boots? Oh yes. Walking through the mud that morning. Yes. My boots stuck in the mud—when I pulled them out: Phloop! The flavor of apricots.

Natalya   Mr. S.—This way of . . . perceiving things. Has this been with you always?

Alexei   What way of perceiving things?

Natalya   Tasting sounds. Hearing colors. Your senses are a jumble.

Alexei   That's what Vasily says. But is that bad?

Natalya   Does it get in the way of your work?

Alexei   I don't think so.

Kreplev   It most certainly did! It got him into trouble on the job.

Natalya (*a look to* **Kreplev**)   Of course. (*Back to* **Alexei**.) It was your editor who referred you, was it not?

Alexei   Yes, Utkin. (*A bit embarrassed.*) I annoy him.

Natalya   Dear me. Exactly how?

Alexei (*cheerfully resigned*)   Like fingernails on the chalkboard, he says.

Natalya (*patiently*)   What have you done that offends him?

Alexei   It's what I haven't done. No notes.

Natalya   No notes?

Alexei   Such a strange thing—he asked to see my notes and of course I didn't have any. Why would I?

Natalya   Most people do take notes. I still have mine from university.

Alexei   I never went to university. I started at art college. Meant to be a draftsman. But it was so noisy—with all the colors. Magenta especially. It's like the roar of a train. Just saying it gives me a headache. Words are easier than colors—they come in pastels, usually. Except when Vasily talks—then the words are—phew—they almost glow! I notice that is true of other men of conviction. Like electric signs!

Natalya *ponders how to deal with him.*

Alexei   You haven't noticed that?

Natalya   I can't say I have.

Alexei   Comrade Kirov especially. His words had a green kind of glow. Like a watch dial. Sad what happened to him.

Kreplev (*this is a discovery*)   Kirov! (*Pacing.*) He covered Kirov!

Natalya   Among other things.

Kreplev *studies the file.*

Alexei   At any rate, I never take notes. But I never forget anything, either. Yet Utkin took offense! Said he'd never met such a lazy reporter. Now was that necessary? To insult me so? My old editor never minded. Of course, my old editor was drunk most of the time. (*A beat.*) Are you going to test my memory?

Natalya *considers.*

Natalya   I'll tell you what. I will write a series of numbers on a note card—at random. (*She begins to write rapidly.*) And you will look at the card—for 20 seconds, say?

Alexei (*eagerly*)   A game?

Natalya   Of a sort.

Alexei   I love games.

Natalya   After which you will tell me what you recall of the list. No need to be nervous. Here you go.

Alexei *looks at the index card as* **Natalya** *starts to time him. He hands the card back before the time is up.*

Natalya   You have more time.

Alexei   19, 68, 23, 99, 17, 47, 36, 84, 32, 44, 71, 25, 16, 10, 22, 11, 87, 38, 5, 63.

Natalya   That's—

Alexei   You want it backwards?

Natalya   The—

Alexei   63, 5, 38, 87, 11, 22, 10, 16, 25, 71, 44, 32, 84, 36, 47, 17, 99, 23, 68, 19. Good?

A beat.

Natalya   Yes. Thank you.

He waits as **Natalya** *chews her thumb and ponders the next step.*

Alexei   Shall we do another?

Natalya   Not right now.

Alexei   Is the examination over, then?

Natalya For now, yes. Thank you.

Alexei (*after a beat*) Will there be a report?

Natalya A report?

Alexei For my editor.

Natalya I can tell him there is no pathology in your history. Nothing here to treat. I could conduct more tests, I suppose—but to what purpose, I'm not sure. You seem to function perfectly well as you are.

Alexei I still annoy Utkin.

Natalya Then perhaps you should take a few notes. For the sake of getting on, you see.

Alexei Whether I need to or not, you mean?

Natalya Exactly.

Alexei I had not thought of that. What an excellent suggestion, Doctor!

He bows to her formally.

Alexei I shall apply your advice. (*Pumping her hand.*) Thank you, Doctor. Thank you so very much!

Natalya Not at all, Mr. S. Not at all.

Alexei *bows and leaves.* **Kreplev** *returns as the scene transforms to his office.*

Kreplev These are significant details you left out of your paper, Comrade Doctor. Where he worked. Where he grew up. His brother's political activities . . .

Natalya They had no relevance to my studies.

Kreplev They have relevance to the state. A man with such a gift—in a position of influence—

Natalya Influence?

Kreplev The state press is a very powerful influence. A shaper of opinion and understanding.

Natalya He wrote about parades and flower shows.

Kreplev He had a connection to Kirov!

Natalya He covered some of Kirov's speeches. I don't think he knew the man personally.

Kreplev   The leader of the Communist Party in Leningrad. And he never once approached the man?

Natalya   I don't know, perhaps he did. But what has this to do with my paper?

Kreplev   Kirov's murder is where it all began! We can agree to that, can we not?

Natalya   Where what began?

Kreplev   Mass arrests. Deportations. Executions!

Natalya (*panicked*)   I don't know anything about that.

A beat. Seeing her fear, **Kreplev** *shifts tactics.*

Kreplev   Forgive me, Comrade Doctor. But in matters such as these, nothing is immaterial. Whether it ends up in your paper or not . . . I must have every detail. (*Back to business.*) Now: Who else knew about this?

Natalya   My director, of course.

Kreplev   Director of the Hospital?

Natalya   Director of my unit. Dr. Freundlich.

Kreplev   Dr. Freundlich. Of course.

He looks at her manuscript.

Kreplev   What happened after that? You say that you sent him away, finding—how did you put it? No pathology in his history?

Natalya   That's correct.

Kreplev   Yet you called him back again.

Natalya   About a month later.

Kreplev   Why?

Natalya   It's not every day you encounter a case like this.

A light shift and **Alexei** *bursts into* **Natalya***'s office.*

Alexei   Doctor! It was such excitement to receive your note.

Natalya   I hope it's not an inconvenience, Mr. S.

Alexei   Not at all! I'm very pleased to have another test.

Natalya   It may turn out to be a series of tests. I have hopes of working with you over a period of time. I think Dr. Freundlich explained that?

Alexei Oh yes! (*Almost laughing.*) And why not? It's not like I've got anything better to do.

Natalya Have a seat.

He does so happily. **Natalya** *hands him an index card. He studies it briefly as* **Kreplev** *circles the scene to observe.*

Natalya (*to* **Kreplev**) As before—we began with a sequence of lists.

Alexei *focuses on the card.*

Natalya Each time, he repeats the material exactly as it has been presented to him. I increase the number of elements—

She hands him more cards.

Natalya Thirty, fifty, seventy, a hundred, five hundred—words, phrases, numbers. It's always the same:

Alexei *closes his eyes, moves his lips, and then, in a rush:*

Alexei Door, egg, knob, bottle, pea, carton, cantelope, horse, clock, handle, chair, river, // (*softly, underneath*) flea, apple, hat, snake, tile, tree, symptom, element, porridge, sandal, basket, ottoman, buffalo, seedling, wine bottle, pencil, floor lamp, pickle, samovar, seagull . . .

Natalya (*over him on //*) It doesn't matter whether the words are gibberish or not—whether I read the list to him—or he reads it to himself. All he needs is a moment's pause between each element—and he gives it back exactly as I'd given it to him. His memory seems literally to have no limits.

Alexei (*completing the list*) . . . leaflet, termite. Good?

Natalya Fine.

Alexei Shall I give you the original, Doctor?

Natalya The original?

Alexei 19, 68, 23, 99, 17, 47, 36, 84, 32, 44, 71, 25, 16, 10, 22, 11, 87, 38, 5, 63.

He beams at her.

Natalya That was weeks ago.

Alexei I recall it vividly—you were sitting right there—holding your clipboard and chewing your thumb.

Natalya My thumb?

Alexei You chew your thumb when you concentrate.

Natalya I do?

Alexei And it gives off the smell of ripe melons. You were wearing a light grey suit—like the one you have on now—except it had a different cut to the skirt. Quieter than this one—this particular grey is a little squeaky. But very flattering to your figure. The other one sighed. Softly. And tasted of . . Mmm . . . brown sugar.

Natalya (*to* **Kreplev**) It wasn't just that he could remember with great precision—

Alexei (*proudly, tapping his forehead*) Once it's in there, it stays.

Natalya (*to* **Kreplev**) It was that his senses were engaged all at once. So the smells, the sounds, the textures. All of that together made the moment—indelible.

Alexei Shall we do another?

Natalya *crosses to pick up a book.*

Natalya So I gave him a dictionary.

She hands **Alexei** *the book.*

Natalya Start with letter A.

Eagerly, **Alexei** *dives into the book. He moves out of the scene.*

Natalya Is this . . . the kind of detail you need, Comrade Kreplev?

Another beat.

Kreplev (*walking into the scene*) Dr. Berezina. Please understand. I'm not the only reviewer in this bureau. I need to ask these questions so that I can defend your work. Any discrepancy could raise suspicions.

Natalya What suspicions?

Kreplev It's a rather fantastic tale, you must admit. Someone might think you invented it from whole cloth.

Natalya Comrade Kreplev, I assure you—

Kreplev And without the ability to sit down with this man myself—

Natalya Comrade—

Kreplev It's extremely difficult for me to verify any of this.

A beat.

Kreplev   And if I cannot verify it—

Natalya   That's—that's why I've brought my notes. And a timeline of our sessions. If I may?

She takes the file and produces another document that she sets before **Kreplev**.

Natalya   As you can see . . . here—I've laid it all out.

Kreplev *studies the document with interest.*

Natalya   Every meeting—what took place, what was said.

Kreplev   You had quite a few meetings together.

Natalya   Every Wednesday. For more than a year.

Kreplev   Until the 9th of March. 1938.

Natalya   Yes.

Kreplev   And then?

Natalya   He went away to the provinces.

Kreplev   Where in the provinces?

Natalya   I don't know. We lost touch.

Kreplev   He left without a word? After working with you for a solid year—no warning, no goodbye?

Natalya   I was taken ill.

Kreplev   Right. (*Beat.*) What was it that laid you up again?

He waits for the answer.

Natalya (*avoiding his eyes*)   Tuberculosis.

Kreplev   Terrible disease. (*Making a note.*) So you were in confinement, then?

He waits for the answer.

Natalya   For two years.

Kreplev   Such a shame. (*Beat.*) But I'm confused by one point, Comrade Doctor. If you lost touch with Mr. S.—how do you know he went to the provinces?

A long beat.

Natalya I don't understand these questions, Comrade Kreplev. You've asked nothing of my methods—nothing of the science. I'm not sure you even care about the science.

Kreplev Truthfully, no. The science is rarely my concern. My task is to ensure that your paper contains no material that could compromise the state.

Natalya How could it possibly?

Kreplev You describe a man who could be a great asset to the people. Or a great liability.

Natalya Liability?

Kreplev A potential subversive.

Natalya Alexei?

Kreplev A man with a precise memory. In an important position—but unhappy in his job.

Natalya But he—

Kreplev With no political convictions—

Natalya He couldn't—

Kreplev Such a man could be easily turned.

A beat.

Natalya He could barely get across the street. Said honking horns smelled like fried onions. And every horn kicked out a different color. He stopped to count one day. Nearly got run over. *(Pleading.)* If he is a liability, it's only to himself.

Kreplev That is not how my supervisors will see it.

A beat.

Natalya I see. You think memory is like a camera. Taking pictures to be stored away. It's not a camera.

Kreplev *(amused)* More of a canvas, then?

Natalya Yes, more like a canvas. Our minds . . . paint impressions upon it.

Kreplev Fuzzy, in other words?

Natalya Imprecise. But over time, the impressions change. Because we change.

Kreplev (*a shift in tone*) As we grow up, you mean? A man sees things much differently than he did as a boy.

Natalya The function of memory is not to document experience, Comrade Kreplev. It's to tell us what it means.

Kreplev And what about a man whose memories *never* change?

Natalya It's not the gift you think it is.

A light shift and **Alexei** *enters again with urgency.*

Alexei Doctor! I am so glad to see you.

Natalya Alexei. Do come in.

Alexei It's been such a week!

He paces.

Alexei I could hardly wait for our session.

Natalya You seem a bit . . . agitated.

Alexei It's Utkin.

Natalya Still having difficulties at work?

Alexei Oh so many. Just yesterday—

Light shift—the office transforms to the newspaper office. **Alexei** *picks up a manuscript and begins to mark it up with an assignment.* **Natalya** *steps back to observe the story.*

Alexei I was at the office, wrapping up an assignment. When Utkin came barreling in.

Utkin *enters.*

Utkin Where's the story?

Alexei *hands him the manuscript.*

Alexei (*to* **Natalya**) An advance on the International Workers' Day Celebration. Parades, carnivals—greasy food—speeches, speeches, speeches! Every year, the same thing. You could run the exact same story, no one would care.

*As **Utkin** picks up a pen.*

Alexei   Recalling your advice, I said: (*to* **Utkin**) Do you want my notes?

Utkin   Your notes?

Alexei   I took notes. Just as you wanted. Here they are.

Utkin   I don't need your notes, Alexei Ivanovich. I need the art for this story.

Alexei   This is what the librarian gave me.

*He produces a photo. He watches as **Utkin** examines the picture.*

Alexei   But there is something wrong with it.

Utkin   This is fine. The crowd is huge; the day is sunny.

Alexei   But someone's missing from the picture.

Utkin   Who's missing?

Alexei   Comrade Bukharin. He spoke at the celebration last year.

Utkin   You're confused, Comrade.

Alexei   Oh no. He was definitely seated. Waiting his turn. And he was a bit bored, I think, or nervous perhaps, 'cause he kept looking down, rubbing his hands together. Gave off the smell of turpentine. And that was odd—because he didn't do that the other times I'd heard him speak.

A beat.

Utkin   Are you daft?

Alexei   I was there. (*To* **Natalya**.) And Bukharin's words—my God—they don't just glow like a watch dial, they spin across the room.

Utkin   Comrade. How is it you do not understand me? This is the approved photograph. It came from the Central News Bureau.

Alexei   That's so strange. Why would the Central News Bureau approve a mistake?

Utkin   It is not a mistake! This is the photo we are to use. Use it!

Utkin *goes off, with the photo.*

Alexei (*to* **Natalya**)   He can be difficult that way. So sharp—his words smell like vinegar. And fall out of his mouth like little bits of flint. (*Beat.*) My theory? He needs a sweetheart. Vasily would put it more crudely, but you get what I mean.

Utkin *returns.*

Utkin   Comrade. This business about Bukharin? He did not speak last year.

Alexei   But I wrote it up—I quoted him extensively—

Utkin   He did not speak last year.

Alexei   Shall I find it for you in the archives?

Utkin   The archives are being re-organized. New directives are on the way. Bukharin did *not* speak last year. He did *not* speak here—and you did *not* cover his speech. Take all that business out of the story and have it on my desk by 5 o'clock.

Utkin *starts to go, stops.*

Utkin   It's for the good of the people.

Alexei (*unsure*)   All right.

Utkin *goes out.*

Alexei (*to* **Natalya**)   Though I can't see how. But I didn't think I should argue with him—not when he's in that kind of mood.

Natalya   That sounds wise.

Alexei   Still, it bothers me. Of course I recall Bukharin's speech: "My fellow citizens—friends and comrades. On this day, the anniversary of a great sacrifice by working men and women . . ." (*Off* **Natalya**.) I won't repeat it all, but he goes on to talk about how wonderful things will be. One day. When the Revolution is realized . . . The usual stuff. I don't see why you would want to wipe that out of the record.

Kreplev, *now circling the edge of the scene, catches her eye.*

Natalya   Perhaps it is as your editor suggested. For the good of the people. And we ought not to question.

A beat as he considers.

Alexei   Perhaps you're right.

Natalya   After all.

(*Directed at* **Kreplev**.) So much good has come of the Revolution.

Alexei   Till next time, Doctor?

Natalya   Next time.

She extends her hand to shake his, but **Alexei** *takes her hand and kisses the back of it instead.*

This throws her a bit; he withdraws.

Natalya (*covering her embarrassment*)   Old world manners. I found it charming.

Kreplev *crosses into the scene with the folder of notes.*

Kreplev   And once again: Your paper says nothing of this exchange. You say only that he had conflicts at work.

Natalya   Which he did.

Kreplev   Did you report this incident to your director?

Natalya   He wasn't interested in those kinds of details.

Kreplev   Someone was. There's an item about it in your file.

She pales.

Natalya   *My* file?

Kreplev   Yes, your file, Comrade Doctor. We all have files. As I'm sure you know.

Kreplev *retrieves a different folder. He opens it and reads:*

Kreplev: "Berezina's patient load includes a reporter for the State News Service. Known to be uncooperative." The reporter, not you. (*Back to the file.*) "This relationship bears close watching as there may be improprieties involved."

He closes the folder.

Kreplev   You're surprised?

Another beat.

Kreplev   Sadly, your file does not explain what the improprieties were.

Another beat.

Kreplev Perhaps you'll shed some light on it?

Natalya I don't know what you're talking about.

Kreplev Do you want to tell me again why your studies were interrupted?

Natalya You know why, if you've seen my file.

Kreplev Indeed. Sorry mess, that was. But you were lucky, Comrade Doctor. Only two years in a labor camp? Most people in your shoes got ten.

A beat.

Natalya Am I under arrest?

Kreplev Goodness, no, Comrade Doctor! Nothing of the kind—

Natalya Then I'd like to go, please.

Kreplev But we've more to talk about.

She prepares to leave.

Natalya I have nothing more to say. If my paper is not ready for publication—

Kreplev My dear doctor—

Natalya I shall withdraw it.

Kreplev Please do not mistake me. I called you in this morning so that we could speak freely. (*Confidentially.*) So that we could help each other.

Natalya Help each other? How?

Kreplev Comrade Doctor: I know you paid dearly for sins committed by others.

He watches for her reaction.

Kreplev If you had to make a few *moral* compromises in order to get by . . . Who could blame you?

She turns away.

Kreplev You weren't the first prisoner to curry favor with the camp's commandant.

Natalya *begins to weep.*

Natalya   I did what I could to survive.

Kreplev   As anyone would.

Natalya   And these favors you speak of, they were not volunteered.

Kreplev   Of course they were not. (*Beat.*) How you begin to rebuild your life after that, I cannot imagine.

Natalya   It took me ten years—more than ten years—just to get back to where I'd begun. Do you know what I did in the meantime?

Kreplev   I understand you're an excellent typist.

Natalya *weeps anew.*

Kreplev   Dr. Berezina, I tell you these things not to frighten you, but because I'm in a position to help you. But it's essential that you be truthful with me. So that we can trust each other.

Natalya   I've told you what I know.

Kreplev   You met with Alexei every week. Your sessions, surely, were not confined just to the study of his memory.

Natalya   Of course we spoke of other things. (*Off* **Kreplev**.) Nothing political. Family matters, mostly.

Kreplev   Family matters? What did he say about it?

Natalya   After his fight with Utkin, things took an ugly turn.

Kreplev   Ugly in what way?

Natalya   Something to do with his brother.

A light shift. **Natalya** *observes as the scene transforms to* **Alexei**'s *room in a communal house in St. Petersburg.*

Enter **Alexei**. **Kreplev** *transforms to* **Vasily** *as* **Natalya** *moves off to observe.*

Vasily   What possessed you to shoot off your big mouth?

Alexei   There'd been a mistake.

Vasily   It's Bukharin. You do know what's happened to Bukharin don't you?

Alexei   Got into some kind of trouble, didn't he?

Vasily   Some kind of trouble? He's a traitor. A saboteur. Because of him, we've got production break-downs all over the country. We have a backlog of orders down at the paper mill—orders I can't fill because we can't get the pulp—we can't get the pulp because someone up the line has been paid off. Why would anyone want to see his picture anyway?

Alexei   What's Bukharin got to do with the paper industry?

Vasily   For someone who makes a living writing news reports, you are incredibly ignorant of current affairs.

Alexei   I don't pay that much attention to politics.

Vasily   You work for the state press! How can you not pay attention to politics?

Alexei   Have you ever heard a politician speak? The words are like rubber balls. Bouncing around, bouncing and glowing and throbbing and shaking—I can't make sense of it.

Vasily   Oh my head.

Alexei   I'll get you an aspirin.

Alexei *retrieves an aspirin and a glass of water for* **Vasily**, *who downs them both quickly.*

Alexei   Are you staying to supper?

Vasily   How did you leave it with Utkin? Are you in trouble again?

Alexei   He gets mad, then he gets over it.

Vasily (*quietly*)   Listen to me. Things are heating up. You understand?

Alexei   Heating up. Let me think: Heat. That word tastes sour, but it's awfully bright-colored.

Vasily   Let's have a little music, shall we? Radio?

Alexei   Oh surely if you like!

Alexei *crosses to the cupboard. He turns on the radio. An orchestra plays—a Tchaikovsky concerto.* **Alexei** *listens—and looks above him. He's seeing colors all around and finding them delightful.* **Vasily** *is used to this routine. He puts his arm around* **Alexei** *and leads him to the center of the room.*

Vasily   Heating up. (*Softly*.) It's a metaphor, Lyosha. You turn up the gas under a pot—the pot gets hot. Turn it up some more, the pot boils away. You understand?

Alexei   The pot boils. Surely.

Vasily   If I don't get the pulp I need—I can't meet my orders. Someone might think I want it that way. You see?

Alexei   Who would think that?

Vasily   No one should. But if word got around that my own brother has been booted out of the News Bureau because he's corrupting the coverage—

Alexei   Who's corrupting? I just asked a question.

Vasily   Stop asking questions. When they tell you to do something, just do it.

At the door, **Mother** *enters with a shopping basket. Hearing the music,*

Mother   Ah. The Philharmonic!

Alexei *takes the basket from her and carries it to the table.*

Alexei   Vasily wanted music.

Vasily (*with a kiss on the cheek*)   Mama. If you don't mind.

Mother   It's lovely. Just a bit loud.

She turns down the volume.

Mother   What luck I had at the market today. The saints smiled upon us.

Vasily   Did the saints send cigarettes?

Alexei   His head is bad again.

Mother   Then I will make you some tea. Look.

Alexei (*at the basket*)   Fresh beets!

Mother   The last of them—and rather tatty. But they'll do for soup.

Alexei (*finding a brown paper package*)   What's this?

Mother   That's for you. From your Uncle Nikolai.

Alexei   For me? What a delight!

Alexei *unwraps the package, revealing a commemorative book about his home town.*

Mother He's had it for years. Thought you might like to have it.

Vasily Uncle Nikolai isn't usually so generous with his collectibles.

Mother It was published to commemorate the new church in Pochinok.

Alexei St. Anselm's.

Mother You were baptized there.

Alexei Who could forget?

Vasily Pft!

Alexei It was terrifying—pushed into the water that way.

Mother Your great-grandfather built the original St. Anselm's—and your father and uncle helped build the new one.

Alexei That man there. Looks a bit like the Tsar.

Mother It's his brother, the Grand Duke. He came to dedicate the church—that's how influential your family was at the time.

Alexei And there's Papa. With Nikolai!

Mother They were both on the church council. That photograph with the Grand Duke was taken right before your uncle left for St. Petersburg.

Vasily What are you doing with that Mama? Truly? Nikolai should know better.

Mother It's just a memory book. And Lyosha will enrich those memories for us. Won't you my dear?

Alexei What do you want to know, Mama?

Mother Take me there. Take me back to Pochinok. Make it come alive again. Make me see it and smell it the way you did—you describe things so wonderfully.

Alexei The bookseller and the bakery next door—words dancing off the page—and the color of bread in the air—you could taste the crowds on a Saturday morning—salty and sweet at the same time. And everyone in a rush and yet—everyone had plenty of time.

Mother We all had time in those days. It's true.

Alexei And Nikolai on a Saturday morning would come round to collect us. Take us fishing—though Vasya never liked it much.

Mother Because he could never get any fish.

Vasily Mama. Nostalgia is a dangerous indulgence.

Mother Later then—when your brother is not here to be offended by pleasant memories.

Vasily I'm serious, Mama. Don't let anyone see this. Wrap it up and hide it under the mattress.

Mother Nonsense. We'll keep it on the book shelf where it belongs.

Vasily Mama. Not everyone in this book is in favor right now. And the cause it celebrates is certainly not in favor. If Nikolai gave it to you—it's because he didn't want to be caught with it himself.

Mother Such talk, Vasya.

Alexei I think Vasya is upset because things aren't going well at the mill.

Mother No?

Vasily Did I ask you to tell her that?

Alexei She worries about you.

Vasily There's nothing to worry about. Things are fine at the mill. It's all under control.

Natalya *transforms to their neighbor* **Demidova**.

Demidova Sonia Mikhailovna!

She crosses off to knock on the door to their rooms.

Vasily Demidova. That old hag.

Demidova (*off*) Sonia Mikhailovna?

Vasily Don't let her in.

Mother I have to let her in, Vasya. She does us favors all the time.

Alexei Blueberry preserves last week.

Demidova Sonia? I know you're in there.

Vasily *puts the picture book on a chair and sits on it.*

Vasily She's a miserable gossip.

Alexei They were lovely preserves.

Vasily *pulls a small paperback out of his jacket as* **Mother** *opens the door.*

Mother Maria Stepanovna. Good evening to you.

Demidova   Sonia, my dear, we need to speak—oh, hello Alexei.

Alexei   Good evening, Madame Demidova.

Demidova   Vasily. Good evening.

Vasily *grunts, does not look up.*

Mother   Before I forget! I have your mending.

She brings a folded dressing gown to **Demidova**, *who examines a seam carefully.*

Demidova   My dear. What fine work! Such delicate stitches.

Mother   It's nothing—a simple repair.

Demidova   You are too kind. And now, I have something for you.

Demidova *unfolds a towel to reveal a handful of dried fruits.*

Demidova   Too many for me. Thought I'd share.

Mother   Currants! Goodness!

Demidova   And this.

She presents a lemon.

Mother   A lemon! How delightful! But how did you manage it?

Demidova   The Nagorskys moved out last night. Left everything.

Alexei   They've gone?

Vasily *perks up.*

Vasily   What do you mean, left everything?

Demidova   Everything. Furniture, clothing—the food in the cupboard.

Mother   They never said a word to us.

Demidova   And you were so friendly with them, too. Though just between you and me, Sonia? I thought they were a bit off.

Mother   Mister Nagorsky was a lovely gentleman.

Alexei   He lent us books.

Mother   Just the other day—

Vasily   But you returned them.

Demidova   He was lovely, it's true. But I did not much care for Madame Nagorsky. She talks too much.

Vasily *snorts.*

Demidova   And she always left the kitchen a mess.

Mother   I never noticed that.

Demidova   Goodness! She slopped all over the place. Especially when she made that dreadful goulash—oh, the odor lingered for days. A supreme lack of consideration. That was her problem.

You don't think so, Vasily?

Vasily   What do I know? They aren't my neighbors.

Demidova   Yes, what do you know, Vasily?

Vasily   Only what I need to know. I think that's the best policy, don't you?

Demidova   So polite that one.

Mother   His head. It's bad tonight.

Demidova   Reading will only make it worse. (*a beat*) What's that you have there, Vasily? Poetry?

Alexei   Looks like Gorky.

Demidova   Gorky! Ah Gorky! Did I tell you? I saw the Lower Depths when it first played the Art Theatre. And do you know? Chekhov was in the audience that night! Did I tell you Sonia—did I tell you Alexei? How I flirted with Chekhov at the interval? I must have told that story 100 times.

Vasily   A hundred and fifty.

Mother   Do tell it again. I so like hearing it.

Demidova   Such a man. Not just a great artist—of course I did not know—none of us knew—how ill he was, but still. When he walked across the room toward me—I could barely breathe. Such regal bearing, such a gentlemanly manner—such intelligence in those wonderful, warm eyes. He kissed my hand! And I felt the blood rushing to my cheeks.

Vasily   You don't say.

Demidova   I'll have you know I kept him very entertained for a full 15 minutes—a few minutes more and I'm convinced he'd have written a part just for me. Instead of that awful Olga Knipper. Insufferable woman! But then the lights dimmed, he went back to his seat, and that was that.

Mother Fate turns on such slight moments, doesn't it.

Demidova Indeed. I swear if it had been a different circumstance—I might be the widow of a great playwright now. Instead of a lighting man.

Vasily You'd still be living in a communal apartment.

Mother Vasya.

Demidova Really, Sonia. I don't know what to say. I'll come back another time, when your son is feeling better.

Mother Please don't take offense, Maria. He's always been unmannerly—I have tried with him, believe me. But he's a grown man, so what can I do?

Demidova I am sorry for you, then. I'll see you another day, my dear.

Mother Thank you again for the fruit.

Exit **Demidova**. **Mother** *shuts the door.*

Mother What's to be gained by this display?

Vasily Why do you indulge that woman?

Mother She just likes to talk.

Vasily How did she get into the Nagorsky's rooms?

Mother I'm sure she spoke to the manager.

Vasily And I suppose he stood watch, too, while she helped herself to more than currants and lemons.

Mother Vasya. Such an accusation!

Vasily You shouldn't accept gifts from her, Mama.

Mother (*softening*) How is your head, Vasya? Still hurting?

Vasily Still attached to my neck.

Mother I'll put some water on. A cup of tea and you'll feel better. You're staying to supper?

Vasily If I may.

Mother Of course you may. Sweetheart. You're always welcome.

Vasily Next time, I come. (*Brighter.*) I'll bring sausages.

Mother That would be lovely.

She takes a kettle and goes out. **Vasily** *goes to the door, makes sure it is closed.*

Vasily (*quietly*)   What did you hear last night? Anything?

Alexei   Some noise in the hall. But I didn't think much of it. Some of the other tenants often come in drunk.

Vasily   Did you see anything?

Alexei   No. But when I left for work this morning, I had a strange, terrible feeling as I passed their rooms. The door wasn't open, but there was a hollow sound coming from inside—and the light around the door—it was all wrong. It wasn't until I got to work that I realized—the curtains were still drawn! (*Beat.*) Mr. Nagorsky was ever so pleasant. Maybe it's a mistake, Vasya—maybe they've just gone on holiday. Should we return the fruit?

Vasily (*pulling him aside*)   Listen to me. The Nagorskys are not on holiday; you know they're not on holiday. And they didn't go on their own.

Vasily *turns up the radio. He draws* **Alexei** *back to the center of the room.*

Vasily (*quietly*)   I can't get Mama to understand this—but if either of you has an opinion about the Nagorskys, you must keep it to yourselves. And keep your head down from now on.

Alexei   My head down.

Alexei *ponders the phrase.*

Vasily   Don't call attention to yourself. If people say things that aren't exactly as *you* remember—just look past it.

Alexei (*trying to understand*)   Look past it.

Vasily   Forget it ever happened, Lyosha.

Alexei   All right, yes. I see. Yes.

Vasily *turns down the radio and picks up the lemon.*

Vasily   A little lemon in the tea is a pleasant thing. Might as well use it, I suppose. Like a cup?

Alexei   Yes, thank you.

Vasily *leaves the room.*

Alexei   Just look past it.

Alexei *gestures the action. The movement generates a wash of color across the room and* **Alexei** *is delighted.*

Alexei   Ah. Tangerine.

A light shift; **Alexei** *leaves and* **Kreplev** *and* **Natalya** *return to the scene.*

Kreplev (*moved by the story*)   That's a very detailed account, Doctor Berezina. I appreciate your willingness to be so forthcoming.

Natalya   What else can I tell you?

Kreplev   You can tell me where he is.

Natalya   As I said—

Kreplev   No harm will come to him. I promise you. And no one will know you told me. That I can guarantee.

Natalya   How?

Kreplev   No one knows you're here today. After you go, there will be no record of this interview.

Natalya (*after a beat*)   I see.

Kreplev   Help me with this, Comrade Doctor, and I can help you. In ways you had never dreamed.

Natalya   By approving my paper?

Kreplev   By purging your record.

Natalya   Purging my . . . ?

Natalya   Comrade Kreplev, please.

Kreplev   Oh, paperwork goes missing all the time in a bureaucracy. You'd be surprised at the number of people who've dropped from sight. Kulaks and dissidents who've reinvented themselves as party loyalists. Party loyalists who've vanished into the woodwork. You think they don't exist?

A silence.

Kreplev   It was once much easier, it's true, to reinvent yourself. In those chaotic times. But even now, one can make arrangements.

Another beat.

Natalya   Why should you do that for me? And put yourself at risk?

Kreplev   There's risk in everything.

Natalya (*sharply*)   And what would you get out of it?

Kreplev   Peace of mind.

Natalya   Peace of mind?

Kreplev   I told you: I'm plagued by a traumatic memory.

Natalya   The boy with bloody hands.

Kreplev   Exactly so. It disturbs my sleep, Doctor. It intrudes upon my waking thoughts—it weighs upon my soul.

Natalya   I'm sorry for that. If it's true. But what has Alexei to do with any of it?

Kreplev   I'll tell you: It's a rather fantastic tale. (*Braced for it.*) But I knew a boy long ago. In a village far to the north. A strange boy with a strange way of seeing things. He smelled colors and saw sounds. And his memory was legendary. He had an older brother who was in my class at school. When I came across your paper I was ecstatic—I was certain this boy and your Mr. S. were one and the same. The name is Sobolevsky. Not Alexei—but Aleksandr—Aleksandr Ivanovich Sobolevsky.

Natalya *looks away.*

Natalya   And you think somehow, he can help you resolve this trauma?

Kreplev   If anyone can.

Natalya   Did he witness it?

Kreplev   I don't know.

Natalya   Then how could he help you?

Kreplev   He would know who the boy was. And he would remember other details—the street he lived on, the people next door.

All of that could jog my own memory. So much of it is buried, you see. Blocked.

Natalya   Then perhaps you should leave it that way.

Kreplev   But that's not what your profession teaches. The only way to escape the past is to confront it. Isn't that so?

Natalya   But it's the patient who must do the work. Not someone else.

Kreplev (*simmering*)   You don't believe me.

Natalya   As you say, it's a rather fantastic tale.

Kreplev   You want proof of the connection? Is that it?

He grabs the file and violently shoves it at her.

Kreplev   The teacher's name. Did he tell you? Is it in there? Find it!

Natalya *sifts through the notes.*

Kreplev   I can tell you without looking. Markayevna. Ludmilla Markayevna. She was there for two years.

Natalya   Yes, Markayevna.

Kreplev   Proof enough?

Natalya   You could have gotten that from his records.

Kreplev   After she left teaching, she helped to organize the deportation of kulaks from our village.

Beat as he studies her.

Kreplev   Perhaps he mentioned something about that?

Natalya (*it sounds familiar*)   Perhaps he did—

Kreplev (*jumping on it*)   So we agree then? This boy and your Mr. S. *are* one and the same!

Natalya (*after a beat*)   It's possible.

Triumphant, **Kreplev** *takes the file of notes from her hand.*

Kreplev (*with a smile*)   Well, then. Now we're getting somewhere.

Another beat.

Natalya   But even if you could find him, Comrade Kreplev: I'm not sure he would be of much help to you.

Kreplev   And why is that?

Natalya (*carefully*)   Because . . . as time went on . . . our work together took a markedly different turn.

Kreplev   What turn?

Natalya   One evening, early in 1938, he came for his usual session.

A light shift as enter **Alexei**.

Alexei (*with a bow*)   Dr. Berezina.

Natalya   But he had a peculiar request.

Alexei   All my life, Doctor, I've taken such pride in my great memory. But now . . . I am tasked with learning how to forget.

Natalya   Learning how to forget?

Alexei   I must erase my memories.

Alexei *makes the same gesture of release that he made earlier, but this time, the color of resignation does not delight him.* **Natalya** *looks to a stunned* **Kreplev**. *A beat, then a tableau—fade to silhouette as the image of Stalin returns to the window. Then darkness.*

End of Act One.

Act Two

Lights rise on **Kreplev**, **Natalya**, *and* **Alexei**. *Scene takes up exactly where it broke at the end of Act One.*

Natalya   You want to learn how to forget?

Alexei   Not everything. Just certain things.

Natalya   I hardly to know where to begin.

Alexei   Surely you have some ideas, Doctor.

Kreplev (*intruding*)   You expect me to believe this? That someone with a vast memory like his would want to destroy it?

Natalya   Not destroy it. Control it.

Kreplev   I am astonished, Doctor, that you would entertain such a request.

Natalya   I could hardly refuse. It presented such an exciting opportunity.

Kreplev   Exciting? It ought to be an affront.

Natalya   Comrade Kreplev. The study of memory is not just about what you retain. It is also about what you let go of.

She motions for **Alexei** *to take a seat.* **Kreplev** *steps aside.*

Natalya   This was a chance to take the work to an entirely new place.

Alexei   Surely you have some ideas, Doctor.

Natalya   Are you struggling with intrusive memories?

Alexei   Intrusive . . . No I don't think so.

Natalya   So you're not troubled by them?

Alexei   Troubled?

Natalya   If the memories are uninvited. They break into your ordinary thoughts and arouse anxiety . . . or anger.

Alexei   Nothing like that.

Natalya   What is it you need to forget?

Alexei   Bukharin.

Natalya   Comrade Bukharin?

Alexei Now that his trial has started.

Natalya You're not the only one who'd like to forget about that.

Alexei It's terrible. I saw it on the newsreel: His hands shook when he spoke. And the color of his words . . . I suppose I should forget his speeches, too.

Natalya You've memorized his speeches?

Alexei Not intentionally.

Natalya Of course not.

Alexei And I should like to forget the way he rubbed his hands together. The dreadful smell it gave off. Like turpentine.

A beat.

Natalya Alexei. When memories are troublesome—it's often because of blocked emotions.

Alexei Oh?

Natalya Some buried trauma. Something terrible we've hidden from ourselves, because it's too painful to face. (*Beat.*) Does Bukharin have some meaning to you? Some . . . personal connection?

Alexei Personal? Oh well, you know—Bukharin. He's—he was once the editor of *Izvestia*. So, being in the news business . . . in a kind of remote way . . . I suppose he might be considered a colleague.

Natalya And how do you feel about the fact—now that it's come out that he's . . .

Alexei Oh, a saboteur you mean? (*Pondering it.*) I don't know. It's sad. Yes. A sad thing. I'm sorry for him.

Natalya Not angry?

Alexei Should I be angry?

Natalya That he's caused such trouble for everyone.

Alexei Yes, it is trouble, isn't it? It's frightening. Vasily says I need to wipe Bukharin out of my memory—and I think he's right.

Natalya Erase him from your mind. Like a figure on a blackboard?

Alexei Yes, exactly like that!

Kreplev *bursts into the scene.*

Kreplev   What nonsense!

Natalya   Comrade—

Kreplev   It's not necessary to erase anyone. Just don't talk about them. (*Calmer.*) That's . . . that surely is what the brother meant. Learn a little discretion?

Natalya   That's what I advised at first. His response was so completely in character.

Back to **Alexei**

Alexei (*blankly*)   You mean I should *lie* to people?

Natalya   Not at all. But it's not necessary to point out the contradiction, is it?

Alexei   I was trying to be helpful.

Natalya   Not everyone appreciates that kind of help.

Alexei   I should simply keep quiet, then?

Natalya   That would be best.

Alexei   But if I can't keep quiet, it would be better to forget, wouldn't it?

Natalya   Do you have trouble keeping quiet?

Alexei   Vasily says I do.

Natalya   What you present is not a problem of memory, but self-control. Perhaps we can work on that.

Kreplev (*returning to the scene*)   This does not sound like research to me, Comrade Doctor.

Natalya   He asked me for help. I tried to help.

Kreplev   Your charge was to study him, not transform him.

Natalya   He was not a happy man.

Kreplev   His happiness was not your concern.

Natalya   It became my concern.

Kreplev   Obviously. Because by now you had developed a friendship.

Natalya   I would not go that far.

Kreplev   But you were fond of him, were you not? Found him likeable. Even attractive in his own, odd way?

Natalya Our dealings were strictly professional.

Kreplev Did he know he was under a microscope?

Natalya Of course he knew. I never hid my intentions.

Kreplev But that's not why he kept coming back, week after week.

Natalya He came because he trusted me.

Kreplev So you were his confidante? A keeper of secrets?

Natalya He had to have someone to talk to.

Alexei Doctor Berezina—it's taken me a while to understand this—but not everyone remembers things the way I do. Like Vasily. He can't remember the day he was born.

Natalya Most people can't.

Alexei But I do. Very clearly. (*Sadly*.) I suppose that makes me a bit of a freak.

Natalya Not a freak. A little unusual.

Alexei And when I ask Vasily what he remembers—about Pochinok. It changes all the time.

Natalya How so?

Alexei When he's in a good mood, he recalls the bakery. The sweets in the window. Ballgames in the park. A girl he had a crush on. But when he's worried or annoyed, he talks about our father. What a tyrant he was— and how brutal to our mother.

Natalya And that troubles you?

Alexei Papa never raised a hand to Mama. And the girl Vasya had a crush on? She did not like him back. When I remind him of that, he gets angry.

Natalya Perhaps we should talk about why you feel such a strong need to be right all the time.

Alexei But I *am* right all the time.

Natalya It's not making you many friends.

Alexei I suppose not. But there's another reason why I must learn to forget, Doctor. (*Beat*.) I have this terrible sensation that my brain is filling up.

Natalya I'm sorry?

Alexei I'm not very old. If I live only as long as my mother—I won't have room up there to remember anything new. I should like to forget a few things. So shouldn't I start with Bukharin?

Natalya Suppose we try an experiment. Close your eyes and think of Bukharin at the May Day celebration. At the exact moment when you first noticed him. What do you see?

Alexei Walking up to the stage. In his fine grey suit.

Natalya And he takes his seat.

Alexei He takes his seat. Among all the other dignitaries. And a man tests the microphone. Bukharin is looking at some papers. It's his speech.

Natalya Let's imagine a cloth moving across that image, wiping away the papers in his hand.

Alexei Just the papers?

Natalya Just the papers. (*A beat.*) Now open your eyes. Most people, you see, don't forget that important public figures existed. What they forget are the details.

Alexei What they had in their hands?

Natalya Exactly. They might recall that they heard Bukharin speak—but they won't remember where. Or exactly what he said.

Alexei They don't recall the speeches.

Natalya Generally not. Or if they do, they recall only a sentence or two.

Alexei (*closing his eyes*)   Bukharin is still on the stage. But now—I can't see his hands. There's some kind of cloud over them. Like a beetle has crawled over the picture. (*Opening his eyes.*) But his speech is still in my head. I need to empty my mind of his words, too. What do you advise, Doctor? How should I go about it? Erase the words, one by one? With a cloth?

Natalya I hardly know what to advise.

Alexei *observes as she make a notation.*

Alexei Doctor. When you write things down. Is it to help you remember? Or allow you to forget?

Natalya Allow me to forget. That's an interesting way to phrase it.

Alexei If you don't have to keep things in your head.

Natalya It jogs the memory to be sure. But I suppose it does save it as well.

Alexei So if I wrote things down, would it save me from having to remember them?

Natalya Now there's a thought.

She takes a piece of paper from her clipboard and puts it on the table.

Natalya Why don't we try it?

She hands him a pen.

Alexei Shall I write out Bukharin's speeches?

Natalya Just one to start with. The May Day speech.

Alexei *sits and begins to write eagerly as* **Kreplev** *crosses into the scene.*

Kreplev This, I presume, was the first of many such exercises?

Natalya First of a few. But he took it a step further. After he'd written out the speech:

Alexei (*eagerly, to* **Natalya**) I should burn it.

Alexei *crumples the paper and exits with happy determination.*

Kreplev What a story. Tossing the words into the fire—to erase them from his mind.

Natalya Why should I make that up?

Kreplev To throw me off. Persuade me he can no longer remember anything—and it's no use pursuing him.

Natalya I'm not that calculating.

Kreplev No? Why then, does your paper say nothing about this?

Natalya It's not material to my paper.

Kreplev And no mention of it in your notes, either. Why is that?

Natalya It would have been dangerous to write that down.

He can't argue with her logic.

Kreplev So these sessions in forgetting . . . they were all . . .

Natalya Not part of the record.

Another beat. **Kreplev** *returns to the notes, weighing his next move. This is not going his way.* **Natalya** *observes him.*

Natalya   Why don't you tell me the real reason you called me in?

Kreplev *turns a page.*

Natalya   On a Sunday morning when no one else is here?

Kreplev *turns a page.*

Natalya   You don't really have the authority, do you?

Now she has his attention.

Natalya   I could walk out of here right now . . . you couldn't do a thing about it.

Kreplev   I can keep you from publishing. And I don't need a reason.

Another beat. She sits.

Kreplev   Curious thing, these notes of yours. (*Beat.*) How is it that you have these at all? Why were they not seized when you were arrested?

Natalya   I was arrested at home.

Kreplev   The 2 a.m. knock. Did no one think to search your office?

Natalya   I don't know what they searched. When I returned from . . . When I could finally get back . . . I discovered them in the archives.

Kreplev   The archives?

Natalya   That's all I know.

Kreplev   Of the Leningrad Hospital?

Natalya   Yes, Leningrad.

Kreplev   How did they come to be there? One of your loyal colleagues saved them for you?

Natalya   I suppose.

Kreplev   You suppose? You don't know?

Natalya   I didn't ask. You find that incredible? I was just grateful that my work had been preserved.

Kreplev   What I find incredible is that you fished these notes out of archives that don't exist.

Natalya I—

Kreplev Bombed to pieces during the siege. Hospital burned to the ground. Like much of the city.

Another beat as he studies her.

Natalya That's true, but . . . obviously . . . some of the records survived. (*Warming to it.*) They must have been transferred to safe storage. Before the invasion.

Kreplev (*with a smile*) Perhaps.

Natalya That must be what happened.

Kreplev Very possible. Except for one thing.

Another page. Another beat.

Kreplev And this is a truly curious thing, Doctor. Your notes are typed so neatly. And though the paper is yellowed with age—the ink seems hardly faded at all.

He looks to her for an answer.

Kreplev How do you account for that?

A beat.

Natalya It's dim in here. You might have a different impression in daylight.

Kreplev *considers his next move.*

Kreplev Believe me, Doctor. I would certainly understand if you had a need to reconstruct the record. Even to embellish the record.

Natalya I'm sorry, Comrade, if you don't find my notes helpful. But I don't know what else to tell you.

Kreplev Tell me his name.

Natalya You already know his name. Or so you say.

Kreplev The name he uses now.

Natalya I don't follow.

Kreplev He's using a different name now. Not Sobolevsky. Something else.

Natalya I don't know about that.

Kreplev   It has to be. Because he's disappeared, you see. Not a trace of him, not one, in a vast store of personal records, to which I have *almost* unlimited access. Not. One. Trace. In nearly 20 years. So he's either dead—or he's reinvented himself. And I believe you know which.

Natalya   How could I know? I haven't spoken to him since the night of my arrest.

Kreplev (*a bit thrown*)   You saw him the night you were taken?

Natalya   Isn't that in my file?

Kreplev   No.

A beat as he regroups. **Natalya** *calculates.*

Natalya   The 10th of March. A Thursday evening. He came to my apartment.

Kreplev   Your apartment?

Natalya   We often met there. It was more convenient—closer to his work place.

Kreplev (*at the notes*)   It's not on your timeline.

Natalya   It wasn't scheduled.

Kreplev   A surprise visit? Why?

Natalya   He was in an agitated state. Another fight with his brother.

Kreplev   And what did you advise?

Natalya   That's a confidential matter.

Kreplev   Confidential. There's that word again.

Natalya   I promised him: Whatever he told me would not leave the room. He was frightened.

Kreplev   It was you he should have feared.

Natalya   Me?

Kreplev   You were the keeper of his secrets.

Natalya   I've never betrayed a patient.

Kreplev   Just your colleagues, I suppose? And only those who were already compromised?

Natalya They asked what people were working on. I told them. I didn't see the harm.

Kreplev You thought they were just making conversation?

Natalya It was the middle of the night—I was exhausted. I could hardly think.

Kreplev What did you tell them about Alexsandr Ivanovich?

Natalya Nothing.

Kreplev You told them all about your research, but never mentioned your prize subject?

Natalya I did not betray Alexei. I did what I could to help him. Up to the very end.

Kreplev Let me tell you something about that "help," Comrade Doctor.

Kreplev *grabs a different file.*

Kreplev Aleksandr Ivanovich did as you advised. Writing voluminously in that notebook.

*Scene transforms to the communal apartment—***Alexei** *enters, with a tablet. He sits and writes out* **Bukharin***'s speech.*

Kreplev But it didn't provide relief. Instead, it set a trap for him.

Natalya *moves aside as* **Kreplev** *tells the story.* **Alexei** *returns to the table, writing in his notebook.*

Alexei (*as he writes*) "My fellow citizens—friends and comrades. Among the working class and within our party we find comrades whose attitude towards the peasantry resembles narrow craft unionism":

A beat.

Alexei Unionism. That tastes like a turnip. Oh but the texture is—is that burlap?

Kreplev *moves out of the scene as:*

Alexei (*back to the speech*) "What, they ask, has the countryside to do with us?"

A knock off.

Alexei "This way of thinking must be abandoned . . ."

A more urgent knock. He gets up and opens the door. **Demidova** *sweeps in with a basket.*

Demidova   Ah, Alexei! So sorry to disturb.

Alexei   Madame. Good evening. Mama is not home yet.

Demidova   I'm sorry for that.

An awkward silence. She puts the basket down.

Demidova   I've brought you some potatoes.

Alexei   How very kind. Mama will be so pleased.

Alexei *retrieves a pot and puts the potatoes in them. He returns the pot to a shelf. Then he sits down and goes back to his task.* **Demidova** *waits.*

Demidova   You won't mind if I wait for her?

Alexei   I am sure *she* would not mind.

A beat.

Demidova   May I sit then?

Alexei   Certainly.

He goes round to pull out a chair for her.

Demidova   Thank you.

She sits. A beat. They regard each other politely.

Demidova   When is your mother expected?

Alexei   I don't know.

A beat.

Demidova   What's that you're doing there?

Alexei   Clearing my mind.

Demidova   A journal? I used to keep a journal, when I was a young girl. I would rush home from a party to record every wonderful detail: What every girl was wearing, what every boy had to say.

Alexei *turns a page, keeps writing.*

Demidova   What possessed you to start a journal, Alexei?

Alexei   It's an assignment from my psychologist.

Demidova   Your psychologist? Truly? (*Another beat.*) What is his name? Is he prominent?

Alexei   Dr. Berezina. A lady.

Demidova   I don't believe I know of her.

Alexei   She works at the Leningrad Hospital.

All the while, **Alexei** *is steadily writing, intently.*

Demidova   And what, may I inquire, caused you to consult with her?

Alexei *stops writing.*

Alexei   I don't take notes.

Demidova   Oh?

Alexei   My editor doesn't like it.

Demidova   And for this you need a psychologist?

Alexei (*as he resumes his work*)   He thought so.

Another beat.

Demidova   I don't suppose you have any tea?

Alexei *puts down his pen.*

Alexei   You want tea, Madame?

Demidova   I shouldn't mind.

Alexei   I shouldn't mind either.

Alexei *crosses to the cupboard to find some tea.* **Demidova** *glances discreetly at the notebook.*

Demidova   Where is your brother this evening? Has he gone out?

Alexei   Vasya doesn't live with us.

Demidova   One would get the opposite impression. One might think he had moved in. As often as he's here.

Alexei   It's just Mama and me.

He sets out some teacups.

Demidova   I'm glad to hear it. Because there are rules. Did you know that on the ground floor, that fellow in the back room—with the dirty overcoat—what was his name?

Alexei Monsieur Tatarov.

Demidova Tatarov, yes. Tatarov. He had someone sharing who wasn't on the books! Six months he had that boy there. How he did that I can't imagine. But that was under the old manager—and I suspect there was some money changing hands.

Alexei Money changing hands.

He puzzles over the phrase, studies his hands.

Demidova So tell your brother: If he has any ideas about moving in, there's a protocol. Seniority, first of all.

Alexei Vasya has a room near the mill.

Demidova Oh yes, the mill. He's foreman now. Isn't that so? And how is he getting on down there? With so many shortages?

Alexei *draws a breath.*

Demidova Doesn't talk about work?

Alexei He prefers that I not talk about it.

Demidova He's certainly the secretive one.

Alexei How do you take your tea?

Demidova A little sugar would be nice. If you have any.

Alexei Sugar.

He searches for sugar; but comes up short.

Demidova He must be missing his quotas. I imagine if he were meeting them, he'd be over here bragging about it.

Alexei Vasya doesn't brag.

Demidova Oh, I've heard him once or twice. Talking about how he's rising in the party—

Alexei I never heard that.

Demidova —how he's becoming a real influence at the council.

Alexei Now that's very odd, Madame. Just now your words have taken on a stale odor. Like a dirty old sock.

Demidova What a thing to say.

Alexei "Influence." It's a rather dusty word. Kind of chalky.

Demidova's *hand goes to her mouth.*

Alexei Like in the newsreels.

Demidova Whatever are you talking about Alexei?

Alexei The other night I went to the pictures with Mama. The newsreel came on—and there he was—Comrade Bukharin! Confessing. To the most awful things. His words were exactly the color of yours just now.

Demidova I'm afraid I don't understand.

Alexei Comrade Bukharin. When he made his confession. His words lost all their color. I've noticed that before. When Vasily doesn't want to be bothered explaining something to me, he'll toss something off and it'll be the color of wet chalk. And I'll know he just made something up.

Demidova Are you saying that Bukharin has made a false confession?

Alexei I just noticed his words changed color as he spoke. Dustier and dustier. The way yours did just now. When you said you heard Vasily bragging. Come to think of it, Madame, your words take on that same dusty color every time you tell that story about Chekhov.

Demidova *stirs in discomfort.*

Demidova I see. Well! (*Tightly.*) Now I understand why you've consulted a psychiatrist.

Alexei Psychologist. (*With a smile.*) I'll put the kettle on.

As he moves to the door.

Alexei Will you have milk in your tea?

Demidova If you don't mind.

Alexei I think I do mind, because we're short of milk, too.

Alexei *goes out. A beat.* **Demidova** *gets up and walks around the table. Another beat as she flips opens his notebook and reads.*

Demidova What on earth?

She flips another page, not sure what she is seeing, but realizes it's not good. She considers what to do. She carefully removes a page from the notebook, then folds the page into her pocket. She looks back at the notebook again as **Vasily** *enters—and she moves quickly away.*

Demidova Vasily.

Vasily   Madame Demidova. (*Sourly*.) What a pleasant surprise.

Demidova   I was here to see your dear mother. But she's gone out.

Vasily   Frighten her away?

Demidova   How funny you are, Vasily, no. She was already gone. Your brother is here, though. He's in the kitchen just now.

A beat. She edges toward the door. He blocks her way.

Vasily   And how are you enjoying your new rooms?

Demidova   Whatever do you mean?

Vasily   The Nagorskys. You've got the whole space now.

Demidova   I have seniority.

Vasily   Did you inherit any furnishings as well? They had a few nice pieces, last I saw.

Demidova   Such manners.

Vasily   And all those books.

She again tries again to leave; he blocks her again.

Vasily   Strange that it should go to you. When they have family in Leningrad.

She moves away.

Demidova   And how are things down at the mill? Meeting your quotas?

Vasily   Fine.

Demidova   I hear differently.

Vasily   Do you?

Demidova   Just now. Alexei and I were chatting. He said—he implied—you're under tremendous pressure.

Vasily   That's interesting.

Demidova   And I said, Alexei! You shouldn't gossip about your poor brother. I'm sure he's doing the best he can.

Vasily   What else did he tell you?

Demidova   He spoke in confidence. I can't betray a confidence.

Vasily *moves in.*

Vasily   You'd betray your best friend for a bar of chocolate.

Demidova   Really, Vasily. I should speak to your mother about you.

Vasily   All right, I'll find out from him what he really said. And unlike you—Alexei won't lie.

He opens the door.

Vasily   Kind of you to stop by.

Offended, **Demidova** *makes her exit.* **Vasily** *slams the door behind her. He tosses his cap onto the table and sits down, exhausted.*

Vasily   That bitch.

Then he notices the notebook open in front of him. A beat as he studies it. **Alexei** *enters.*

Alexei   Vasya. Where's Mama?

Vasily (*weary*)   I couldn't find her. (*Beat.*) Lyosha, what's this?

Alexei   Homework. For Dr. Berezina.

Vasily (*patiently*)   Lyosha, how many times do I have to tell you? When people come by, put your writings away.

Alexei   It was only Demidova.

Vasily   Her especially. Will you please be more careful?

Alexei   I'm sorry, Vasya. I'm making tea. Like some?

Vasily (*rubbing his temples*)   You've read my mind.

Scene freezes as **Natalya** *crosses into the scene.*

Natalya   Where did you get that story, Comrade Kreplev?

Kreplev   From the record.

Natalya   Really?

Kreplev   Every building in St. Petersburg had a witch like her—trading confidences for favors.

Natalya   That is not the story that Alexei told me.

Kreplev   He didn't have the whole picture. He didn't understand what had happened in his own home.

Natalya   He understood very well. He was terrified of his brother.

Kreplev   That's a lie.

Natalya   It's true. Vasily was brutal—ambitious—not to be trusted.

Light shift. Now **Natalya** *tells the story.*

Natalya   When he found the notebook . . .

Kreplev *transforms to* **Vasily** *and returns to find the open notebook.*

Vasily   What's this?

Alexei   My notebook.

Vasily   No, what is *this?* This writing—here?

Alexei   Oh. It's Bukharin.

Vasily   Bukharin?

Alexei   I'm erasing him. Just as you asked. You see, I write his speeches down—

Vasily   His speeches?

Vasily *grabs the notebook.*

Vasily   Are you out of your mind?

Alexei   Give me that.

Vasya pushes **Alexei** *away,* **Alexei** *responds with surprising force, shoving* **Vasily** *into the wall.*

Vasily   Get off me, you freak!

Alexei   I'm not a freak Vasya!

Vasily   Get off!

This time **Vasya** *punches him and he reels back, losing his balance.*

Vasily   You keep shit like this around and we'll all be on a train to the East.

Alexei   I'm not a freak.

Mother *enters to find* **Vasya** *standing over* **Alexei**.

Mother   Vasya? Lyosha? What is this?

Vasily   Just a joke.

Mother   Then why is he bleeding?

Vasily We were fooling around. Got out of hand.

Mother (*to* **Alexei**) What happened?

Alexei He took my notebook.

Mother That's nothing to fight about. Vasya.

Reluctantly, **Vasily** *hands the notebook back to* **Alexei**.

Vasily (*to* **Alexei**) Remember what I said.

Mother Lyosha. You need a compress for that eye.

Alexei I'm all right.

Vasily Where've you been?

Mother I went to see Nikolai.

Vasily All this time?

Mother He's been ill. I made soup.

Vasily Mama?

Mother (*breaking*) He's been taken.

Alexei Nikolai?

Vasily When?

Mother A few hours; I don't know.

Vasily What happened?

Mother I went to his apartment. You know he's been ill. They were there when I arrived. Three men. In dark coats.

Vasily Did they take your name?

Mother (*looking away*) I wasn't raised to be rude, Vasya.

Vasily Your address too, I suppose.

Mother They barked all these questions—

Vasily What else did you tell them?

Mother I don't remember.

Vasily Mama!

(*Grabbing her*.) What else did you tell them?

Alexei (*jumping up to block him*)   Stop badgering her.

Vasily   Stop interfering.

Mother   Vasya! (*Indicating the walls*.) The others.

Vasily   The others. (*Moving away*.) Now you think about the others!

Mother   They asked me a few questions. I don't know what I said. I was frightened.

Alexei   It's all right, Mama.

Mother   Nikolai said they wouldn't be long. So I started cleaning. Sorting. But they never came back.

Alexei   Don't worry, Mama. We'll get it straightened out. We'll go to the police—

Vasily   No! No police.

Alexei   We have to—

Vasily   You want to get us all shot?

Vasya *grabs a valise and starts to put clothes into it.*

Alexei   What are you doing, Vasya?

Vasily   You can't stay here.

Alexei   Why are your hands shaking?

Mother   Boys. Can't you be kinder to each other? I worry about you.

Vasily   Mama, listen to me.

Mother   Both of you need to find nice girls. And settle down.

Vasily   It isn't safe here.

Alexei   It's some kind of mistake, Vasya. What could Nikolai have done?

Vasily   It doesn't matter if it was a mistake. They took him, they'll come for us. You have to pack.

Mother   Not another move. No. It was hard enough when we came here.

Vasily   A few clothes, that's all. I'll be back in an hour.

Mother   Where are you going?

Vasily To see a friend. (*Quietly.*) Someone who owes me a favor.

Mother Apologize to your brother before you go.

Vasily (*aside to* **Alexei**) Don't let anyone in—and don't let her go out.

Vasily *slams out.*

A beat.

Alexei We better start packing.

Mother (*grabbing his hand*) No, you sit with me. Sit with me—and tell me one of your memories. Easters in Pochinok, the beautifully colored eggs. Bring it back for me.

Alexei Not now, Mama.

Mother When your grandmother was alive—and organized the whole meal. Wasn't it wonderful?

Alexei No, Mama. Vasily is right—it is not good to think about the past. You must put it out of your mind.

Mother Lyosha.

Alexei I have to go out for a while. Please start packing.

Mother Get some ice for that eye.

He grabs his notebook and goes out, leaving **Mother** *alone. A beat. She stands and begins to pack. A light shift; the scene fades to darkness as* **Stalin**'s *eye peers through the window.* **Mother** *exits;* **Kreplev** *and* **Natalya** *return.*

Natalya And that's when he came to me.

Natalya He was shaking from the cold—or so I thought. Then he came into the light—and I saw his face.

Kreplev *crosses away as the space transforms to* **Natalya**'s *apartment.* **Alexei** *enters and sits as she applies an ice pack to his eye.*

Alexei I don't know what happened. He's never done that before.

Natalya Hold still.

Alexei I've never done that before.

Natalya *Keep it still.*

Alexei He was so scared—it scared me.

Natalya Does he know you're here?

Alexei Vasya? I don't think so.

Natalya You didn't tell him you were coming here?

Alexei I didn't tell anyone. Not even Mama.

Natalya Good. That's good.

A beat.

Alexei Strange things are on going on. No one speaks and yet, the silence is so very dark . . .

Natalya Everyone is on edge these days.

Alexei I think it's more important than ever that I learn to forget.

He takes the notebook out of his coat.

Alexei I filled 40 pages tonight. Bukharin's address to the Agricultural Bureau. And here—

Now he notices a page is missing.

Natalya What is it?

Alexei There's a page missing.

Natalya *examines the notebook.*

Natalya What was on it?

Alexei Start of a speech—about the New Economic Policy . . .

Natalya Could it have fallen out?

Alexei It's been torn.

A beat.

Natalya Who had your notebook last?

Alexei Vasily . . .

A moment.

Natalya Alexei—

Alexei I don't want it to be possible.

Natalya But you must consider it—

Alexei What could he want with it?

Natalya I think we both know.

Alexei I should burn this.

Kreplev *charges into the scene.*

Kreplev No! He couldn't believe that. Not of his own brother.

Natalya Who else but the party loyalist?

Alexei Dr. Berezina. (*A beat.*) I think . . . I think I should not go home tonight.

Natalya Stay here.

Alexei Here?

Natalya Just for a few hours. I have a friend who may be able to help.

Kreplev You are the one.

Alexei *presses her hand.*

Alexei I have to get word to Mama.

Kreplev You are the one who taught him to be afraid.

Natalya He came to that on his own.

Alexei She'll be frantic.

Natalya When you are safe. Then I will get word to her.

Alexei *bows and leaves.*

Kreplev Vasily was impatient with him, it's true. But he was devoted to his family.

Natalya I only know what Alexei told me. He was afraid to go home.

Kreplev Did he stay with you that night?

Natalya I sent him to a friend.

Kreplev What friend?

Natalya Dr. Freundlich. I don't know what became of him after that.

A beat.

Kreplev Perhaps we are telling the same story after all, Comrade Doctor. (*Beat.*) Alexei did not go home that night. His mother was indeed frantic: Vasily went out to look for him. The newspaper office, the movie houses, Nikolai's apartment—up and down the canal path, even, against his better judgment, the police station.

A light shift and **Mother** *appears as if in the communal apartment, with the memory book of* **Pochinok**. *She has an ink pen and is blacking out an image in the book.*

Kreplev   And when he returns, to tell his mother that he cannot find Alexei anywhere, he finds her with Nikolai's gift in her lap.

Natalya   The memory book of Pochinok.

Mother   Vasya. Any word?

Kreplev   One by one she blacks out the faces of the disgraced. First her husband's—

Mother   Did you find Lyosha?

Kreplev   Then her brother-in-law's—Nikolai—

Mother   Where did you go?

Kreplev   And finally her infant son's . . . As if by blotting out their faces, she could exonerate herself.

Kreplev *transforms to* **Vasily**.

Vasily   I've been everywhere, Mama.

Mother   Go back to the newspaper office. See if he's come in yet.

Vasily   I've been there twice.

Mother   I'll tell you what I think. I think he's met a girl. Yes, I do.

Vasily   Mama.

Mother   Boys do silly things sometimes when they have a sweetheart.

Vasily   Mama: We have to prepare ourselves for the worst—

Mother   Vasya. Patience. He'll come walking in any minute.

Vasily   I don't think we can wait much longer.

Mother   The idea. We can't go without your brother.

A beat as he watches her, realizing he has no choice but to go out again.

Vasily   No. Of course you're right.

Vasily *kisses her on the cheek.*

Vasily   If he comes in, you tell him to stay put.

Vasily *transforms to* **Kreplev**. **Mother** *continues her task.*

Kreplev Sonia Mikhailovna was alone in that room for only a few hours more.

Sound of the 2 a.m. knock—a cold pounding.

Mother Lyosha?

More pounding—violent, terrifying.

Mother Lyosha is that you?

She stares at the door. A beat. The door flies open on its own. Shadows of the secret police fill the hallway. **Mother** *retreats.*

She vanishes in the dark. Stalin's staring eye returns to the window. The image in the window fades to the view from **Kreplev***'s office.* **Mother** *is gone.*

Kreplev When Vasily comes back to his mother's room, the door is hanging off its hinges—and the contents of every drawer scattered across the room. His heart breaks at the sight: What else is there for him to do, but flee?

Natalya What else could he do?

Kreplev That's the question that eats at me. What else could he have done?

Natalya Had he stayed, he would have been arrested himself.

Kreplev We can agree then? The brother is not to blame? If he was brutal—at times—it's because he was frightened. We can agree on that?

A beat.

Natalya Comrade Kreplev. You spoke to me earlier of a childhood trauma. A memory that intrudes on you.

Kreplev The boy with bloody hands.

Natalya A boy you knew in Pochinok. Where you grew up. With your younger brother. Alexsandr.

A long beat.

Kreplev So, Comrade Doctor. Now we know each other's secrets.

Natalya Do we? Do we know them all?

Kreplev Doctor Berezina, I beg you: I have nothing else. No other stories to tell. If Alexsandr is still alive, I want to find him. Is that so hard to understand?

Memoirs of a Forgotten Man   197

A beat.

Natalya   Vasily. If that is really your name. I so wish to believe you.

Kreplev   Do you need more proof? Something only a brother would know?

Natalya   Tell me.

Kreplev   He was afraid of lightning.

Natalya   Yes, I recall. He jumped away from the windows.

Kreplev   He was left-handed.

Natalya   True.

Kreplev   His handwriting was a fine, delicate kind of script.

Natalya   Almost feminine.

Kreplev   He hated boiled eggs. And he sometimes forgot to tie his shoes.

Natalya   Nearly tripped a few times.

Kreplev   Did he ever speak of me?

Natalya   With great admiration. And affection.

Kreplev   That's how he spoke of you.

A beat.

Kreplev *crosses to his desk and sits down. He takes a form from a drawer and begins to fill it out.*

Kreplev   I'm approving your paper, Comrade Doctor. You should be hearing from the editor soon.

He clips the form to **Berezina**'s *manuscript and sets the manuscript aside.*

Natalya   Thank you.

Kreplev   And may I commend you for your efforts. It's very good work.

Natalya   That's . . . that's very kind. (*A beat.*) Am I free to go?

Kreplev   You were always free to go.

She picks up her coat and puts it on.

Natalya   You are right, Comrade Kreplev. My notes are indeed reconstructions. The originals were lost long ago.

Kreplev   Then I am very impressed, Doctor Berezina. These are very convincing forgeries.

Natalya   I had some help.

Beat.

Kreplev   Aleksandr did not go to the provinces after all?

Natalya   Oh he went. Long ago. And I lost track of him, exactly as I said.

Kreplev   How did you find him?

Natalya   He found me. A few years ago . . . when a traveling carnival came through town.

Kreplev   A carnival?

Natalya   He finally found an occupation that suited him.

Kreplev   Dr. Berezina. My earlier offer still stands.

Natalya   That is very kind. But I would prefer to work through official channels.

Kreplev   Where is he?

Natalya   Right now? I don't know. But . . . I can tell you where he is likely to be. Next week—when the curtain rises.

*Lights shift, then fades to a pinspot on **Kreplev** and the sound of a train on the tracks.*

Kreplev (*to the audience*)   I leave Kiyevsky station before dawn. A twelve-hour journey through villages and towns, fields of green rye under a sun so pure it's impossible not to think of Pochinok. I have this strange sense that I am moving backwards in time, the years falling away and the boy emerging: the idealist who once believed that a revolution was possible, that human nature could be remade, and all selfish impulses pounded out of us. Then, finally, would Russia be the nation it was destined to be. What did it matter if one face or another disappeared from the history books? If it meant that this bright future could come into being?

Light shift and lights rises on the impression of a carnival tent.

Kreplev   I arrive near dusk. The kind of small-time circus that makes a yearly circuit through the provinces. Acrobats and aerialists—horses leaping through hoops of flame.

Lights up on **Alexei**, *now known as* **Azarov**, *in his circus uniform—tuxedo, top hat, white gloves and blindfold. In the window we see the same display we saw at the beginning. About 30 random words in various hands, as if each word is written on a blackboard by different people.*

Kreplev *watches as if from the wings.*

Kreplev   Here, the Amazing Azarov is the star.

Azarov *takes a bow to enthusiastic applause.*

Azarov   Thank you. Thank you, ladies and gentlemen!

Kreplev (*to the audience*)   I knew that such a reunion required great care.

Azarov *removes his blindfold; more applause.*

Kreplev   So I gave no hint of my true mission, but presented myself as Pavel Kreplev, a low-level bureaucrat.

Azarov *crosses to* **Kreplev** *as if he is in his caravan after the show. He removes his gloves.*

Kreplev   Certain that he would recognize me immediately.

Azarov   Pochinok you say?

Kreplev   Yes, Pochinok. (*Beat.*) I went to school with your brother.

Azarov   My brother?

Kreplev *hands an envelope to* **Azarov**.

Kreplev   I have a letter of introduction.

Azarov (*amused*)   From my brother?

Kreplev   From Dr. Berezina.

A beat as **Azarov** *examines the letter.*

Kreplev   As the letter explains, I'm charged with reviewing her paper.

Azarov   She's going to publish. How nice.

Kreplev   I want to assure you of complete confidentiality. But given the circumstances—and the fact that we come from the same village . . . I thought it prudent to meet with you. And . . . to see you in performance.

Azarov *folds the letter away.*

Azarov How did you like the show?

Kreplev Very entertaining.

Azarov I've gotten much better at it over the years. Used to be quite nervous. Stage fright.

Kreplev I can imagine.

Azarov But now it works very well, I think. (*Beat.*) So you're from Pochinok too.

Kreplev Yes. Perhaps I look familiar to you?

Azarov *studies him.*

Azarov I'm not very good with faces.

Kreplev I can hardly believe that.

Azarov Oh, it's true. I have an amazing memory for useless details—as you have seen. But when it comes to faces, I'm hopeless.

Kreplev Is that by design?

Azarov (*laughing*) Perhaps. I've had to train myself to let go of an awful lot over the years.

Kreplev Otherwise your head fills up?

Azarov Exactly! Five shows a day, six days a week—pfuh! No room for anything more. In fact—that's the next thing I've got to do. Erase the lists from tonight's show.

Kreplev How will you do that?

Azarov Oh it's a little exercise I've worked out. Trade secret.

Kreplev And what exercise do you use to erase faces?

Azarov Do you need this for the paper?

Kreplev You truly don't recognize me?

Azarov (*after a moment*) Should I?

Kreplev We were quite close as children.

Azarov We were?

Kreplev Played together. Sometimes fought.

Azarov (*puzzling*)   I'm sorry. It's been a long time.

Kreplev   Wouldn't you recognize your own brother if you saw him?

Azarov   My own brother? It's so funny that you keep talking about my brother. I haven't got a brother.

Kreplev   Vasily Ivanovich.

Azarov   I'm an only child. You must have me confused with someone else from the village.

Kreplev   Your brother was Vasily, your mother Sonia—

Azarov   My mother was Sonia, but I have no brother. I'm sorry, what is all this about?

Kreplev (*grasping*)   Do you recall a family with a nasty little dog?

Azarov   There were quite a few of those.

Kreplev   Little yellow thing. The dog was so awful—it yapped all the day long. We had to shut the windows even in the warmest weather.

Azarov   *We* had a dog like that.

Kreplev (*a revelation*)   You had such a dog?

Azarov   Yes, but not for long. Father made us get rid of it.

Kreplev   How?

Azarov   Gave it away I suppose. Well, now let me think.

Kreplev   There was a boy with bloody hands.

Azarov   Boy with—oh, wait. Yes.

Kreplev   Sitting on the stoop.

Azarov   Oh yes. I do recall that. Sitting on our front stoop and crying.

Kreplev   Your front stoop?

Azarov   Because his father had forced him to kill the dog. He told the boy—get rid of it, or live in the street. So the boy grabbed a carving knife and cut the dog's throat—just for spite.

Kreplev (*it comes together*)   Who was he, this boy?

Azarov   Oh. Well—it's funny, I don't know. I recall the way he wept. His cries were the flavor of blood oranges. But his face is a blur. As if a beetle has crawled over it.

Kreplev I am that boy!

Azarov You?

Kreplev It has to be! You were too little—it had to be me. I'm the one who did it.

Azarov Mr. Kreplev.

Kreplev I'm the boy with the bloody hands!

A beat.

Azarov Mr. Kreplev—

Kreplev My name is Vasily. I'm your brother. Vasily Ivanovich.

A beat as they lock eyes.

Kreplev Surely you know me!

Azarov Vasily Ivanovich. Your voice is familiar—and yet ... I'm sorry—I can't place you at all.

Exit **Azarov**. *Lights fade to a pinspot on* **Kreplev**.

Kreplev This is how a man makes accommodation. By rewriting his own history. (*Studying his hands.*) And so a boy who bent to his father's cruel impulse—invents a different boy to take the blame. Is this madness? Or is it what memory is meant to do? To shape us and relieve us of the impossible past? But what if those memories are immutable and still—pasted indelibly into the mind like snapshots in an album? How does that man make accommodation? If his mind is just a catalog? (*A beat.*) Or perhaps he really did remember.

Perhaps Alexsandr Ivanovich had not erased me at all. No, what he had learned to do—finally agreed to do—after all these years . . . was lie. (*Liking the idea.*) Surely that is it! When survival depends on that kind of accommodation. (*With a smile.*) I like that story so much better. So that is the one I will tell.

Lights fade on **Kreplev**.

End of play.

Notes on the Play

Memory is not merely a collection of images or facts, but the construction of a narrative. It is a way of creating ourselves. Over time, memories change. They evolve as we evolve and continue to create ourselves, to create meaning in our lives. But if you cannot tell stories to yourself, then the memories do not change—and we cannot create our own story. So perhaps the gift of total recall is no gift at all—because it means we never gain any understanding of ourselves.

A personal story. It's how to stay sane. When our agreed upon narrative is disrupted—so that I deny your suffering, your sacrifice. Deny your very existence—we lose our bearings. We lose our way. Our very sanity. It becomes a form of national madness. It played out in Stalin's Great Purge, and it plays out on the American political stage when argument gives way to propaganda. How do we find our way back to the sane center?

D.W. Gregory's plays frequently explore political issues through a personal lens. The *New York Times* called her "a playwright with a talent to enlighten and provoke" for her most produced work, *Radium Girls*, about the famous case of industrial poisoning. Other plays include *Molumby's Million*, nominated for a Barrymore award by Philadelphia Theatre Alliance; *The Good Daughter, October 1962*; and a new musical comedy, *The Yellow Stocking Play*, with composer Steven M. Alper and lyricist Sarah Knapp. Gregory also writes for youth theatre and makes occasional appearances as a teaching artist. Her drama, *Salvation Road*, was the winner of the American Alliance for Theatre in Education's Playwrights in Our Schools award and developed through New York University's new plays for young audiences program. Her work has received the support of the National Endowment for the Arts, the National New Play Network (NNPN), the Maryland Arts Council, the Alfred P. Sloan Foundation, the New Harmony Project and the HBMG Foundation. A member of the Dramatists' Guild, Gregory is an affiliated writer with the Playwrights' Center in Minneapolis and an affiliated artist with NNPN. More information can be found on her website at www.dwgregory.com.

Interview with Playwright D.W. Gregory

*Researched, interviewed and edited by Sharon J. Anderson,
CATF Trustee*

You have said that a recurring theme in your work is "to explore political questions through personal stories." What political questions are you exploring in Memoirs of a Forgotten Man*?*

One of the questions that I'm wrestling with in the play is the power of propaganda and the conflict that arises when people begin to see the conflict between their experience and the official party line. A mundane example is in the workplace when management puts out stuffy memos about how great everything is when people in one department or another know that it's not true. A profound example is what we're wrestling with in the play—a regime that's literally rewriting history. You have the memory man, Alexei, who has the ability to remember very precisely and to know very precisely where things are going off the rails. He also apparently has the inability to keep quiet about it.

I finished the first draft of this play in the summer of 2016 before the last election. The results of that election give the play a greater urgency. I'm struggling with the price you pay when you decide that your political agenda is more important than your adherence to the facts and truth. There are such things as verifiable facts. Stalin literally erases his political enemies from the record book. In an effort to rewrite the record, he Photoshops enemies out of the photographs and then erases them in reality when he has them murdered.

For a long time, we've been in a place in our democracy where we are not on the same page as to what the facts are, the *fundamental facts*. A huge media machine—particularly Sean Hannity and Fox News—is basically churning out propaganda. If we can't be on the same page about the fundamentals of verifiable facts, then we are in a state of madness.

That is precisely what you write in your notes at the end of your play: "When our agreed upon narrative is disrupted—so that I deny your suffering, your sacrifice. Deny your very existence—we lose our bearings. We lose our way. Our very sanity. It becomes a form of national madness."

We're losing our grip on reality because we can't agree on the fundamentals of facts themselves. I'm an old-school journalist who grew up in the mainstream media, and I've been appalled for a long time by this narrative that every major newspaper and network in this country is somehow swimming in liberal bias. This narrative undermines the press. At one point Trump called the press, "The enemy of the people"—a line straight out of Stalin; straight out of *Animal Farm*. The first step in the direction of tyranny is undermining the press.

In his book On Tyranny, *historian Timothy Snyder writes that Americans have settled for a "a self-induced intellectual coma." How much as we to blame? Are we accommodating?*

We've accepted the erosion of some foundational norms, but we still have a free press. We still have—despite efforts to undermine it—a democracy. We still have the principle that no one is above the law, not even the President of the United States. It is frightening to see the degree to which Congress, particularly the Republicans in Congress, have completely capitulated and given up their Constitutional responsibility to act as a check on the Executive Branch of government.

When your party is in power and you don't question when the Executive is overreaching and going beyond Constitutional authority, then you're responsible for giving up that ground. A completely compliant Congress is not at all what the Founders had in mind.

Are we responsible for it? We are *all* responsible. I've taken a lot of heart from what I've seen recently of engaged and active young people; for example, the Parkland students who organized the "March for Our Lives" protest. These young people know that they must be physically engaged because we no longer have the luxury of not paying attention. These students are not intimidated. They are not allowing themselves to be silent.

Why did you set this play specifically in the period of Stalin and his Terror campaign to rewrite public memory?

I kind of backed into this play when I came across a book, *The Mind of a Mnemonist*, by A.R. Luria—a Soviet neurologist. The book is the author's account of working with a young man who had a limitless memory as well as synesthesia—turning sounds into vivid visual imagery. I was intrigued and thought he would make a fascinating character and his story would make a fascinating play, but I didn't really have a handle on what the play would be.

I was also intrigued by what Luria left out of his account. He was working with his patient in the 1920s and 1930s and even into the 1950s, but there is almost no reference to the world outside. This made sense because in that time and place, the less you said about that world, the better. Here was someone with a novel memory for vivid detail, time and dates, how things tasted, smelled and looked, living in a time and place where the regime was trying to rewrite history and public memory and that someone is unable to forget anything. The juxtaposition of those two things ultimately took me to writing this play.

How much does your personal experience come into this? In a 2009 interview you shared that a childhood memory that explains who you are as a writer was the sexual abuse you experienced at the hands of your oldest brother.

Everybody has some kind of a driving life narrative that drives her or him again and again to recurring themes. Albee seemed to write a lot about adoption and displaced characters apparently because of his personal experience of having been adopted.

What happened to me as a child has definitely driven my interest in certain subjects: the power of denial and the lengths people go to maintain a narrative, a fiction. When you are growing up in an abusive household, the narrative is, "Everything's great." If parents can't deal with it, denial is a coping mechanism so they don't have to face something that would be disruptive if confronted. To survive, denial is the only choice for them.

One character in the play says, "The only way to escape the past is to confront it." Another says, "The study of memory is not just about what you retain. It is also about what you let go of."

Memory works at a couple of levels. There's the organic, the biological—"How is your memory functioning?" If someone has dementia or a brain injury, then her or his memory isn't functioning properly. The other level is the power of our emotional needs; what we need memory to do for us. What memory really does is help us to write our stories so we can make sense of our lives. That's the function of memories.

Can we trust our memories?

Any defense attorney will tell you that eyewitness testimony isn't as reliable as we think. We don't remember things with the precision we think we do particularly about traumatic incidents.

In his Atlantic *article, "How to Build an Autocracy," David Frum writes: "What is spreading today is repressive kleptocracy, led by rulers motivated by greed rather than by the deranged idealism of Hitler or Stalin or Mao.*

Such rulers rely less on terror and more on rule-twisting, the manipulation of information, and the co-optation of elites."

To maintain power in this country today, more and more resources are going into fewer and fewer hands. The erosion of the American middle class is something that goes hand in hand with the erosion of democracy and the assault on public education. To have a strong democracy, you have to have an educated population and a mechanism where the average person can have a voice in political system, which means having enough money to buy ads. If you don't you do drift toward kleptocracy.

We've been here before, for example, with the laissez-faire capitalism in 1890s that Lincoln Steffens wrote about in *The Shame of the Cities*. The whole Progressive Era was about trying to overcome those imbalances and instituting systems that would tamp down corruption.

I'm really aghast at the assaults on the "Deep State"—going after the civil service. Civil service was instituted to replace patronage jobs. Before the civil service, the President basically handed out jobs in the Federal government to his supporters and friends. When Lincoln was in the White House, people wanting jobs were lined up out the door and down the block. Civil service got rid of that patronage system and replaced it with a system that emphasized skill and qualifications.

People must begin to understand why we have certain systems in place today and why they were established. Every regulation that's in place is in response to a problem, a serious issue such as air and water pollution. If industry is going to dump all sorts of pollutants, then they need to be held responsible.

The fact that so many people are simply not tuned into this history is also the function of grossly underfunded public schools.

In an online article for The New York Review of Books, *Russian-born journalist Masha Gessen described the commonality between Trump and Vladimir Putin this way: "Lying is the message. It's not just that both Putin and Trump lie, it is that they lie in the same way and for the same purpose: blatantly, to assert power over truth itself."*

I completely agree.

Dead and Breathing

Chisa Hutchinson

For Aunt Veronika.

With a muthafuckin' k.

Cast of Characters

Veronika, *40-something, black, boisterous*
Carolyn, *68, black, wealthy, prim but only to a point*

Setting

Present day in Carolyn's lovely home in a town where it's acceptable for black people to have lovely homes.

The master suite of an old-money home, where **Carolyn**—*old and sick and not at peace with either*—*sits grumpily in a claw-foot tub full of water. She is being carefully bathed by* **Veronika**—*a robust woman in her forties whose loud and loose mouth is miraculously incongruous to the delicate deliberateness of her hands.*

Veronika   Yes ma'am, I saw a lot of weird stuff in the ER, but that tops 'em all. In fact, that's right about when I decided to get into caring for the elderly. Shit. Old people are generally wise enough to know a watermelon's got no place up their ass. You gotta appreciate the man's sense of adventure, though. I bet he's a real hoot in bed. Or in the produce aisle—ha! If he worked at a grocery store and got an employee discount, that'd be like an endless sale on sex toys for him. That'd be some shit, wouldn't it? You think his coworkers ever suspected him of being food fetishist? Can you imagine? "Mr. Smith, is that a cucumber in your pocket or are you just happy to see me?" HA! That wasn't his name, by the way—Mr. Smith. I changed the name to protect the . . . well I was gonna say the innocent, but I think a watermelon up the ass pretty much precludes you from that category. Hell, the watermelon may've been the only innocent party up in that camp. Still. I wouldn't put the man's business out on the street like that. It's illegal. And unprofessional. And I am nothing if not professional. Spread 'em, sister. I gotta get at your happy flaps . . .

Offstage, a doorbell rings.

Veronika   Aw, just when the convo was gettin' good. That's probably your meds. Listen, if I run and get that, you promise not to pull any crazy old people stunts? You gonna be okay without me for a minute?

Carolyn *just glares at* **Veronika**.

Veronika   Okay then. Don't go slipping off while I'm down there, Ms. Ma'am. (*Shouting as she goes.*) I'm comiiiiiing . . .

Veronika *exits the bathroom.* **Carolyn** *watches her go, heaves a heavy sigh when she's gone. Slowly,* **Carolyn** *slides down in the water until she is fully immersed. She can only stay under for about eight seconds before she pushes herself back up, which takes some effort. She takes a moment to catch her breath before her eyes land on the sink, which is a veritable buffet of pharmaceuticals.*

Carolyn *goes about the business of getting out of the tub. It takes a little while, but once she's out, we see that she has a surgical scar on her* *lower abdomen. She makes a bee-line for the prescription meds. She grabs one of the bottles, tries to read it, can't. She shakes it as best she can so that the pills rattle.*

Carolyn Mmph.

She puts down the bottle, picks up another, shakes it. It produces a decidedly different rattle. The right one, apparently, because **Carolyn** *tries opening the bottle. Fumbling fingers. Failure.*

Carolyn (*to the bottle*) Fuck you.

She looks around some more, catches sight of a hair dryer sitting on the vanity, goes for it, plugs it in. She makes her way back over to the tub. She's just about there when the plug is yanked out of the outlet. She looks back at the unplugged plug, sighs and rolls her eyes. Just then, we hear **Veronika** *returning.*

Veronika (*off-stage*) Ooooo-wee! Guys applying for delivery man jobs must send pictures in with their resumes, because being fine as hell is clearly a prerequisite for employment . . .

At this, **Veronika** *has opened the door. She takes a moment to register the sight of* **Carolyn** *standing over the bathtub with a hair dryer in her hands. Then she just continues doing what she was going to do—opening the box of new prescription meds, arranging them on the sink, and talking about the delivery man.*

Veronika Maybe it's just the uniform. I don't know what it is about men in uniform—that seems to be a universal aphrodisiac. Generally. But *that* man? Specifically? Mmph! He does that uniform a few different favors.

Veronika *has finished arranging the meds and is moving toward* **Carolyn**. *Over the following,* **Veronika** *takes the hair dryer from* **Carolyn**, *puts it back on the vanity and starts to help the old woman back into the tub.*

Veronika I imagine he don't look too bad out of uniform either . . . heh!

Carolyn (*resisting* **Veronika**) Enough.

Veronika Hmm?

Carolyn I said enough. I've had enough.

Veronika Ooo girl, we ain't wash the most important bit yet, though. Just two more min—

Carolyn That's not what I mean and you know it, you lowly hussy. *Enough.* Enough of all of it. Of you and . . . and . . . that *dumpster* you call a mouth. Of being sick. Of this *life.* This stupid, useless life that insists on *extending* itself despite me. I'm sick of it. And anyway, I don't know how I feel about you being so eager to get at my *happy flaps,* so let's not and say we did.

Pause.

Veronika Well, go 'head, Ms. Ma'am! That's the first time you said more than two words to me since I started here! Good for you! I was starting to think you had cancer of the throat, too. But you alright! And if you don't want to keep your breadbox clean, that's fine with me, but we both know your immune system is shot to shit, and that you're susceptible to infection in the darndest places. Hmph, if you think living is so intolerable now, just wait 'til you're living on the toilet, pissing shards of glass.

A moment before **Carolyn** *grudgingly starts to get back into the tub.*

Veronika *tries to help, but* **Carolyn** *waves her off. Once she's seated,* **Veronika** *gets back to the business of washing* **Carolyn**. *They are quiet for a moment.*

Carolyn Mike or Kelvin?

Veronika Hmm?

Carolyn The delivery man.

Veronika (*smiling*) Ooo girl, the last thing I was looking at was his name tag.

Carolyn Italian, or bald and black?

Veronika I guess he could've been Italian. He certainly wasn't bald and black. That would've been just too much.

Carolyn He is too much. Kelvin. Too bad he's a homo.

Veronika . . . The fine ones always are. Okay. Up . . .

Carolyn *stands and gets out of the tub with little assistance from* **Veronika**.

Carolyn Mmph. He is nice to look at, though. Which is about all somebody like me could do anyway.

Veronika (*re:* **Carolyn** *getting out of the tub*) Look at you! High-steppin'! Go 'head! They told me I would have to lift your little, weak ass out of the tub, you know. Shows how much they know. You alright!

Veronika *dries* **Carolyn** *off.*

Veronika And homo or no homo, I bet you could rock Kelvin's casbah if you put your mind to it. And a couple of other parts—ha! Shit, you look damn good. I ain't even gonna qualify that with "for your age" or "for someone in your condition" because look, I know folks younger and healthier than you that got nothing on all this you got going on.

Carolyn Oh, you're just being polite now.

Veronika Really? I strike you as the polite type?

Veronika *holds up two bottles of lotion.*

Veronika You want the shea shit or the lavender shit?

Carolyn Shea. Lavender makes me smell even older than I am.

Veronika *rubs lotion into* **Carolyn**'s *skin, puts a robe on her and sits her on a stool in front of a vanity over the following:*

Veronika Lucky you don't *look* as old as you are. Not nearly. You look a little like Eartha Kitt. Anybody ever tell you that?

Carolyn My husband used to tell me all the time. It used to annoy the shit out of me. I started to feel like that was the only reason he married me—because I looked like somebody I wasn't. Then he stopped telling me, and I missed it. Figure that. And then he died. Probably because I started looking less and less like Eartha Kitt and he couldn't bear the thought of living without her.

Veronika *gets a brush from a drawer and begins brushing* **Carolyn**'s *hair.*

Veronika HA! Well that's bullshit because he clearly married you for your sense of humor. You're a sharp one, Ms. Carolyn. Funny and sharp. Who knew?

Carolyn There's nothing funny about me. And if I were so sharp, I'd remember your name.

Veronika You know my name: Veronika!

Carolyn Veronika. That's right. Veronika. (*Beat.*) You're not at all like the others. You don't talk to me like I'm five or like my shades are half drawn. You haven't cried at all yet . . . you're stronger than that . . . (*Beat.*) You won't flee like the others, will you, Veronika?

Veronika No, ma'am. You're stuck with me 'til the end.

Carolyn   Whenever that is. (*Beat.*) What else did they tell you about me, Veronika?

Veronika   Why do I feel like every time you say my name, you're trying to pull a Jedi mind trick?

Carolyn   What else did they tell you?

Veronika   Carolyn Elizabeth Whitlock, sixty-eight years old. Diagnosed with Stage III uterine cancer five years ago. The mass was removed; you were treated with chemo, but relapsed a little over two years later. You've spent the last two years in hospice care in your lovely home.

Carolyn   Two years in hospice. Doesn't that strike you as just the cruelest irony? And do you know how many nurses have been in and out of this lovely home in those two years?

Veronika   A lot.

Carolyn   Sixteen. You'll make seventeen.

Veronika   Well, you can quit counting because I already told you I'm in it for the long haul.

Carolyn   Hell, how much longer are we anticipating the haul to be?

Veronika   Well—

Carolyn   You know they gave me six months to live . . .

Veronika   Yes, I—

Carolyn   Two years ago.

Veronika   . . .

Carolyn *very deliberately makes eye contact with* **Veronika** *in the vanity mirror.*

Carolyn   I'm tired, Veronika.

Veronika   I think I know where you're going, Skywalker, so you can just quit now while you ain't too far behind.

Carolyn   I'm *tired* and I'm too weak to do anything about it.

Veronika   You ain't weak. I just watched you do the can-can out of that tub.

Carolyn   Don't play dumb with me, brown cow. (*Beat.*) I've tried plenty, you know. Tried enough times to send sixteen medical professionals running for the hills, compelled by the Power of Liability. The thing is I just can't seem to think of a way to do it that won't give me time to reconsider, a way that's removed enough from my consciousness, *fast* enough . . . I don't have a gun, and even if I did, I'd have to actually pull the trigger. I'm too weak. Weak up here . . .

Carolyn *points to her own head.*

Veronika   That ain't weakness. It's called "will to live." And it don't live up here . . . (*Pointing to* **Carolyn***'s head.*) It lives here . . . (*Pointing* **Carolyn***'s heart.*). There's nothing weak about wanting to live.

Carolyn   There is when you've got nothing left to live for.

Veronika   Bullshit.

Carolyn   Dead husband. Never had any kids.

Veronika   What about Kelvin?

Carolyn   Pff.

Veronika   What about me?

Carolyn   You're not my type.

Veronika   You don't know what kind of impact you're having on me right now. You could be changing my life as we speak. You don't know. And you don't always have to know. Just because you aren't aware of your reason for living doesn't mean you don't have one.

Carolyn   What a disappointment you are. I dared to hope that I'd finally found the one strong enough to help me. But now I see that you're just as stupidly sentimental as the rest.

Silence. **Carolyn** *stares blankly, seemingly resigned.*

Veronika   Oh, I see. You now return me to my regularly scheduled program of disdainful silence . . .

Silence. **Veronika** *just shakes her head and continues brushing* **Carolyn***'s hair.*

Veronika   Hmph. You are too much, Ms. Carolyn.

Silence.

Veronika   A gun is too vulgar anyway, don't you think?

Carolyn*'s eyes focus on* **Veronika** *again via the mirror.*

Veronika Pimps and gangstas use guns, not someone of your standing. You'd need something more dignified. More Chanel No. 5 and less Axe Body Spray.

Carolyn You . . . have something in mind?

Veronika I need you to know something about me, Ms. Carolyn.

Carolyn You've killed before?

Veronika Now why the fuck would you go saying something like that right now?

Veronika *begins pinning up* **Carolyn***'s hair.*

Carolyn Well that *is* what we're talking about.

Veronika We had a nice little euphemistic exchange going there and you just go and take a wrecking ball to it.

Carolyn Oh please. *You are* a wrecking ball. Why so "polite" all of a sudden?

Veronika (*overlapping*) No, I've never *killed* anyone. I'm a *nurse* . . .

Carolyn Oh, here we go . . .

Veronika And a Christian.

Pause.

Veronika That's what I need you to know. I'm a follower of Christ's teachings, Ms. Carolyn.

A brief pause before **Carolyn** *bursts into laughter.*

Veronika Ecclesiastes, Chapter 7, Verse 17: "Be not overly wicked, neither be a fool. Why should you die before your time?"

Carolyn *stops laughing.*

Carolyn Shit. You're serious.

Veronika As uterine cancer. I take it you're not Christian.

Carolyn Not remotely. Not even in the popular, superficial, hypocritical way. I certainly never would've figured you for one . . .

Veronika Oh, you must've missed my bumper sticker when I took you for your tests the other day: "Honk if you Love Bumper Stickers About Jesus" . . .

Carolyn Yes. Must have. Well. (*Beat.*) How about you say a little prayer while you hold the pillow over my face, if that'll make you feel better about it.

Veronika "Do you not know that you are God's temple and that God's Spirit dwells in you? If anyone destroys God's temple, God will destroy him. For God's temple is holy, and you are that temple." First Corinthians, Chapter 3, Verses 16 and 17.

Carolyn Oh stop it! What does any of that even *mean*?

Veronika It means you'll go to hell.

Carolyn Oh, is that all? It can't be any worse than this.

Veronika Sister, I've been there. Yes it can. Trust.

Carolyn If I weren't in such a hurry to die, I might ask you to elaborate on that.

Veronika I just . . . I know what it's like to—(*Beat.*) Look: it's not the killing you I have a problem with. Truth be told, I ain't that attached.

Carolyn Well, thank you.

Veronika I don't even fear that God will strike me down for doing it. He can see into my heart. He knows that I'd be doing it at your behest, to end your mortal misery, and I know He'd forgive me.

Carolyn Great. So what's the hold-up?

Veronika You. Your soul. You can't repent once you're dead. It'd be your final sin and it'd be irrevocable and I will've helped you commit it. I can't be responsible for sending your soul to damnation.

Carolyn Mmph. Liability, after all.

Veronika Moral. Not legal.

Carolyn What difference does that make to me? I'm suffering.

Veronika *pushes a hairpin in with a little too much vigor.*

Carolyn Ow!

Veronika You're malingering.

Carolyn Excuse me?

Veronika *forces* **Carolyn** *up by the elbow and walks her out of the bath half of the suite and into the bed half over:*

Veronika Nothing. Come on, princess, let's hurry up and go get you situated in your big, fluffy bed with all those big fluffy pillows. Wouldn't want you to miss *The View*.

Carolyn You think I'm *malingering*? I HAVE CANCER.

Veronika (*mimicking the commercial*) "But it doesn't have you!"

Carolyn I thought *I* was a bitch.

Veronika You *are* a bitch. Only difference between your breed of bitch and mine is that your breed can afford to be bitchy.

Carolyn *stops and pulls her arm away from* **Veronika**. *It is about as close to an act of violence as* **Carolyn** *can get. She glares at* **Veronika**, *straightens her robe.*

Carolyn So that's what this is all about. Money.

Carolyn *walks the rest of the way to her bed on her own.* **Veronika** *just watches.*

Carolyn You think that just because I've got money, I've had an easy life. That I couldn't possibly know what real suffering is even if I am *dying of cancer*. I couldn't possibly have any complaints.

Veronika Did any of those words come out of this mouth?

Carolyn You're not looking out for my soul. Who are you kidding? You don't want me to have any peace. You *want* me to suffer. That unflappable nature of yours? That isn't patience. That isn't strength. It's sadism. It's the private joy you take in knowing that you get to watch as the mighty fall. You get to have your sense of fairness—your notion of *good Christian justice*—validated. A bitch like me dies a slow, horrible death, it gets added to the balance and the scales tilt in your favor. Praise the Lord. Amen.

Pause.

Veronika Jeremiah, Chapter 29, Verse 11: "For I know the plans I have for you, declares the Lord, plans for welfare and not for evil, to give you a future and a hope." (*Beat.*) I'm going to go make you an omelet now. And it's gonna be the tastiest fuckin' omelet you've ever had. That's how good the Lord is. So rejoice and stop wasting the precious life you have left.

Veronika *exits, leaving* **Carolyn** *to contemplate what she's just said. It's unclear if it penetrates at all because* **Carolyn** *is scowling something* *awful. After a few moments, she grabs a remote from her nightstand and turns on the television across the room.* The View *is on.*

Carolyn   Mmph.

Carolyn *changes the channel. One of those won't-you-please-save-the-children commercials is on.* **Carolyn** *watches it for a moment, rolls her eyes, turns the television off. In another room, the sound of eggs being scrambled. A moment before* **Carolyn** *abruptly reaches for the telephone. She attempts to dial a number, but can't really see the buttons all that well and has to find her glasses first . . . are they on this nightstand? No. Maybe that one . . . a graceless skootch across the bed aaaaand . . . nope. Well, where in the . . . oh. There they are. Under one of those fluffy pillows, which* **Carolyn** *flings across the room. Okay. She puts the glasses on, picks up the phone again and gets to work dialing. A moment before:*

Carolyn   It's Carolyn Whitlock. Connect me to Martin . . . I don't care, I'm dying, put me through. (*A moment.*) Martin . . . shut up, I don't care. Listen. I have a beneficiary . . . I know what I said before, but that's the benefit of *now*: it's never *before*. So get a pen and take down this name . . . uuuuhhhh . . .

Carolyn *goes digging through the drawer of a nightstand, rifles through some papers until she finds one with a card stapled to it. She reads off it:*

Carolyn   Veronika—that's with a "k" for whatever reason—Fern . . . f-e-r-n, like the plant . . . yes . . . yes, she's my in-home nurse. Put that. Put "for being the only person in my miserable life who ever truly gave a shit about me" yada yada . . . I don't care . . . Well whatever, you're the lawyer, lawyer it up . . . Everything . . . No, I'm not fucking with you. When have you ever known me to fuck with you, Martin? *All of it. Everything.* Except your agreed upon commission, of course. Wouldn't want to deprive your kids of the latest iPod or iPad or whatever . . . yes . . . yes, right now. Jesus, just use the electronic one. Hell by the time you finally get here with the fucking thing, I might be dead already, who knows how much longer I have? . . . Oh, fuck you, Martin. I'm dying. I'm sorry it's not as fast as you'd like. Just get my papers in order. Say hello for me to that . . . *woman* you married. Goodbye.

Carolyn *hangs up, takes her glasses off, and settles into the fluffy comfort of her pillows. She grabs the remote again, turns on the television and watches* The View *smugly, shamelessly. Just then,* **Veronika** *reenters, carrying a tray with an omelet, some toast and juice . . . typical breakfast fare.*

Veronika Ta-daaaaaah . . . !

Veronika *brings the tray over to* **Carolyn***, sticks a fork in her hand and moves to the bath half of the suite over the following:*

Veronika Now you just shove that in your face, lay a nice buffer for these meds, and try not to kill yourself with that fork.

Carolyn Har har.

While **Veronika** *prepares the meds,* **Carolyn** *pokes at the omelet.*

Carolyn What did you put in this?

Veronika Don't worry, most of it's edible.

Carolyn Mmph.

Veronika Gruyere, tomatoes, spinach, scallions, and a little bit of pesto.

Carolyn Hm. I had all that in the house?

Veronika Yeah, thanks to me.

Carolyn (*tasting finally*) Mmm. That's actually quite good.

Veronika What?

Carolyn I said it's quite good.

Veronika No, it's *fucking* good.

Carolyn What's the difference?

Veronika One's as good as fucking. The other's as good as quite.

Carolyn *laughs a little despite herself.* **Veronika** *comes back into the bed half with the meds all ready. She gives them to* **Carolyn**.

Carolyn Well, I don't remember enough to know if it's as good as all that, but I do know this is the first time I've actually tasted anything in a while. Where did you learn to cook like this?

Veronika Oh, here and there. I was a bit trampy in my twenties.

Carolyn (*popping the pills*) Weren't we all?

Veronika Hmph, I was a bit trampier than most.

Carolyn The hell you say.

Veronika Parents kicked me out when I was sixteen.

Carolyn Really? Why?

Veronika *sits in a nearby chair.*

Veronika . . . They didn't approve of my boyfriend.

Carolyn Ah.

Veronika He was quite a bit older.

Carolyn Quite a bit older, or fucking old?

Veronika HA! Hmph. I was sixteen. He was forty.

Carolyn (*somewhat scandalized*) Oh.

Veronika (*all very matter-of-fact*) I moved in with him when I got disowned, naturally. And it was fine for a while. Until he started bringing his friends around. He liked to *share*. Said that if I was going to stay with him, that was how I could contribute.

Carolyn Hm. So then your parents were right to disapprove.

Veronika In reality, sure. Just not in principle.

Carolyn That makes no fucking sense.

Veronika It does if you don't think about it too hard.

Carolyn Mmph. (*Beat.*) So what did you wind up doing?

Veronika About what?

Carolyn About Mr. Sharing-Is-Caring? Surely you didn't stay.

Veronika . . . No, I moved out. Lied about my age for work, earned slave-wages, eviscerated my credit before I even had any, acquired enough roommates to fill a clown-car . . . that kind of thing. Actually managed to graduate high school despite all the jobs and the nosedive my grades took senior year . . . then night school for nursing aaaaand *poof!* (*Arms up in mock-dazzle.*) Look at me now!

Carolyn Mmm, sorting pills and wiping old people's asses. Living the life. Is this how you imagined it would all turn out?

Veronika Please. When I was a kid, you couldn't tell me I wasn't gonna dance for Ailey.

Carolyn A lovely dream. What happened?

Veronika I took a dance class.

Carolyn HA!

Veronika   RIP, ballerina dreams. Puberty was the nail in the coffin.

Carolyn *laughs so hard, she starts to cough and choke like maybe some pesto went down the wrong pipe. In an instant,* **Veronika** *is up out of her chair and wiping away the food now dribbling down* **Carolyn***'s chin.*

Veronika   Shit, get a load of me. I'm spit-take funny.

Carolyn   Sorry, I just got overwhelmed by the thought of . . . of all *that (gesturing to* **Veronika***'s body)* in a leotard.

Veronika *(feeling some kind of way about this)*   Hm . . . I know, right? Just imagine.

Carolyn   Tell me more. About the dreams you had. I like this.

Veronika   Oh, you don't even want to hear it. Apart from the whole black ballerina thing, it was pretty standard shit. The list . . . you know . . . husband, kids, house, dog . . .

Carolyn   And where do you stand now in relation to those goals? Do you still want all those things?

Veronika   Yeah. I do. But . . . I dunno . . . I just haven't uh . . . met the right . . . you know . . . We can't all be Eartha Kitt.

A moment. A beat.

Veronika   You get enough to eat? You need anything else?

Carolyn   Thank you, no. I'm fine.

As **Veronika** *moves to take away* **Carolyn***'s tray,* **Carolyn** *puts a hand on her arm to stay her a moment.* **Carolyn** *opens her mouth to speak before she knows for sure what to say.*

Carolyn   Dogs are overrated.

Veronika   Yeah. I'm more of a cat person anyway. Be right back.

Veronika *exits carrying the tray.*

Carolyn *smiles a little watching her go. After a moment, the smile fades and she appears to slip into a dark place.*

She sinks a little bit, droops as though she were held up by strings that suddenly went slack. Upon hearing **Veronika** *approach again, she picks herself up a little.*

Veronika   So, Ms. Carolyn, if you don't mind my asking: why didn't *you* ever have kids? I mean you had the husband, the house . . . you have enough money to pay for *my* services out of pocket, so I'm pretty sure that wasn't a consideration . . .

Carolyn   It . . . just . . . wasn't on my list.

Veronika   Hm. I don't know many women your age for whom that's true.

Carolyn (*abrupt*)   Well, it is for me.

Veronika (*realizing this is a sore spot*)   . . . Okay. Begging your pardon.

A moment as **Veronika** *takes a seat.*

Veronika   I actually . . . I was a mother once, you know.

Carolyn   Really? (*A realization.*) Oh.

Veronika   Yeah, she . . . my daughter . . . she wasn't biologically my daughter, I didn't squeeze her out, no ma'am. She was a friend's kid. Biologically. A friend who died young.

Carolyn   I'm sorry.

Veronika   Of AIDS.

Carolyn   Oh.

Veronika   Which she passed on to her daughter. *My* daughter. For six years, anyway. She succumbed eight days before her sixth birthday. And there was nothing I could do to help her.

Carolyn   Oh my. That had to be hard. Is that why you became a nurse?

Veronika   See, I told you you were sharp. Yes, ma'am. It is indeed why I became a nurse. That child was the best thing that ever happened to me.

Carolyn   Hm. (*Beat.*) Well, you ever consider having more? Maybe one of your own? My understanding is that society has advanced to the point where a woman doesn't even need a husband to reproduce anymore, just sperm.

Veronika   . . . I can't.

Veronika *looks like she wants to say more, but doesn't.*

Carolyn   I see. What about adoption?

Veronika   Believe me, I've thought about it. But . . . adoption would be complicated. For starters, look at my life. I'm never home. I'm always working. Which brings me to my second point: I'm not financially prepared for a kid. I mean, it's one thing when you have one thrust on you and you just have to do what you can to make ends meet. But I can't consciously choose to take on that kind of responsibility without the means to see it through. I don't know how to lay a foundation for a kid's future. Shit, from the little I do know about it, I gather that if I wanted to adopt *now* I'd have to start a college fund like ten years ago.

Carolyn (*pouncing on this opening*)   Well . . . what if you didn't have to worry about any of that? What if you didn't have to work or worry about money? Say you were independently wealthy . . . would you adopt then?

Veronika   Well, that would certainly make it easier. (*Beat.*) You know your show's on, right?

Carolyn   So . . . assuming wealth, you would adopt a kid, start a family . . . what else?

Veronika   How wealthy are we talking here?

Carolyn   Lottery winner wealthy.

Veronika   Pick 5 or Mega Millions?

Carolyn   Mega.

Veronika   I'd do a lot of traveling probably. I know everybody says that. Even if they don't have a passport: "I'd like to travel." Original, right? But it's what I'd do, so . . .

Carolyn   What else?

Veronika   Go back to school and study the most obscure, impractical shit I can think of. Russian philosophy, Aramaic, theatre, Comparative Lit . . . everything. I'd spend the rest of my life collecting PhDs. And hunting exotic recipes. And volunteering . . . oh man, there are *so many* causes I'd want to give to . . . Planned Parenthood, AIDS research, youth shelters . . . I could start a foundation or something.

Carolyn   That all sounds wonderful. I'll give you the name of a good financial advisor.

Veronika   That's nice of you to offer, but what's he going to tell me? If I cut the premium cable channels, I could retire by the time I'm 500?

Carolyn   He's going to tell you what to do with all my money.

Pause. **Veronika** *laughs a little.*

Veronika   Okay, I get it. You're rich, I'm poor, joke's on me. Ha ha. You can stop fucking with me now.

Carolyn   Why does everyone think I'm f— my lawyer said the same thing when I called him to change my will.

Veronika   . . . You called your lawyer.

Carolyn   Yes.

Veronika   When?

Carolyn   When you were making me that tasty fucking omelet.

Veronika   . . . You changed your will?

Carolyn   Yes. Veronika-with-a-k Fern-like-the-plant is now my sole beneficiary.

Veronika   Beneficiary of what?

Carolyn   A lady never discloses her net worth. Suffice it to say you could adopt a small army of children and never need a single cent of scholarship money to put them through college.

Pause. **Veronika** *looks doubtful.* **Carolyn** *picks up the phone and holds it out to* **Veronika**.

Carolyn   Call my lawyer if you don't believe me. Just hit redial and ask for Martin. They'll try to tell you he's in an important meeting—just be insistent. He's probably sitting at his desk with his pants around his ankles, jerking off to internet porn. I actually caught him at it once. He's an excellent lawyer, but the man's got an addiction. Doesn't help that his wife's got a tundra between her legs. Frigid bitch. You know, I'm really starting to like that I can just say this kind of stuff around you. There aren't many people I can talk to like this.

Veronika *stands and starts to walk away.*

Veronika   Okay, crazy lady. I'm going to clean out your tub now.

Carolyn   Twenty-seven million.

Veronika *stops in her tracks.*

Carolyn   Give or take a few hundred thousand. I don't have anyone else to give it to. You wouldn't be competing with any children or ambitious young gigolos. Martin gets 3 percent, but otherwise it's all yours.

Veronika *turns back to* **Carolyn**.

Carolyn The thing about a will, though . . . somebody's got to die for it to kick in.

Pause.

Veronika Wow, I was so wrong. You're not Skywalker. You're Vader. You're bribing me now?

Carolyn I'm offering incentive.

Veronika Twenty-seven million?

Carolyn That's not even counting the house. This wouldn't be such a bad place to raise a few kids.

Veronika Oh sure. "And this is the room where I killed sweet old Ms. Carolyn so I that could inherit everything we have today, kids . . ."

Carolyn So sell it. Burn it. Whatever. I won't care, I'll be dead.

Veronika You're serious.

Carolyn As AIDS.

Veronika . . . That's fucked up.

Carolyn Well, we can't all pull off jokes about deadly diseases with the same aplomb as you.

Veronika Just so I'm clear: you're telling me that if I assist your suicide, I'll inherit twenty-seven million dollars?

Carolyn Plus the house.

Veronika Twenty-seven million dollars plus the house.

Carolyn All verifiable. I'll show you my latest account statements.

Veronika (*weighing it in her mouth*) Twenty seven *million* dollars . . .

Carolyn But actually that's not what I'm trying to tell you. What I'm *really* trying to tell you is if I'm not dead by the end of your shift, I'm going to have to make another call to Martin.

Pause.

Veronika Wow, I was so wrong. You're not Vader. You're Satan.

Carolyn Oh come on. You're missing your own point. You asked me to consider the possibility that I'm having an impact on your life, right? That I may be of some *use* to you. Well, now I'm asking you to consider the possibility—the *very real and immediate possibility*—that I may be of more use to you dead.

Veronika *takes a deep breath. She sits at the foot of* **Carolyn***'s bed.*

Carolyn   What if *this* is all part of God's big plan for me? For *you*? If you refuse, you'd be denying me peace *and* purpose. You'd be denying God's will.

Veronika *is deep in thought.*

Carolyn   Not to mention what you'd be denying yourself: a family, a wealth of worldly experiences, the means to do good, to help people in need . . .

Veronika   Please stop talking for a minute. I'm . . . (*Another deep breath.*) I need to think.

Pause.

Carolyn   Would it help if I hummed the *Jeopardy* tune?

Veronika   For real, shut up.

A pause before **Carolyn** *grabs her remote and turns the volume up on the television.*

Veronika   Seriously, bitch?

Carolyn   It's a big house. Go think somewhere else.

Veronika *stands, grabs the remote from* **Carolyn** *and turns the television off.*

Carolyn   The next words out of your mouth had better be either "Yes, I'll do it," or funnier than anything Chelsea Handler might be saying right now.

Veronika   How do I know you're not just saying this to get me to off your miserable ass?

Carolyn   I told you, call my—

Veronika   And even if you're totally on the level, how do I know that the police won't come after me? You put me in your will and then die all in a matter of hours that just happen to be during my shift . . . that's suspicious as hell.

Carolyn   Did I mention Martin's an exceptional lawyer? And anyway, I'm *in hospice*. Everyone's expecting me to die.

Veronika They've been expecting it for two years.

Carolyn No one's going to bother you about it. Not the police, the DA . . . no one. They wouldn't touch anyone I've tapped on the shoulder. I may not look like much, but I'm still a pretty formidable force in these parts.

Veronika Yeah, until you're not.

Carolyn I assure you, no one's going to throw any flags on the play. You'll be free and clear. You just have to trust me.

Pause.

Veronika Hand me the phone.

Carolyn *does.* **Veronika** *presses redial and waits.*

Veronika Uh . . . hello, yes. Can you connect me to Martin, please? This is Veronika Fern, I'm Carolyn Whitlock's nurse . . .

Carolyn *makes a gesture encouraging* **Veronika** *to steamroll through this.*

Veronika It's urgent. *Very* urgent. Thank you . . . Hello, Martin? Yes, I was told I should call y—. . . No, she's . . . still alive . . .

Carolyn Mmph.

Veronika Well, sorry to disappoint, but she's still sitting here, staring at me, waiting for my head to explode. She actually told me that she— . . . Oh yeah? Well, I'll take that as a compliment, she's quite a spitfire . . . (*Placing a hand over the receiver, addressing* **Carolyn**.) He says it sounds like you've met your match . . . (*Back into the phone.*) . . . I'm sorry, congratulations on what . . .? Okay, that's actually why I'm calling. I mean, is that even kosher? You know she's crazy, right? You know probably better than most . . . Believe me, it's not that I can't use the money . . . Yes, she told me how much sh—. . . No . . . No . . . Yeah, I'm starting to get that impression . . . Yes . . . yyyes . . . rrriiiiight. Okay, well . . . thank you, then. I'll, uh, let you get back to business. Buh-bye.

Veronika *hangs up the phone.*

Veronika You're real slick, you know that? (*Beat.*) Part of me was hoping you were lying.

Carolyn And the other part?

Veronika The other part needs to go pray.

Veronika *moves to the bathroom.*

Carolyn (*calling after her*) Put in a good word for me while you're at it.

Veronika *closes the door that separates the bath half from the bed half. She paces for a moment, then puts the lid down on the toilet and has a seat to have a chat with God.*

Veronika Okay, God. What kind of shit is this you're trying to pull? Are you testing me to see just how much I can take before I get back in bed with the Devil? Or is this a legit mission you want me to accept? I mean it's not like you give signs like you used to . . . burning bushes and whatnot? That's unmistakable shit. But what do I have to go on? I'm *willing* to do *your will*. Know that. Even if it means budgeting for the rest of my life, turning down twenty-seven *millio* . . . you know what, I'm not even gonna say that out loud any more. It's just . . . it's cruel. If your will is that I say no to all that, it's cruel, but . . . it's *done*. Just *please*: let me know. I'll admit, "Thou shalt not kill" . . . that's pretty clear. But not too long before that mandate, you were commanding your disciples to take out their own fam, so clearly there's a gray area. Is that where I am right now? The gray area? Is the gray area supposed to feel like an episode of the *Twilight Zone*? Look, I know you probably get this a lot, but as this really is a matter of life or death, I don't think one little sign is too much to ask. God . . .?

Silence. Punctuated by a wicked loud fart. It surprises **Veronika** *even though it came from her. Yup. One of those.*

Veronika Really? Don't tell me that's it! How am I even supposed to interpret that? You know what? Forget it. Forget I asked. I'm just gonna . . . I'm just gonna spray some . . . spray some spray shit and keep moving and all will be revealed. I have faith. I do. Watch how faithful I am . . .

Over all this, **Veronika** *has retrieved a can of aerosol from somewhere and is spraying to cover up the fart. Now she's going for the cleansers and a scrubby, which she uses to begin cleaning out the tub. Vigorously. She becomes increasingly agitated as she scrubs.*

Veronika (*talking more to herself at this point*) I'm just gonna keep on doing what I was doing until you show me I should be doing otherwise. I'm gonna . . . I'm gonna scrub the *fuck* out of this tub, for starters. And I'm gonna rinse it when I'm done scrubbing, and when I'm done rinsing, I may just scrub it again if it'll keep me from putting that old spider-bitch in a choke-hold and giving her what she's been asking for . . .

At this point, **Veronika** *tries to spray some cleanser and nothing comes out.*

Veronika   Oh come *on*!

Carolyn (*shouting to* **Veronika**)   You know, if you play the hand I'm trying to deal you, you'll never have to scrub another tub in your life.

Veronika *looks down at the scrubby and cleanser, then up, then throws the stuff down and marches back into the bedroom. She stands at the foot of* **Carolyn**'s *bed, just looking at her and breathing funny for a moment.* **Carolyn** *waits patiently for maybe the first time in her life. A pause. A decision.*

Veronika   I'll do it.

Carolyn *clasps her hands together in quiet appreciation.*

Veronika   I'll do it. But under one condition . . .

Carolyn *nods and listens ever so expectantly.*

Veronika   That you accept Jesus Christ as your Lord and Savior.

Pause.

Carolyn   Done. Okay so . . . how are you going to do it? Do you need me to—

Veronika   Wait wait wait wait wait NO. *Done?* You think that you can just—? No. It doesn't work that way.

Carolyn   Well, what am I supposed t—

Veronika   You didn't even *say* it.

Carolyn   Say what?

Veronika   That you accept Jesus Christ as your Lord and Savior.

Carolyn   I just did!

Veronika   No, you said "done." Which might be fine if I asked you how you want your steak cooked.

Carolyn   First of all, I would *never* order my steak well done. That's just uncouth.

Veronika Oh, of course.

Carolyn Second, how does one just *declare*—

Veronika Simple, bitch! Say, "I accept Jesus Christ as my Lord and Savior."

Carolyn Fine! I accept Jesus Christ as my Lord and Savior!

Pause.

Veronika Well that's bullshit.

Carolyn I don't know how I'm supposed to convince you otherwise.

Veronika *opens her mouth to respond, but then realizes the sense in what* **Carolyn** *just said.*

Veronika Huh. I don't either. But I'm not doing this thing until I know for sure that your soul will be in the hands of the Lord.

Veronika *begins pacing.*

Carolyn This is . . . this is just . . . I don't even have *words* for what this is . . .

Veronika Then maybe you should shut the fuck up and let me think some more, how 'bout that for a plan?

Carolyn *indignantly shuts up.*

Veronika Okay. Okay. Let's start with . . . let's start by going over what you already know about Jesus. Ready . . . *go*.

Carolyn Are you serious?

Veronika How are you supposed to accept Him as your Savior if you don't know thing one about Him?

Carolyn Why not? Plenty of Christians do.

Veronika Then live long and prosper, bitch.

Carolyn I know what everybody else knows. That he was a guy who was supposedly born to a virgin over 2,000 years ago, and went around preaching peace and helping the poor and all that shit. And then he got nailed to a cross because ancient Romans hated Democrats.

Veronika Wow, that's . . . I could really feel the love you have for the Lord just now.

Carolyn Well, that's what I know.

Veronika Okay then. *How* do you know it?

Carolyn I wasn't raised a heathen, you know. My mother actually did take me to church when I was a child.

Veronika What denomination?

Carolyn Catholic.

Veronika Mmph.

Carolyn It was the only one noble enough for our bourgie side and ritualistic enough for our black side.

Veronika I'm not judging.

Carolyn Everybody judges Catholics. Even Catholics.

Veronika Psh. Especially Catholics. What made you stop going to church?

Carolyn I developed critical thinking skills.

Veronika *gives her a look to let her know that ain't gonna cut it.*

Carolyn I got the sense that the priest was enjoying confession a little too intensely.

Veronika Mm. (*Beat.*) Well, did you *like* anything about church? Was there anything about Catholicism that . . . I dunno . . . *moved* you?

Carolyn Not particularly. I mean, it was all pretty gory stuff . . . even Communion made me gag, and everybody *loves* Communion. Eat my flesh? Drink my blood? This is an invitation? No thank you. None of it ever really appealed. (*Beat.*) Except . . .

Veronika Except . . . ?

Carolyn It's silly. Never mind.

Veronika No really, what?

Carolyn . . . The smell.

Veronika . . . Okay.

Carolyn It was the books mostly. I liked the smell of the hymn books and the bibles and things. I used to thumb the edges of the pages so the smell would waft up to my face. It smelled sweet and sacred and safe, like someplace you'd want to be in a thunderstorm and . . . and I felt like

... if I breathed it in deep enough, I could be filled with God and tradition and ecstasy and all those wonderful things that the priest would preach on and on about and the people would pray and pray for . . . but me? I'd found a shortcut. Through my nose. That's ridiculous, right?

Veronika   Not at all. It's kinda lovely actually. Spirituality through olfactory osmosis. I dig it.

Carolyn   Does that mean I passed the test? Is that enough for a good Christian death?

Veronika   Ms. Carolyn . . .

Carolyn   Listen, can we—? I'm really not trying to be a bitch here, but I just don't see what this is going to accomplish. If Jesus is my way out of this awful existence, then He is, in fact, my Savior. It doesn't get more sincere than that.

Veronika   Then let me come at this from another angle: why do you want to die?

Carolyn   What part of "I have cancer" doesn't feature with you? I don't *want* to die, I—

Veronika   Exactly. Nobody wants t—

Carolyn (*overlapping*)   I *am dying*.

Veronika   Dear, I've come across a lot of dying people. I haven't met one of them yet that didn't really wish they had more time.

Carolyn (*incredulous*)   Right.

Veronika   I mean the kind of time you've been having. Any of them might've killed for that kind of time, given their circumstances. But not you.

Carolyn   Well. We already know I'm extraordinary.

Veronika   Extraordinary, yes. And ungrateful. Incredibly, offensively ungrateful. You've *had* more time. You might *still* have more time. Do you know what a gift you've been squandering? Two years? *Two years* you let go by without acknowledging the miracle of it. Seven hundred and thirty days. That's seven hundred and thirty miracles. You let seven hundred and thirty miracles go by without even noticing, Carolyn. Without even giving them credit for being miracles. Jesus would not approve.

Carolyn   Maybe not. But He would forgive. (*Beat.*) I have to pee.

Veronika *automatically moves to help* **Carolyn** *out of bed.*

Veronika   Of course you do. Just when we're starting to clock some real Tea.

Carolyn (*genuinely baffled*)   Just when we're starting to what some what?

Veronika   Nothing. Forget it. Come on.

Off they go to the bathroom.

Carolyn   What does tea have to do with anything?

Veronika   You don't need to concern yourself with the tea, sweetie.

Carolyn   Don't call me sweetie. Call me cunt before you call me sweetie. My husband used to call me sweetie.

Veronika   Did you even love your husband, Miss Ma'am?

Carolyn   Of course I did. He was my husband. Why would you even ask that?

Carolyn *pees.* **Veronika** *unrolls some toilet paper.*

Veronika   It's just whenever you bring him up, you have a tone.

Carolyn   A tone?

Veronika   Yeah like . . . an edge.

Carolyn   Hm. It's obvious you've never been married.

Carolyn *has finished peeing and* **Veronika** *tries to go in for the wipe, but* **Carolyn** *swats her away, and snatches the wad of toilet paper.*

Veronika   Front to back.

Carolyn *pushes herself forward on the seat and wipes herself.*

Carolyn   Did you know that I wiped myself for decades before you came along?

Veronika *chuckles a little as she helps* **Carolyn** *off the seat. She glances into the toilet bowl.*

Veronika   Huh. That's some good pee right there.

Carolyn   Ew.

Veronika   No, really. It's not as yellow as it's been. More of it, too.

Carolyn   Great. Now my piss is a miracle, too.

Veronika   See? Like that there? Edge. I don't have to have been married to recognize edge when I hear it, sweetie.

Carolyn *gives* **Veronika** *a look.*

Veronika   Sorry. Cunt.

Veronika *flushes.*

Carolyn   I loved my husband, Veronika. Very much. It's marriage I wasn't too keen on. Excuse me if I don't romanticize it the way a proper widow should.

The two make their way back to the bed.

Veronika   Well, as an aspiring widow, I have to ask: what was so bad about it?

Carolyn   Oh, you know: the snoring, the piss on the floor around the toilet, the general feelings of claustrophobia and personal effacement.

Veronika   Ooo, tell me more about those last ones. They sound interesting.

Carolyn   Nothing to tell. It's simple fractions, really. You get married, you get half the space you used to have. You go from being a whole person to half a couple. If you're lucky.

Veronika   Were you lucky?

Carolyn   I don't feel like lying up in bed right now. I want to sit in the chair.

Veronika *walks* **Carolyn** *over to the chair.*

Veronika   Well . . . ?

Carolyn   Well what?

Veronika   Were you lucky in your marriage? I mean, you know, given that it was a marriage.

Carolyn   Don't you think that asking me questions about my life might be a bad idea? Seeing as I'd like you to end it and all.

Veronika   Actually, I was trying to get a sense of all this suffering I'm supposed to be ending.

Carolyn   *Actually*, you're not trying to get a sense of *shit*. What you're really trying to do is convince me that all life is worth living.

Veronika   I just want to understand why yours isn't.

Carolyn *opens her mouth to respond, but gets cut off.*

Veronika   And please stop giving me the cancer crap. The fact of cancer doesn't need to affect your opinion of life.

Carolyn (*waving a dismissive hand*)   Agch.

Veronika   From where I'm standing—

Carolyn   I don't care about the view from where you're standing.

Veronika (*overlapping*)   You seem determined to be miserable, cancer or no. I mean, were you ever *not* miserable? Have you ever experienced happiness in the whole of your sixty-eight years? 'Cause if so, maybe we just need to find a way to replicate that shit.

Carolyn   No.

Pause.

Carolyn   Is that what you want to hear? No, I have never known happiness. I may not be able to point to a concrete, legitimate reason to be miserable, but I think that a life utterly devoid of joy in and of itself is reason enough to want to end it.

Veronika   Devoid of joy? You haven't enjoyed *anything* in life?

Pause.

Veronika   With all that you have? And I'm not referring to your wealth so much as your access. You've had so much access to all the things that seem to make so many others happy—traveling . . .

Carolyn   Traveling's a hassle. So much hassle and for what? See some old buildings, eat food prepared in kitchens of questionable hygiene and spend most of your trip with one end or the other aimed at the toilet . . .

Veronika   Culture . . .

Carolyn   How many times can you see *La Boheme* and still give a shit?

Veronika   Education?

Carolyn   Paper in frames gathering dust on the wall of the study.

Veronika   Love?

Pause.

Veronika   You did say you loved your husband.

Carolyn   I know what I said.

Pause.

Veronika You're withholding like a muthafucka. (*Beat.*) What was his name, your husband?

Carolyn What does it matter? He's dead. There's no *replicating him*.

Veronika Give me the first letter. Can I buy a vowel?

Carolyn You can't afford my vowels.

Veronika Yet. Shall I guess? Let's start with A-names . . . Aaron? Adam? Andrew. Arnold . . .

Carolyn Stop.

Veronika Stop, it was Arnold or stop, it's not an A-name?

Carolyn Stop *stop*.

Veronika Moving on to B's then . . . Barry . . .? Benjamin. Bernard, Bob, Brandon, Brendan, Brent? No, Brent's too contemporary . . . Bartholomew?

Carolyn Who would ever marry anyone named Bartholomew?

Veronika C's: Cal, Calvin, Cecil, Cedric, Chris—

Carolyn Leonard, alright?! His name was Leonard.

Veronika Oh, that's a sweet name. Did you call him Lenny for short?

Carolyn No.

Veronika What did you call him?

Carolyn I mostly just stuck to "hey you."

Veronika *gives her a look like, "Come on . . ."*

Carolyn I'm not trying to be a smart-ass. It was . . . it was a little inside joke. Dating back to the days before we were married. We would keep running into each other at social events and friends' parties and things and he always remembered my name, but it took several meetings for me to remember his, so I would just say, "Hey you." He never did let me live that down. Even after we were married. In jest, I'd greet him with, "Hey you," and he would say, "Woman, you married me and don't even know who I am."

A moment as **Carolyn** *drifts a bit.*

Veronika That's cute.

Carolyn Right. Cute.

Veronika Sounds like he was a nice guy.

Carolyn (*facetious*) Sure. He was a sweet-sweet-sweetie-sweet-sweetie-sweet-*sweet*.

Veronika There it is again. Edge.

Carolyn What do you want? You want me to say he was abusive? That he beat me? Well, he didn't. Never laid a hand on me. You want me to say he was unfaithful? Tell you what a womanizing bastard he was? Nothing could be further from the truth. He wasn't a drunk, he didn't gamble, he was kind and generous and the best friend I ever had.

Veronika Okay . . .

Carolyn I had a good man in my life for thirty-six years and now I don't.

Veronika Alright. I get it. I'm sorry. (*Beat.*) Is that why you don't see the point of living anymore?

Carolyn You haven't heard a damn thing I've said, have you? Not a damn thing. I am so sick of your sanctimonious bullshit. Life isn't a gift to everybody, you know! That's something only poor people think because they spend the majority of their "precious time" meeting the basest of needs. They scrape enough money together to buy some sandwich meat and pay the heating bill and that's a good day. Time well spent. Something bad happens and it's easy for them to say, "Well, at least I'm still alive," because they don't know any better. Truly! They are just completely unaware of any other sort of fulfillment. That! *That* is what they mean when they say ignorance is bliss. Because if they knew—if they really knew!—what life is like when it's impossible to be *just happy to be alive*, the world would not be as absurdly populated as it is!

Pause.

Veronika I guess it's a good thing I can't have kids then, hunh? Sure would hate to contribute to the absurdity of things with my poor, blissful offspring.

Pause.

Veronika Fine. Fuck it. Just give me some time to think out the best way to go about doing this, okay? You'll be dead before you can say "indentured servitude." Meanwhile, allow me to spruce up your deathbed.

Veronika *silently begins removing the bedding, checking the sheets, replacing the protective covering . . . the business of nursing.* **Carolyn** *watches her for a moment, then grabs a book off a nightstand. Then she remembers: glasses. They're not on the nightstand . . . oh right. She left them in the bed. Which means they're now somewhere in the folds of that mess of bedding down there. She moves toward the rumpled bedding at the foot of the bed and starts feeling around. When the bedding slides to the floor,* **Carolyn** *stiffly follows. Some grunts accompany her efforts. They draw* **Veronika***'s attention.* **Veronika***'s automatic response is to go help* **Carolyn***, but she stifles that impulse and just watches for a moment. She melts a little watching* **Carolyn** *struggle so mightily with such a minor task, cringes when she sees* **Carolyn** *wince at having to extend her body at one point. Eventually, though,* **Carolyn** *emerges with the glasses and hoists herself up.* **Carolyn** *turns toward* **Veronika***, waggling the glasses in a small gesture of triumph, but* **Veronika** *has gone back to changing the bedding as if she didn't just witness any of that. A bit crestfallen that her tiny victory has seemingly gone unnoticed,* **Carolyn** *heads back to her chair, sits and puts her glasses on. She attempts to read the book for just a few seconds before:*

Carolyn   I'm not going to apologize.

Veronika   I don't expect you to.

Carolyn   Good.

Veronika   Apologizing to the servants will only affirm their humanity and give them funny ideas about freedom.

Veronika *silently finishes making the bed.* **Carolyn** *just watches for a moment before remembering the pillow that she threw across the room. She gets up and retrieves the pillow and shoves it at* **Veronika***.*

Carolyn   Hm.

Veronika *takes the pillow, unceremoniously slaps it in place and fluffs it.* **Carolyn** *hovers.* **Veronika** *notices* **Carolyn** *hovering.*

Veronika   Oh, was that supposed to be a poignant, reaching-across-the-class-barrier moment? Did I fuck that up? Here, give me my cue again . . .

Veronika *snatches the pillow out of place and turns toward* **Carolyn** *as if she's just received the pillow from her.* **Carolyn** *retreats to the chair over:*

Veronika (*feigning hard*)   Oh, Ms. Carolyn! You don't have to do that! Mighty kind of you, Ma'am! You not at all like them other mean, rich people I done worked for. Such a pity you ain't long for this world, Missus! Why oh why do the good ones got to die . . .!

Carolyn *throws her book at* **Veronika**. **Veronika** *looks up at* **Carolyn**, *a bit stunned.*

Veronika   Old woman, you don't want to fuck with me.

Carolyn (*mock-frightened*)   Oooooo! What are you going to do, kill me?

Veronika   No. No. I won't.

Carolyn   Pardon?

Veronika   Either you start acting Christian—*acting* mind you, no lip service—or you continue to die at the agonizing rate at which you have been with no assistance from me.

Carolyn   Oh, this is good fun for you, isn't it? Playing me like a yo-yo. Making a cancer patient dance. Is that something Christians do? Because if it is, I really don't think I want to kill myself trying to be one, so to speak.

Veronika   Good Christians don't kill themselves! They leave the killing to tsunamis or to faulty airplane mechanics or to emotionally disturbed misfit teenagers—

Carolyn   Or to cancer!

Veronika   *They leave it to God!* Repent. *Repent.* That's all I'm asking. You think you have legitimate reasons to throw your life away? Alright. Maybe I'm naive or hypocritical to try to judge. But I won't be your tool unless I know that you've made your peace with God, and you can't do that if you're still blaming Him for whatever it is you think you didn't get out of life.

Carolyn   And by "made peace with God" what you really mean is come around to your way of thinking. However you spin this, it still comes down to you and this power trip you're on.

Veronika   Don't try to twist this all around! You're the one trying to pull my strings, dangling your millions in front of me—

Carolyn   And the house.

Veronika   Fuck you. You think working-class folks can't afford to have principles, but before you're done living, you're going to know otherwise, *sweetie!*

Carolyn *picks something else up off the nightstand—a pen maybe—and throws it at* **Veronika**. *Then a notepad. They fall short of their mark.*

Veronika Bitch, you better quit this shit before you burst a seam!

Carolyn's *going for the lamp, when* **Veronika** *charges over to her to restrain her.*

Veronika I ain't playin' with you!

As **Veronika** *tries to wrangle the lamp away from* **Carolyn**, **Carolyn** *is doing whatever she can to push* **Veronika** *away.*

Veronika You better act like you got some sense or I'll do you like them crazy nuns at St. Benedict's. They taught us more than reading, writing and 'rithmetic. Trust.

Suddenly, **Carolyn** *stops everything and stares at* **Veronika**. *A beat.*

Carolyn St. Bene . . . wait . . . you went to St. Benedict's?

Veronika *pauses, caught.*

Carolyn But that's all-boys, isn't it?

Carolyn *looks as though she's very actively putting something together.* **Veronika** *looks uncharacteristically sheepish.*

Carolyn You're . . . are you . . . ? *You're a man?*

Veronika No, I'm a woman. With extraneous parts.

Carolyn You're a man. You're a man! *Oh my God!*

Veronika I'm transgender.

Carolyn You're disgusting is what you are! I can't . . . I can't believe . . . !

Veronika There's nothing to believe. I am what I am. I'm the same person I was two minutes ago. This doesn't mean—

Carolyn No.

Veronika This doesn't mean anything has to change. I'm still—

Carolyn No no no no NO! I can't! I *can't!*

Veronika I'm—I'm sorry, but—

Carolyn *looks pretty panicked.* **Veronika** *reaches out to calm her, but:*

Carolyn *Don't touch me!* Don't you *dare* touch me!

Veronika *backs off.*

Carolyn You lied to me.

Veronika No, I didn't.

Carolyn You misled me, deceived me, *betrayed* me, whatever you want to call it—you *lied*!

Veronika What could I possibly hope to gain from deceiving you? What *benefit* did I get from being a woman? I'm not *trying* to deceive anybody. I *can't* deceive anybody because what you see really is what I am. I can't betray anybody when it's my own body betraying me.

Carolyn (*overlapping after "trying"*) No! No no no no no no no no *no* . . .!

Carolyn *puts her hands over her own ears.*

Veronika Ms. Carolyn . . .

Veronika *tries to physically remove* **Carolyn**'s *hands from her ears.*

Veronika Carolyn, please . . .

Carolyn *swats wildly at* **Veronika***, lands a slap or two on her face.*

Veronika *backs off. A moment.*

Carolyn You bathed me! You *bathed* me . . . you . . . *ugh*!

Pause. **Carolyn** *looks as though she may start to cry.*

Veronika I'm sorry.

Carolyn Yes, you are. Sorry. Just sad, sorry, and *confused*, aren't you? God, I cannot *deal* with this right now! I have *cancer*!

Veronika Let's get this straight: I am not confused. I am far from confused.

Carolyn (*overlapping*) Sick then. You're sick, not all there . . .

Veronika On the contrary, there's more of me here than I'd prefer.

Carolyn Don't do that. Don't try to joke your way back into my good graces. You're a liar and a freak.

Veronika Look: I know that you're old and set in your ways and that nothing I say is going to appeal to your reason . . .

Carolyn My reason? This is not a reasonable matter.

Veronika (*overlapping*) . . . but I'm going to try anyway. If there were ever any doubt in my mind about who I am, don't you think I would've exploited it for all it's worth?

Carolyn I don't want to discuss this any further.

Veronika (*overlapping*) Don't you think I would've just gone ahead and passed as a man if I had *any* doubt? That would've been much easier, don't you think?!

Carolyn THERE'S SOMETHING WRONG WITH YOU!

Veronika (*losing her shit*) With *me*?! Ha! Okay! Sure! You "normal" people—*huh!*—you go right on ahead then! Go on beating me, raping me, trying to kill me because you don't like the look of me. Ram a bottle up my ass, shove your dick in my mouth while calling *me* faggot. Laugh while I choke on semen and irony. Go on disowning your own flesh and blood when they need you most. Go on feeling that your *whole way of life is threatened* because I'm in love and want to get married. You got yourselves convinced that my happiness must be at your expense and then legislate accordingly. You neglect your children, abuse them, try to flush your newborns down the fucking *toilet*. Meanwhile, I risk my own health trying to resuscitate an infected five-year-old, but you won't let me adopt. And that's alright? Aaaaaaall that's totally fucking normal, right? Huh! Please. If there's something wrong with me, then FUCK. YOUR. NORMAL.

A tense moment. **Carolyn** *moves toward the phone, picks it up.*

Veronika What are you doing?

Carolyn I'm calling your supervisor. I'm telling her to send someone to replace you as soon as possible. This is ridiculous.

Veronika Are you serious right now? After all that?

Carolyn *starts to dial.*

Veronika If this is a ploy to really get me to kill your ass, it's *this* close to working.

Carolyn Oh God.

Carolyn *stops dialing. A revelation.*

Carolyn Death by Tranny.

A laugh escapes **Carolyn**'s *mouth. Then another. She is laughing uncontrollably now. She laughs so hard, she has a hard time breathing.*

Veronika *can't help moving to help* **Carolyn**, *but when* **Veronika** *touches her,* **Carolyn** *jerks away, viscerally repulsed. She stops laughing and glares at* **Veronika** *for a moment before sitting on the bed, looking totally forlorn.*

Carolyn   Your God has a real shitty sense of humor, you know that?

Veronika *sits on the other side of the bed.*

Veronika   Yes, I do know that.

Carolyn   Pff. Of course, you do. Look at you. Look at . . . what He did to you.

Veronika   So you concede that I didn't have a choice. That God Himself made me this way.

Carolyn   I'm not conceding shit. And that was meant to be an insult, not validation, you know.

Veronika   I know.

Carolyn   This . . . this is something. This is a test. It has to be. I mean, Lord knows I want this to end—I never worked so hard for anything in all my life. Never had to. You are . . . you're the first person to ever make me work for something I want.

Veronika   Well shit, I've been working too. Trying to get you to this very point, actually. All that effort to keep you alive, and all it took was just me being me.

Carolyn   Oh, don't get me wrong, I still want to die, but . . . like *this*? At the hands of . . . ugh.

Veronika   I'm trying real hard to not be offended by this.

Carolyn (*caught up in her own thoughts*)   No. No. Not like this. I couldn't stand it.

Veronika   Hm. Maybe you'll live long enough to write a book about how hate made you want to live. Times Best-seller right there.

Carolyn   Thanks to millions of hateful Christians, no doubt.

Veronika   Hm.

Pause.

Carolyn   That must be hard.

Veronika   What?

Carolyn Knowing that the group you most strongly identify with thinks you're an abomination. How do you reconcile that?

Veronika By remembering that Christian ain't a group, it's a faith. I don't do so well with groups . . .

Carolyn Hmph.

Veronika But faith . . . faith I've got in spades.

Carolyn I think you just have a thing for paradoxes.

Veronika That explains a lot, actually. (*Beat.*) Huh. I just got read by a homophobic, atheist, suicidal sociopath.

Carolyn I'm not . . .

Veronika . . . Not . . . what . . . ?

Carolyn Hm.

Pause.

Carolyn Boy, that'd make for a real fucked up epitaph, wouldn't it?

Veronika The worst.

Pause.

Carolyn Come over here.

A moment before **Veronika** *stands and walks over to* **Carolyn**. *She waits while* **Carolyn** *stares at her.*

Veronika What?

Carolyn I see it now.

Veronika Yeah, oxycodone'll have you seeing a lotta shit.

Carolyn No really. I don't know how I missed it before.

Veronika (*sitting in the chair*) Oh hon', don't even take it personally. Many a trained eye before yours couldn't tell.

Carolyn I suppose you find that flattering.

Veronika I suppose you find that horrifying.

Carolyn I do, in fact. (*Pointing to* **Veronika**'s *breasts.*) And those?

Veronika Hormones.

Carolyn   Mm. Are you . . . did you . . . you know . . .

Carolyn *makes a scissoring gesture.*

Veronika   That . . . is . . . not something I really care to disclose. Not to you.

Carolyn   No, I don't suppose you do.

A moment. **Carolyn** *takes a deep breath.*

Carolyn   There is a tranny in my bedroom.

Veronika   I'm gonna need you to either get over it or get back on that phone and make good on your threat to replace me.

Carolyn   I'm—

Veronika   Good luck finding a new Angel of Mercy.

Carolyn   I'm trying to work through something here.

Veronika (*facetiously*)   That so?

Carolyn   YES. FOR ONCE IN MY LIFE . . . I'm . . . trying to do something . . . different. Okay? Don't . . . don't . . . just . . . be patient with me. Please.

Veronika (*caught off-guard by the earnestness*)   . . . Okay.

A pause as **Carolyn** *just looks at* **Veronika**, *her face contorted with consideration.*

Veronika   What exactly is it that you're trying to do?

Carolyn   I'm trying to get past the fact that you're . . . transgender.

Veronika   Girl, you were over it twenty minutes ago.

Carolyn   I didn't *know* twenty minutes ago.

Veronika   Exactly. Didn't know. Didn't care. And we got along just fine because it didn't matter.

Carolyn   . . .

Veronika   Yes, Tin Man, you had a heart all along.

Carolyn   Agch. I hate that movie.

Veronika   Really? You're the first I ever met.

Carolyn   I could say the same to you.

Pause.

Carolyn About the tranny thing, not the movie thing.

Veronika Yeah, I got that.

Pause. **Carolyn** *stares at* **Veronika** *some more.*

Carolyn So *this* is what an Angel of Mercy looks like. Heh.

Veronika I like to think all angels look like me.

Carolyn Would you really . . . still help me?

Veronika I said I would.

Carolyn But . . . if there were no money . . . would you still go through with it?

Veronika . . . The money helps.

Carolyn I know . . .

Veronika But to be honest . . . I don't know.

Carolyn Hm. The money wins again.

Veronika It's not just about the money. Ironically, the money is the only thing resembling a right reason I have for wanting to do it at this point. You've given me a couple of others since that one, and trust me: nowhere near right.

Carolyn . . .

Veronika That was a joke. A terrible, totally inappropriate joke. You know that's the only kind can make. I don't want to kill you. I just don't. I . . . I actually think you're pretty fucking cool despite yourself. And . . . you know . . . despite what you think about me. I don't want you to die. And I've been trying like hell to understand. I have. But I don't. Not totally. But maybe it isn't for me to understand. Mysterious ways and all that . . . I don't know. So. I'll still help. If you need me to. (*Beat.*) Do you need me to?

Carolyn Have you . . . thought about how you might do it?

Veronika I was thinking maybe the old *fsss* (*gestures injection*).

Pause.

Carolyn Is that supposed to mean something to me? *Fsss*?

Veronika Bitch, I know you watch enough *Law & Order* to know what the *fsss* is. Air embolism? Through injection? *Fsss.*

Carolyn Oh. Right. Okay. That's . . . is that safe?

Veronika What the fuck kinda question is that? Of course not. *It will kill you.*

Carolyn I mean for you. Is it safe for you? Untraceable?

Veronika What do you care? I'm just a lying freak.

Carolyn Well, whatever you are, you're still a *person,* I guess.

Veronika Thanks.

Carolyn And anyway, everybody's a lying freak. You just got caught at it.

Veronika So you won't die hating me?

Carolyn I need you too much to hate you.

Veronika Wow. Very Machiavellian of you.

Carolyn And I don't know you well enough to hate you. But I do know you well enough to not hate you, so . . . no. I don't suppose I'll die hating you.

Veronika That's . . . that's actually kind of sweet. Coming from you.

Carolyn I try.

Veronika Wow. You must really wanna go if you'll accept Death by Tranny.

Carolyn I passed the test, I guess.

A moment during which **Carolyn** *tries to look at* **Veronika**, *but is uncharacteristically sheepish about it.*

Veronika Embolism should be inconspicuous enough, I think. If I getcha behind the ear, the puncture mark won't even be visible.

Carolyn Are you sure you've never done this before?

Veronika It's not that I've never considered it. Hospice will have you thinking about these things more than you'd ever want to admit. But no, I've never done it. (*Beat.*) My last patient had stomach cancer, had to take all his drugs, get all his fluids and all his meals intravenously because he couldn't keep anything down. He was in so much pain in the end. We kept having to up his morphine . . .

This seems to have an impact on **Carolyn**, *who is very quiet for a time.*

Veronika   His last words—the last coherent ones, anyway—were, "I never did go skiing."

Pause.

Veronika   I'd like to go skiing. Like right now, actually. (*Beat.*) Is there anything you'd want to do? Before?

Carolyn   Not really. I hate skiing.

Veronika   What really kills me is that you look healthy enough to ski. I swear. If I didn't know any better—

Carolyn   Well, it's a good thing you do.

Veronika   No one you want to call? No . . . no foods you want to try? You can't die on an empty stomach. I can fetch you some truffles. I make a diabolical filet mignon in a red wine reduction . . .

Carolyn   Stop.

Pause.

Veronika   You're the most alive person I've worked with in a long, long time. You have so much *life* in you.

Carolyn   And that really is a shameful waste. I know that that bothers you. I understand that you value life. Which—despite the fact that you're a less than honest sexual deviant—actually makes you a better Christian than most. A better *person* than most. But now I need you to understand something about me: I'm not a nice woman.

A brief pause.

Veronika   If that was supposed to be earth-shattering insight, I'm afraid it fell a little short of the mark.

Carolyn   I'm serious. I'm . . . I'm a truly awful person. I have been all my life. I've used people. Treated them like trash or, at best, like furniture. My husband included. And he was never anything but kind to me. I manipulate. I'm a terrible manipulator. I'm also vindictive. And vindictive people oughtn't be allowed to have as much money and power as I have. You have no idea how many lives I've ruined. How many dreams I've crushed. I considered crushing yours. Whenever you threatened to not go through with the plan, I thought about how I could just call up your supervisor and tell her that you've abused me . . .

Veronika *I* abused *you*?

Carolyn You called me a bitch, jabbed my scalp with hairpins . . . you manhandled me, insisted on touching my "happy flaps" . . .

Veronika Oh wow . . .

Carolyn I wouldn't even have to lie to get you fired. To rob you of your license, your livelihood. I would've threatened you into submission. And to top it off, I wouldn't have had to give you a single dime. I could've called Martin and told him I was just fucking with him after all. You would've truly wanted to kill me if I'd taken it that far, wouldn't you've?

Veronika . . . Why didn't you?

Carolyn I found myself wondering the same thing. Truly. I'd done it hundreds, maybe thousands of times before. You have no idea.

Veronika I'm starting to get the picture.

Carolyn And it just dawned on me. Really. Just now. It dawned on me how much I *need* you to understand *why*. Why the death wish. I'm . . . it's not that I want to die and it's not that I *am* dying, it's that I *deserve* to die. That's it. I know you think I'm "pretty fucking cool," but the reality is I don't have a single redeeming quality. I haven't contributed a single positive thing to this world. And not only that, I'm toxic. I poison. I annihilate. I'm not tired of living, I'm tired of destroying. The thing is, I'm too old to learn how to do anything thing else.

Veronika Bullshit. You just learned to love a tranny in like ten minutes.

Carolyn Only because I urgently needed to. I don't have the time to make it right. But you do. You have the time, you have the heart, and when I'm gone, you'll have the resources. That's the best I can do at this point.

Pause.

Carolyn Do you understand?

Veronika . . . Yes.

Carolyn Good.

A long pause.

Veronika Okay, so . . . now?

Carolyn Now. Please.

Veronika *somberly moves to the bathroom and grabs a syringe from the tray of pharmaceuticals. She walks back over to the bed. She pauses, takes a good long look at* **Carolyn**.

Carolyn Oh God, the suspense is killing me. But not fast enough, so let's go.

Veronika *holds the syringe up to the light and fiddles with the plunger.*

Carolyn That's . . . that's a big bubble.

Veronika It's gotta stop your heart, not give you hiccups.

Carolyn Won't that . . . will it hurt?

Veronika I wouldn't know. But . . . I'm pretty sure that if you do feel any pain, you'll be dead before it really starts to bother you.

Veronika *finishes prepping the syringe.*

Veronika You ready?

Carolyn *nods.* **Veronika** *takes a deep breath.*

Veronika Okay . . .

Veronika *moves in and examines the space behind one of* **Carolyn**'s *ears. She about to go in with the needle, but balks.*

Veronika "Will it hurt?"

Carolyn What?

Veronika You want those to be your last words?

Carolyn What the hell does it matter? You're the only one who's going to remember them anyway.

Veronika What, I don't deserve better? You're *trying* to traumatize me?

Carolyn *huffs.*

Carolyn Fine. How about: "What a long, strange journey it has been . . ."

Veronika Really?

Carolyn I don't know. Shit. How many people have to choose their final words.

Veronika Pretty much anyone who's about to be executed. Or commit suicide. And oddly enough, you fall into both categories, so . . . I think what you ought to be asking is, "How many people *get* to choose their final words?"

Carolyn Hmph. Another gift?

Veronika It's rare.

Carolyn So are third nipples. Doesn't make them gifts.

Veronika *huffs.*

Carolyn Fine. My last words will be . . . (*Actually sincere.*) Thank you. Thank you for what you're about to do.

Pause.

Veronika You're not a bad person, Carolyn Elizabeth Whitlock. I'm going to pray for you every day, okay? Starting today. God have mercy on you.

Veronika *tries to resume the task of sticking* **Carolyn** *behind the ear, but has to wipe away tears first. Suddenly,* **Carolyn** *stays* **Veronika***'s hands.*

Carolyn Wait.

Their eyes lock for a moment. **Veronika** *opens her mouth to say something. Just then the phone rings. Both women exhale heavily.*

Veronika Should I . . .?

Carolyn Yes!

Veronika *puts down the syringe and picks up the phone.*

Veronika Hello . . .? Yes, may I ask who's calling . . .? Uh . . . okay, just a sec . . .

Veronika *hands the phone to* **Carolyn***.*

Carolyn This is Carolyn Whitlock . . . oh, hello . . . yes . . . uuuuh yes . . . mmm-hmm . . . *what?* . . . That's . . . are you sure . . .? . . . No, I . . . *Seriously?* That's . . . that's something else . . . I . . . yes, absolutely . . . absolutely, I understand. Yes. Uh . . . thank . . . you . . . see you soon.

She hangs up the phone.

That was Doctor Thomforde. He says . . . he says . . . those last tests that I went in for? They all came back clean. They can't explain it. They can't explain it, but they couldn't . . . they couldn't find any evidence of cancer. None. I appear to be cancer free. C*ancer free.* They want me to come back in just to be sure, but . . . huh . . .

Pause.

Veronika   Oh Jesus. Are you serious?

Carolyn *smiles an odd little smile, nods an odd little nod. A moment. Suddenly,* **Carolyn** *starts to laugh. Hysterically.* **Veronika** *joins in. They laugh and laugh and laugh.* **Veronika** *looks up, and lifts her arms in praise.*

Blackout.

End of play.

Chisa Hutchinson's plays, which include *She Like Girls, The Subject, Dead & Breathing,* and *Somebody's Daughter* among others, have been presented by such venues as Atlantic Theater Company, SummerStage, the Lark, the National Black Theater, the Contemporary American Theater Festival, and Second Stage. She's won a GLAAD Award, a Lilly, a New York Innovative Theatre Award, a Helen Merrill Award, and the Lanford Wilson. She's been a Lark Fellow, a Dramatists Guild Fellow, a New York NeoFuturist, and a staff writer for the Blue Man Group, and is starting her sixth year as a resident at New Dramatists. Currently, she's working mercenary-style on two film projects with producer Stephanie Allain (*Hustle & Flow, Dear White People*) as well as two indie film projects. She's also gearing up for two NYC productions, one of which is a staged production of a radio drama she was commissioned to write for Audible, and starting a revenge-horror play for South Coast Rep. BA Vassar College; MFA NYU. For more info, visit www.chisahutchinson.com.

Interview with Playwright Chisa Hutchinson

Researched, interviewed and edited by Sharon J. Anderson, CATF Trustee

Whenever you describe the play Dead and Breathing *you say, "It's a comedy. Swear." What's funny about being in a hospice for two years dying of cancer?*

Exactly. There's really nothing funny about it. Whenever I tell people what the play is about, it always sounds so heavy and bleak. If you're living in hospice or a hospice worker, you cannot be in that space all the time. It would be exhausting. Hospice workers have to have a sense of humor otherwise they would scratch their eyes out and never come out into the light of day.

Comedy is a defense mechanism. It's the way we survive. If people who are suffering just dwelt on the suffering, it would be totally exhausting and unpleasant. If you plan on living, you've got to have a sense of humor.

One of the characters in Dead and Breathing *is based on your favorite aunt.*

When I finished this play, I was so excited to send it to my aunt to get her stamp of approval. She loves it and has shared it with everybody. She's a nurse who has seen a lot of suffering, yet she is probably one of the funniest women I know. She's got such a wry sense of humor and is relentless with her comedy. She is a joy to be around, and I hope that the audience will find her as enthralling as I do.

Did you follow her around with a tape recorder or a pad and pencil? How much of this play is comprised of her actual words?

It's more that the characters are inspired by her. It's more like I'm asking, "What would my aunt do if she were in this position?" Yes, I'm transplanting her into this fictitious situation, but the character is very real with my aunt's attitude, her humor and her quickness.

You have said that your plays are about three things: race, sexuality and gender. Is this true about Dead and Breathing*?*

I always have an agenda, but I don't like to beat people over the head with it. Whenever you have to give your pet a pill for medication, they won't swallow it. But if you stick the pill in a piece of cheese or wrap a piece of chicken around it, they'll eat it. I feel that way with plays that have messages. If you wrap the message in something else—like a narrative about mortality and morality, faith and forgiveness—it makes a message about race or gender easier to swallow.

Is the play more about the relationship between the two women or about death and assisted suicide?

The relationship is the vehicle that carries the message. How can men in your audience come to care about women? How can you make them give a shit about gender issues? They won't if you don't give them something broader to relate to. How can I write a play about race that people who do not identify as people of color can relate to? The trick is to focus on the human relationships and present another angle to sneak the message in.

Why is someone as young as you dealing with assisted suicide?

I have multiple sclerosis, and I wonder sometimes—and this is kind of morbid—when I'm going to die. I have fears and concerns about how MS will affect my breathing or my heart or some other function that I really need. Right now it's just in my legs. I wonder if it ever got to the point where I was unable to function, if I would decide, "Wow, this is not really the quality of life I want. I really would rather not go on like this." I wonder if I would decide that, but I don't think I have the courage.

Here's an excerpt from a short story called "Go Like This," by Lorrie Moore. The story is about Elizabeth, a married writer with one child who has been diagnosed with terminal breast cancer and announces to her friends and family that she has decided to end her life: "I tell them the cancer is poisoning at least three lives and that I refuse to be its accomplice. This is not a deranged act, I explain. Most of them have known for quite a while my belief that intelligent suicide is almost always preferable to the stupid lingering of a graceless death." What do you think of that description?

Wow. Wow. That is the best articulation of that I have ever heard. This applies directly to *Dead and Breathing* because it is the struggle between this nurse whose job is to nurture life, and the patient who asks her to end it. It goes against what the nurse believes. Her function is to tease out the difference between intelligence—as in intelligent suicide—and ingratitude for life. The nurse feels like this woman who has been in hospice for two years has had two years of life. The nurse can't shake the feeling that this woman is totally ungrateful and has wasted two years' worth of life.

This play is a question: Is there a difference between that intelligence and that ingratitude? Between rationally wanting to end your life and being ungrateful for the life you've been given?

Are you grateful for the life you've been given?

I am absolutely grateful for the life I've been given. Every day. Every day. I sometimes wonder if there will come a time when I'm not grateful or when I will say, "Okay, time for that intelligence. Time for the intelligent suicide that could be a grateful way of going."

In his book The Savage God *(written after the suicide of his good friend, poet Sylvia Plath), A. Alvarez describes suicide as ". . . a closed world with its own irresistible logic." Is* Dead and Breathing *a closed world with its own irresistible logic?*

Yes, I think so because it departs from conventional ideas of morality. It's not necessarily about what's right and what's wrong, but rather what's beneficial and what's not. I think it's definitely a world of its own, but one that I hope is still intriguing for folks to visit for an hour and a half.

I read that one of the things that inspired you to write plays was a debate you heard between August Wilson and Robert Brustein about color-blind casting. I once saw a scene from the play Night, Mother, *by Marsha Norman—about a daughter announcing to her mother that she plans to commit suicide—with two white actresses, and then saw the same scene with two black actresses. The two scenes felt very different to me.*

They should feel different! The black actresses add a whole other dimension. I felt that way when I saw *A Streetcar Named Desire* on Broadway with multi-racial casting. When the sisters are talking about their struggles and struggling in the South, it takes on a whole other meaning. When you cast a black actor in a role that is traditionally white, of course it's going to "color" it differently just because of our cultural baggage which can, actually, heighten the dramatic narrative. It can certainly refresh it.

I also think, though, that it can hurt the actor. Having been in the position of playing a white character, it's hard to fully commit to a role that you know wasn't really meant for you. You're constantly thinking, "I wonder how the audience is feeling about this? Are they taking this differently than the way it was intended?" Black actors should have the option of getting their own narratives out there; to play a role that was actually intended for a black actor, otherwise it's going to be intellectual acrobatics throughout the audience. That is, people will be focused on figuring out what statement the director is trying to make by casting a black chick in this role. I think it does a disservice.

Would it do a disservice to Dead and Breathing *if it featured two white actresses?*

To an extent, yes. There are elements in the play that are distinctly African-American, and I think that they would either be lost entirely or take on a whole different meaning if they were performed by non-black actresses. Not that I'm not open to that, but it is a different interpretation. As a playwright you have to accept that people are going to take liberties. You try your best to make the blueprint as clear as possible, but people may have trouble casting the eight black people and the one white person; they'll have to use a couch instead of a bed, and so forth.

You have said that you write plays to "make yourself and others like you more visible." Why do you need to make yourself more visible?

Why the hell not? If I see one more damn play about a white chick who is restless in her marriage . . . please, just get a divorce and be done with it so I can go home.

African-American culture? It doesn't get more dramatic than our experience. It just doesn't. If you want to put something electric on stage, put black people on stage. First, we have very interesting experiences that go beyond self-indulgent fluff that I really can't get into. Enough already with the whining. If you want a play that's about something bigger, a play about people who struggled mightily with something beyond themselves, put black people on stage. Second, I think about audiences. I've had former students email me out of the blue to thank me for the race-appropriate monologue they performed in my theater class; how it inspired them. There's something motivating, too, about seeing yourself on stage, about seeing yourself in art. It's incredibly validating. It's not just a fluffy, fun experience. When you feel important enough for someone to make art about you, you are motivated to go out and achieve something and contribute to the world.

Is that the singular, peculiar, unique thing about art?

I think so. People for whom going to the theater is a regular Sunday afternoon and who regularly see themselves on stage—those people begin to take this art for granted. For others it is a relatively new thing, "What? There are black people on stage? There are Asian theater companies out there?" For people for whom this type of theater is different . . . they can *feel* it and appreciate it in a way that may be lost on others who've been able to take it for granted.

Some people are going to be shocked and scandalized by the ending to *Dead and Breathing*, but I was not shocked, and I did not write the ending to scandalize anyone. Perhaps I am taking the dramatic narrative for granted.

Why even take the risk of scandalizing an audience?

Again, I honestly did not set out to scandalize the audience. I just didn't. For me, it is what it is. That's all I can say about it.

Alice Walker said that, "Life is better than death because it's a lot less boring and it has fresh peaches in it."

I would have said mangoes.

20th Century Blues

Susan Miller

Time

The present during a TED Talk. And four months earlier over the course of a day in New York City.

Setting

New York City Artist's Loft and Living Space.

A few stage directions are suggested in the text just to establish the geography. But the staging is entirely up to the director, the designer and to the requirements of the space.

Running Time

1 hour, 40 minutes. Without an intermission.

Characters

The four main characters are all women in their sixties. These are funny, passionate, complicated women, each of whom brings a unique history, as well as pressing current concerns, to the table. The often fast paced rhythm of their dialogue should suggest that they talk in ways only people who know one another well can. Even though individually they have different levels of comfort, intimacy, and friction with one another. They are not "polite" in their interactions, nor should their genuine connection to each other fall into the trap of sentimentality. Sometimes the lid blows off. At a cost.

Danny, *attractive, great sense of humor, with an artist's energy and wild strain. Layered with urban angst and a dose of self doubt. Divorced. Has a grown son,* **Simon**. *She's an accomplished, well known photographer at a crucial turning point in her life.*

Sil, *a real estate agent. Separated from her husband. She works her ass off to keep current. And to keep afloat.*

Mac, *a high level journalist. African American. She is witty, smart, opinionated. Lives with her female partner.*

Gabby, *a dedicated veterinarian running her own practice. She lives in Boston with her one and only husband. She doesn't do well with conflict, and wants everyone to be "okay."*

Bess, *Danny's mother, 91. (Can be played by some a good deal younger.) In no way is she a generic "old" woman. She is modern and loving, with former talents of her own, though she is now in the early stages of dementia.*

Simon, *Danny's son, early 30s. Smart, sense of humor. He works for a progressive cable/internet news program. He is close with his mother and grandmother.*

Act One

Lights up on area representing a TED talk—the present.

The TED Global Conference Initiative sign/logo is projected.

After a moment, **Danny** *makes her entrance, her camera slung over her shoulder, securing her headphone mic as she moves across the stage to her designated spot. She catches her breath and takes a moment to connect with her audience.*

Danny   The history of the world.

Beat.

In five hundred words or less.

Beat.

Go.

Beat.

My final exam. Junior year. I was in the throes of trying to impress my professor who I wanted to want me—I know. A *bad* idea. So I pulled an all nighter. With some help from a magic little diet pill every girl in the dorm seemed to have, except me. I was wired with facts and possibilities. I knew this baby cold. I was in the zone. I showed up to the final exam in my pajamas. And, I aced it. A week later I got my grade back and there was a big ugly *F*. With a note from the professor written in red. "USE YOUR WORDS." I was stunned.

Beat.

What did he mean, *use my words*? And then I opened the test and looked at the page. Layer upon layer of *right* answers. *Unreadable*. A drug induced blur of number two pencil. A smudge. I had written all of it, everything I knew, in an eighth of an inch space between two lines on the first page of my bluebook. The history of the world, lost forever. Under an avalanche of my tragically indecipherable, brilliant ideas.

Beat.

I switched to Fine Arts. And started taking pictures. No words necessary.

Beat.

I want to tell you something you don't know. Even if you googled me. I really want to tell you something I don't even know yet. But I'll start with a fact. I was born in the decade just after the Second World War. So when the Museum of Modern Art announced they were giving me a retrospective of my work, I had to deal with it. Being a certain age. And having to think about how I want to be remembered. MoMA, of course, assumed it would be the work I'm already known for. Which they seem to enjoy calling my brand. But, please promise me you won't ever. Anyhow, it completely disrupted any notions I had, if I had any at all, about what I would or should be remembered for. Or which of the photographs I've taken in my career deserves a gallery wall or your attention here today.

The following photographs are projected behind her as she speaks. Her photographic point of view is distinct, artful, amusing.

French Wedding Day

Beat, then next image:

Art School

Beat, next image:

Times Square Or Bust

Beat, next image:

Boys In The Hood

Beat, final image:

Town Council Meeting With Donuts

The projections go blank.

Something about the *group*—I don't know—people in juxtaposition with one another—just compels something in me. Like somehow we all affect the atmosphere together in a way that changes something we'll never really get to see. How it started was I got this gig taking school pictures. You know that thing they do at the end of a year. Miss Gallagher's third grade class. All lined up in rows. And sometimes I'd imagine them grown up. Out in the world. But the truth is once I finish shooting, I never see any of the subjects again. Except for *one* group. One group I've never shown publicly. Even though I've photographed these women once a year, every year, since the day we met forty years ago.

Beat.

In jail.

Beat.

Well, it was the Seventies. You were no one if you didn't spend a night in jail.

Beat.

I can't say what drew the four of us close. Maybe it was something we recognized in each other but didn't yet know. Except that we were young and dazzled by it.

Beat.

So, when I started thinking about the retrospective and my former cell mates, these women I've known through decades and more than one lost political cause, it became clear that they were the ones to represent me at MoMA. They have something to tell you.

Their faces say what I can't.

Maybe they're what's buried under the scrawled answer in my failed history exam. Maybe they're my *A*.

Beat.

So the plan was—well, *my* plan—if everyone cooperated, because these are not cooperative types, let me just say—was to unveil the photographs here. And talk about why they matter in the scheme of things.

Beat.

That was the plan.

Beat.

But then a day can happen that leaves everything up in the air.

Lights change. **Danny** *walks off stage.*

The TED Global Initiative sign goes away and a projection goes up with the words: **Four months earlier***. After a few moments, that sign goes off.*

A projection comes on that suggests an Assisted Living Facility.

Danny, *who has changed some piece of clothing from the prior scene to suggest a different time, walks back onstage as her mother also comes on with her walker.* **Danny** *is visiting* **Bess***, who has mild but growing dementia.* **Danny** *applies lotion to her mother's hands as* **Bess** *looks around her room at the art work (which is not displayed).*

Bess   Those are nice. Those things on the wall.

Danny   They're your paintings, Mom. You made them.

Bess   *I* did?

Danny   And the sculpture.

Bess   I didn't know that.

Not too bad.

Bess   So what's on the agenda?

Danny   All the girls are getting together. Like we do. Sil and Gabby and Mac. It's the day I take their picture.

Bess   That's wonderful. (*Then, not a complaint, just a curious fact:*) You know I haven't had a meal since I came here.

Danny (*jollying her*)   Mom, you've been here a year. I think you must have eaten at least a piece of toast. You'd be wasting away.

Bess (*small laugh*)   Oh. Yes. I guess so.

Danny   Are you hungry? I'll get us some ice cream.

Bess (*a little anxious*)   How do I pay for it?

Danny   My treat.

Bess   *looks at something else that catches her attention. A photograph.*

Bess   That's wonderful of Dad. Did you take it?

Danny *nods yes.*

Bess   Do you hear from him? He was always with me. I don't see him. I don't know if he's still my husband.

Danny   Daddy's always going to be your husband, Mom.

Bess (*her mind taking a quick turn*)   I think he's here somewhere. Probably talking with the other men.

Danny (*reassuring*)   I'm sure he is. I know he is.

Bess   We took a ride to the Poconos yesterday. Dad and I. Nothing special.

Danny   Those are the best kind of rides.

Bess (*troubled*) Honey, do you know where I'm sleeping tonight?

Danny Right here, Mom. In your room.

Bess Oh, this is my room?

Danny It's where you live now.

Bess I'm not really sold on it.

Danny I know. But maybe we can work on how to make it better.

Bess Well, that's something to think about.

A moment.

Do you think you can drive me home? Or should I call a cab?

Lights change. The screen flies up.

Danny *walks into the revealed space of her loft studio. It is now later that morning.*

Danny *pours herself a cup of coffee, as* **Gabby** *enters breathless, with flowers. Although they haven't communicated in person since the last shoot, they talk as if they're picking up where they left off.*

Gabby Did you know you can have a personal guide to walk you anywhere you want to go? I named mine Wanda. She re-routes you if you go off course. Which I did every two minutes. I thought she'd have a nervous breakdown.

She gives **Danny** *the flowers. They hug.*

Gabby I can't believe I'm the first one here.

Danny There's no babka! I was expecting babka.

Gabby Greenbaums is no more. You live here. Didn't you notice?

Danny I'm in denial. I mean, do we really need another nail salon or pharmacy? Or is it a bank? Who are the people who have so much money we need another bank?

Gabby *walks around the studio, taking it all in.* **Danny** *stands back, quiet, enjoying just watching her.*

Gabby What is it about this place? It's like I can see your synapses. And your beating heart.

Danny I miss you. I'm just saying it.

Gabby *stops at a photograph leaning against a wall of elderly people gathered in a large room.*

Gabby This one's new. What is it?

Danny *"Assisted Living."*

Gabby *is affected by* **Danny**'*s study of the residents.*

Gabby Is this—(*Realizing it's where* **Danny's** *mother lives.*) Oh. Danny.

Danny It's my next series. I'm just trying to sort out the images.

Gabby They're beautiful.

Beat.

Gabby How is your mom? Is she adjusting?

Danny (*moves to sit on arm of sofa*)   She stopped carrying her purse. When the women there start leaving their purses behind, it's a kind of capitulation. I don't think they ever adjust.

Gabby Does she recognize you?

Danny So far. She can't place me in time, though. I can leave the room and come back five minutes later, and she'll call out my name like it's the most wonderful surprise.

Gabby Everyone should have your mother.

Danny (*not wanting to dwell, changes the subject*)   So, people are talking about you. There's speculation.

Gabby *takes off her shoes and makes herself comfortable.*

Gabby (*tossing it off, but covering*)   Because I'm staying at the *W*?

Danny Because you aren't known for doing things like staying at the *W*. Are you staying at the *W* alone?

The door opens to **Mac**. **Gabby** *is saved by her entrance.*

Mac (*to* **Gabby**)   She's here! Our wanderer.

Danny No babka, though. If you were counting on it.

Mac (*to* **Danny**)   You don't get out much do you?

Beat.

Our Gabby.

Gabby *moves toward her, as* **Danny** *takes this in.*

Danny   All day I've had this fresh urge towards everyone I've ever loved. It's a surprising development. I'm on the brink of calling people.

Mac (*putting the brakes on sentiment*)   You don't want to do that.

Danny   It's so achingly present. It stings.

Beat.

It passed.

Mac   I'm relieved. (*To* **Gabby**.) You found your way. I'm proud of you.

Gabby   Wanda helped. I couldn't have done it without her.

Danny   Her GPS.

Mac   This whole new relationship you're having with technology. I'm rattled.

Gabby (*sits on a chair*)   Mac, your article. I finally got to read it on the train. What I can't grasp is how the juvenile justice system can even call itself that when they keep putting these kids in solitary. I'm amazed you got anyone to open up.

Mac   The bigger deal is that the paper ran it. Deep reporting is not so much cherished anymore.

Danny   I cherish it.

Mac   And I cherish you for cherishing it.

Mac *moves to sit near* **Danny**.

Mac   Anyhow, as long as Gabby's upset I'll take that to mean she liked it.

Gabby   I like everything you write even before you write it. Just seeing your name! I'll never get used to it. I'm sorry. I'm a fawning fan.

Mac   Lead with that.

Gabby   Still learning the etiquette.

Danny After all these years, you still don't know that if Mac doesn't hear from us, she'll take to her bed.

Gabby I'm glad no one judges my work that way. All a vet has to do is be competent. And kind.

Danny Which you are never not.

Gabby Which is the easiest thing to be with an animal. And for that everyone licks my face. (*Fully.*) It's so good to be here. I missed everyone madly.

Mac Sil had her guest room ready. She thinks you're having an affair.

Danny (*driving it home*) At the *W.*

Gabby (*diverting attention*) Has anyone noticed my hair?

Mac (*like it's no big deal*) It's gray.

Danny It's cool.

Mac I like it gray.

Gabby Because no one said anything.

Mac Why is it a man can go without shaving and he's all of a sudden some kind of tragic figure you want to take home and nurse or a genius artist who has no time for anything except his genius work, but a woman stops coloring her hair and she's completely let herself go. (*To* **Gabby**.) So, do you like staying in a hotel?

Gabby I love amenities. I brought you some shower caps. I never knew how much I loved amenities.

She moves to her purse to retrieve them and hands them to **Mac** *and* **Danny**. *Then, giving in*:

Gabby I'm not having an affair. (*Reluctant.*) It's. More. Like. A trial run.

Beat.

I'm in training.

An anticipatory silence from the others.

For widowhood.

Beat.

I'm practicing to be a widow.

Then, seeing the worried expressions on their faces:

Oh no, David's fine.

I mean, as far as I know. We never know what's taking place in our cells and organs. So, in that sense no one is ever exactly *well*.

Danny So, you're just a lunatic.

Gabby I need to know what it's like to be independent. I want to be prepared so when it happens, I can go right into gear.

Mac As long as you're not already signed up for a bereavement support group.

Gabby I went to one meeting.

My children aren't happy with me, either.

Danny And your husband, who is still very much alive, what does he think?

Gabby He's not exactly in the loop on this.

Danny So you're on the down low. A stealth widow in training.

Mac (*to* **Danny**) I really have never heard of this. Have you?

Gabby's *cell rings. She checks it.*

Gabby Sorry. I have to take this. (*Into phone as she walks out of area:*) Hi, Doris. Uh huh. It's probably her diet. Let's try switching her to Senior low residue. How is her stool?

She walks out of their sight.

Mac Well, that makes two people we have to keep alive. Ruth Bader Ginsberg and Gabby's husband.

Mac *moves to the kitchen area to get some coffee. A moment of quiet as they pour and sip, relishing the ritual.*

Danny So, did you catch Rachel Maddow last night?

Mac I thought we decided /

Danny I know.

Mac (*continuing over*) / we weren't going to /

Danny I know.

Mac (*continuing over*)   / do that.

Danny   There will be no MSNBC or cable news talk of any kind.

Mac   We all agreed.

Danny   It's just I thought when we said we weren't going to discuss things, we were still going to discuss things.

Mac   It's what's in my brain all day. And then I have to write it. And fact-check things that may not even exist in the factual world.

Danny   She should have you on her show.

Moves toward **Mac** *in kitchen.*

Mac   Why? Because we're both/

Danny   Smart.

Beat.

Well, it is kind of a—moment for your people. Connecticut, Maine, Iowa, Alafuckinbama. The whole United States of America. Finally you get the right to marry. But, now if some Evangelical baker doesn't want to sell you a wedding cake, that's *his* right.

Mac   Ah. *Those* people.

Mac *moves to sofa and sits.*

Danny   Well, you can't call it a great moment for your other people either when the white people are still trying to stop them from registering to fucking vote.

Mac (*off handedly*)   You're white, by the way.

Danny   Sadly. Even though I always put *Undecided* on those forms.

Mac   But, you've drawn up a gay map. I'm touched.

Danny   You should be.

Mac   Because of me?

Danny   And a few other humans. But, yes.

Mac (*with humor*)   Well, it's only right since you're the one who turned me.

Danny   And how does that work?

Mac   Are we talking about this?

Danny   It seems.

Mac   Because we don't.

Danny   You opened the door.

Mac   We don't, generally, ever. And I'm fine with that.

Danny   Being here with you. Now. It awakens a need.

Mac   To what?

Danny   To talk about it.

Mac   Can you parse the word "it?"

Danny   You. Me. It.

Mac (*a breath*)   All right. Well. So. After we had that—*moment*, I realized I was probably, most likely, all right definitely going to be gay. I just wasn't gay for you.

Danny   Oh, nice.

Mac   Danny. Come on. It was—That's not—I mean, if it hadn't been so good, I wouldn't have known that's what I wanted. You were my friend.

Danny   I could have been more.

Mac   No. You couldn't.

Danny   I always had a little twinge with every new woman you were with.

Mac   You romanticized my life. We would have lasted a week.

Danny   But, it would have been a *memorable*, week.

Mac   With an unendurably painful breakup.

Danny   Who'd break up with who, do you think?

Mac   You'd leave me, of course. But, instead here we are. In your living room.

Danny   Well, I could've, *might've* been gay for you. And still known it was never going to happen with anybody else.

Mac   And it never has. Right? (*A tad jealous.*) Has it?

Danny   Oh. You'd like that. For me to tell you that you were the only one.

Another thing that's never going to happen.

Gabby *walks back in.*

Gabby What's never going to happen?

Danny (*enjoying this*) Mac and me. Being lovers.

Gabby Is this a new thing? Straight until menopause?

No one says anything.

What?

Long beat.

Stop!

Danny 1982. The shoot on the stairs. Nobody guessed? You couldn't tell we had just been making out?

Gabby With each other?

Beat.

Am I just pathetically out of touch with the sexual vibrations of the universe? Because this is just not something that would ever cross my mind. (*Taking it in.*) So, it was a thing.

Mac It never went far enough to be a thing.

Danny Well, it was not *not* a thing. It might have been a thing.

Gabby I mean, you were always leaning in to each other. Going to the bathroom together. Arms and legs draped across the couch. But, that's kind of how it was. With all of us.

Danny Are you shocked?

Gabby Not that you were—whatever. Just that I didn't know about it. Because maybe it's over for you, but it's just happening for me. Which is not fair.

Beat.

So, who made the first move?

Danny *gestures to indicate it was her.*

Gabby But, you're straight.

Danny Apparently not every minute of the day.

Mac She's straight. It was just a lapse in orientation.

Danny If not judgment.

The sound of the door buzzer.

Gabby That's gotta be Sil! I'll go down and get her. (*Starts to go, then:*) Does *Sil* know?

Mac Go!

Gabby I have more questions.

Gabby *goes out the door.*

Mac (*to* **Danny**) Seriously, no one else?

Danny After you? Or before you?

Danny, *purposefully seductive, approaches her.*

Danny Mac.

Mac What?

A moment. Then **Danny** *stops the tease.*

Danny I'm glad we're here in my living room. I'm glad we never had to break up. Or destroy love letters. Which, had we gotten to the point of writing, would have been heart stoppingly sad and beautiful. I'm glad you found the right person to be with. And I'm glad that you're my friend. (*Beat, then slyly.*) Who I kissed.

Mac (*drawing out the word*) Whom.

She takes a long self-satisfied swig of her drink.

(*Quietly concerned*). So, have you heard anything from Simon?

Danny Not yet. But, I don't think he's going to want to talk to me today of all days.

Mac I don't know another mother and son who talk so much.

Danny Well, maybe not when he's going to meet the person who gave birth to him.

Beat.

You do everything to keep them from hurt, then you deliver it yourself. I knew when he was two days old I'd have to tell him someday that he was adopted. When he started getting really attached to the idea of being in my belly, I knew it was time. I so wanted it to be true, to be the one who carried him.

Mac You did carry him. You carry him.

Danny I *want* him to meet his biological mother. I'm just praying she's a concert pianist. Or a translator at the U.N.

Beat.

Or a teacher. Someone who doesn't disappoint him. (*Something she has worried over many times.*) It could so easily go wrong.

Mac Simon's yours. He'll always be yours.

Beat.

Have you said anything to Gabby and Sil?

Danny No. I don't want today to be about that. It's hard enough to do what he's doing. This needs to be his. And, the best thing for me is to let it be about the work.

Mac See, you do that, though. That thing where you take it on and it seems virtuous or strong, but really it's not. It just keeps you apart.

Danny, *somewhat chastened, has no comeback.*

Gabby *has just opened the door to* **Sil**, *whose head and part of her face are covered by a scarf.*

Sil (*without skipping a beat*)   What the hell, Gabby? I bought Ben and Jerry's. Now I'll be forced to eat it. And I fucking dusted. I put out little soaps.

Sil *and* **Mac** *give each other a hand slap as* **Sil** *walks past her to hug* **Danny**.

Gabby I love little soaps. Don't be mad.

Sil (*to the room*)   Sorry, I'm late. Showing an apartment that nobody loves.

Mac What's the matter with it? Did someone die there or something?

Sil It's a pre-war building. Of course someone died there. Everything happened there.

Beat.

They want crown moldings and granite countertops. People can't find comfort in anything.

Gabby (*to* **Sil**)   Are you really disappointed I didn't stay with you?

Sil No. That's. I mean. It's our little custom. But, you're here.

Danny Gabby's charting out the next phase of her life.

Mac Her solo journey in the wilderness.

Gabby I'm so jealous that you all live in the same city.

Mac That doesn't mean what you think it does.

Gabby And that's code for?

Mac Some grand idea of us.

Gabby Why shouldn't we be a grand idea?

Danny Mac's just busting everyone's balls today, for some reason.

Sil Why solo? You're making me nervous.

Mac Things happen.

Gabby Nothing's happened.

Danny She's preparing. For when it happens.

Mac Spousal abandonment.

Danny By death, mainly. They're okay otherwise. Right? You're okay otherwise?

Gabby We're fine. David's fine. I just need more experience navigating the world without him.

Sil Jesus, Gabby.

Gabby Well, if you look at statistics, women outlive men. And you want to know why? I saw the whole thing play out one day in the park. Adam was maybe two. The kids were running back and forth to this little wading pool, and I was talking to the other mothers. Well, *trying* to. Because women always talk like they'll be interrupted. By a drowning or an accident. Something terrible.

Beat.

Women live longer just to finish their conversations.

Sil O-kay. Well. If you really want to get a jump on life without David, I have a charming little studio I'm trying to unload in midtown.

Mac I heard charming. I think I heard midtown, which is an oxymoron. But, then, I'm having a hard time deciphering your words, muffled as they are by chiffon.

Danny Yeah. I've been straining to figure out the whole look.

Gabby I thought it was chic. But I'm from Boston.

After a moment, **Sil** *removes her scarf. Her neck and areas of her face are a road map of pre-surgical lines.*

Sil (*ready for a fight*) And I don't want to be talked out of it.

Danny Fuck me.

Gabby You're getting a face lift?

Danny Fuck me.

Sil So let's everyone try and adjust.

Mac You're confirming everything the culture reveres.

Sil I need my job.

Mac You disappoint me.

Sil What's disappointing is that you'd see this as a personal injury I'm inflicting on *you*.

Gabby People don't wake up sometimes. From the anesthesia.

Sil (*to all*) I'm not like you. I'm not of your ilk.

Danny I love it when you talk dirty. *Ilk* now. What ilk are we that you're not?

Sil Financially stable.

Her friends take this in, having not considered it.

Gabby I could see doing it if I didn't already know what it's like to have an operation I didn't elect and still worry about having again.

Mac So, in principal you're okay with it?

Gabby I'm just saying. Thinking ahead to the single life and how hard it would be to get back into the dating scene. Given what I see on JDate. (*Anticipating their response.*) I only signed up to read the ads. Some of them are very touching.

Danny Begging the question of who's for or against, what's wrong with your face, Sil? I love your face. I need you to keep this face.

Sil That's only a *little* selfish.

Danny I'm the chronicler of that face. I care very much what happens to it.

Sil If my having work done compromises the integrity of your work, don't put it in the show.

Danny *responds viscerally at what she senses will be more than a tossed off remark.*

Danny (*thrown and with an edge*) That would kind of affect what I'm going for, don't you think?

Sil (*an edge*) You mean the forty years of our gradual decline?

A pause.

Mac Has anyone noticed the disappearance of *What Becomes a Legend Most*?

Gabby Well. Because furs.

Mac It's not only the risk of public humiliation by animal rights avengers, it's because there are no actual legends left. You can't be a legend without something to show for it. Some wear and tear.

Sil I'm not aiming for legendary status. I just want to make a good impression on my clients without perpetually looking like I need a long nap.

Danny There are worse crimes against humanity.

Sil Look at my neck. Look at these bags under my eyes.

Gabby I adore your bags. I wouldn't know you without them.

Danny You think property values will fluctuate in your favor once you look rested? I'm not sure your face has such a direct influence on the economy.

Sil *My* economy. My personal ability to prosper and keep my place in this current climate where everything is scrutinized. So loudly.

Beat.

If I don't make a big sale, I'll be hurting.

Gabby Can't your children help?

Sil Let's not do children right now.

Gabby Because you think I talk too much about mine? Fine.

Sil Am I betraying some binding agreement I didn't know I agreed to that we remain the only women in the modern world who haven't had work done?

Gabby Well, I *am* the only one in my book club.

Mac (*to* **Sil**) It's just everyone we went after. For doing it. The mockery. You, in particular. You were particularly unkind.

Sil When Gabby went to a spa to lose weight, she didn't ask us if we thought she needed to lose weight. She went. She lost. We were scared for her to be a size eight and want to be a size zero. But we didn't gang up on her!

Gabby You were scared for me?

Danny You looked awful. Your ass was almost non existent. You're not meant to be a hard body, Gabs. It's a total contradiction.

Mac We didn't say anything. We should've.

Sil So, how is what I'm doing any different?

Mac It's not. It's the same crowd fed idea that your fortunes will suddenly improve if you look a certain way.

Sil I'm not a role model. No one is going to point to me as an example. I'm just trying to make a living. I don't owe anyone my face.

Danny You *do*, though. We all do. If we want to pass anything on.

Sil I'm scaring clients.

Danny So, you need a complete tear down before you can show a house?

Sil I'm scaring *myself*. I want to look in the mirror and see someone—

Mac Younger?

Sil Someone who looks like me.

Mac Younger!

Sil *Refreshed.*

Gabby Does it really matter, anyway? I mean, do people still look? On my entire walk through this city no one looked at me.

Sil Well, in real estate your face is plastered all over lawns and subway cars and little refrigerator magnets.

Mac Yeah, you don't really have to send me any more of those.

Sil I take my clients to the hip neighborhoods. The buildings with baristas and juice bars. I even get them in to the wunderkind who gives the haircut of the moment. But, it's not enough. A person in my business can't show her age.

Danny   So you should what? Go underground? Only come out at night? Just so you don't offend anyone. With your oldness.

Mac   I'd hate to have to worry about what I look like when I'm writing. But, I still can't turn off my voice. It's there on the page. And it's a voice younger people will instantly recognize as not of their time. Which when they get older is a time that won't belong to them anymore either, though no one ever believes that day will come.

Beat.

I get it, Sil. But, plastic surgery isn't going to change the fact that every generation gets a turn. It's just not ours anymore.

Danny   Well, I have six walls at the Modern and 18 minutes in a TED Talk to prove you wrong. This is my turn. And you're part of it. And, at least for today I own (*to* **Sil**) *your* face, (*to* **Mac**) *your* opinions, (*to* **Gabby**) and *your* tight little ass.

So, Sil, if you could wash those terrifying marks off your face, we could start setting up.

She gets a wipe or tissue from kitchen and gives it to **Sil**.

Danny   And, I need those releases.

Sil   What does it mean that we all of a sudden have to sign something? We never had to sign anything before.

Danny   I never *needed* you to sign anything before.

Sil   That comes by messenger, no less.

Mac   She has handlers now.

Sil   This was always just a thing we did. An excuse to get together. Not something we'd have to consider as part of your career.

Danny   What did you think? That I'd just take the pictures and put them in a little scrapbook.

Mac   Well, you did kind of spring it on us.

Danny   It's a formality. You're just agreeing to let me exhibit the work I've been doing with you for the last forty years.

Mac   I've known you people for forty years?

Danny   And that you won't sue anyone.

Sil   Why would we sue anyone?

Gabby   Are you planning to sell them at the museum? Are we going to be on postcards in the gift shop?

Danny   I own the copyright. No one's going to put anything in the gift shop.

Mac (*not happy*)   You have the copyright to my face? I don't remember signing that away.

Gabby   So, I shouldn't get attached to the postcards.

Sil   I'm uncomfortable. Is anyone else uncomfortable?

Mac   Constantly.

Danny   It's what I strive for. To make you uncomfortable.

Sil   With the idea of public scrutiny.

Danny   It'll be *artistic* scrutiny. And that will be on me. Not you.

Gabby   Is that lovely critic still around? The one who called your work optimistic.

Danny   I was crushed.

Gabby   I thought it was a compliment.

Danny   He might as well have said my show looked like snapshots of people saying *cheese*.

Mac   As much as you'd like to be seen as dark. Have been dark. You have to admit there is something less than shadowy in groups of people assembled for what seem to be fairly benign activities.

Danny   *Seems* to be.

Gabby   Mac, you can't say that the "Council Meeting With Donuts" doesn't imply something about to erupt. (*To* **Danny**.) That's one of my favorites. I don't know if I ever told you.

Mac   Okay. There was an underbelly. I take it back.

Sil   So people get to see my wrinkles *and* my underbelly.

Mac   And what manner of fresh hell have you gotten us into with a TED Talk?

Sil   Not to mention, what the actual hell *is* a TED Talk?

Danny (*can't believe* **Sil** *doesn't know*) Really?

Sil I've never bothered to watch one.

Danny All right. So, it's the kind of thing where a neurosurgeon, say, who had a stroke deconstructs the irony of someone who studies the brain having a stroke. Or a tech genius invents a robot and demonstrates how this robot will improve the world.

Mac To de-construct. Important people share an important message with people who are not as important but would like the secret of how to be.

Gabby (*to* **Danny**) So, what's *your* message?

Danny (*inclusive of everyone*) You're the message.

Sil You're going to trot us on stage like those inspirational robots?

Danny Not *actual* you. Do you think I want people to see your three dimensional selves? And there will be no robots. Just your faces. In the photographs.

Sil To demonstrate what? What are we the bearers of?

Danny (*a beat*) Time.

Sil (*resistant, upset*) I don't want to be a mirror. I don't like the idea of being assessed by how I weathered the years. People thinking the years haven't been kind to her.

Danny (*losing patience*) You got to grow up, work, have kids, go to the movies. Time hasn't been kind to people who don't get time.

Gabby The thing that worries me. Is. What if, you know, critics or whoever go after you for trying to pass off pictures of your friends as maybe not living up to your other work. We'd be the reason for your failure. I don't know if I could handle that.

Mac Something I never would have thought of. Thank you, Gabby.

Sil No. She has a point.

Danny Was I wrong to trust everyone would be okay with this?

Mac If you trusted us, why did you wait until today to give us the releases?

Danny I knew you'd over think it. Like you're doing.

Mac (*building opposition*) You raised the stakes, Danny. It changes things.

Beat.

I mean, those TED Talks go viral. Giant projections of our faces on multi screens. And then all the iterations on modern devices where anyone can brand you with an ugly, soul crushing name.

Sil   How can that be a good thing?

Mac   And aren't you just a little worried that all this attention might resurrect something from the past you don't want to have to deal with again? Because I am.

Gabby   I would not be happy to be reunited with anyone from the senior class of Falmouth High.

Mac (*dryly*)   For example.

Beat.

I broke some stories that caused a shit storm I'd like never to revisit.

Danny   I thought you lived for shit storms.

Mac   Well, not for all the unintended consequences. Why expose yourself?

Danny   We've all done things, Mac. There's always going to be someone out there who's not a fan.

Mac   Or too much of one.

Danny   The thing is, anyone can find you. Every piece of our data is have-able. You, of all people, know this, Mac

Beat.

But, this isn't about that. Is it?

Sil (*hesitatingly opening up a deep seated insecurity*)   It just seems. I'm going to say it. That there's a hierarchy of value in what we do. Gabby saves animals. Mac exposes truths. And Danny makes art. We have journalism and medicine. And art.

Gabby   Sil, for God's sakes/

Sil (*rising anger*)   No. Let me—just hear me out. Which means that someone, a sales person say, I don't know, a food truck owner, someone providing a service without improving or healing anything is pretty low on the ladder of determining who prevails in a situation. I'm expected to yield. For the sake of art. Or the greater good. Speaking truth to power beats selling condominiums.

Danny So this is about me. And not wanting it to be about me.

Gabby Please, let's not spend this day fighting.

Mac No one's fighting.

Gabby I came for the camaraderie.

Mac Sometimes fighting is foreplay. To the camaraderie.

Danny Whereas Mac isn't afraid of a fight. Mac is afraid of *not* fighting.

Mac Perfectly stated. And deeply resented. Don't analyze me.

Sil Sometimes I think—

Danny Let's have it. Let's have the ugly talk. It'll come out later, anyway. When you go home and call each other up. So let's have it.

Sil We're all too enamored. We do what Danny asks us to do. Because we think it has a higher purpose. Or because she's some kind of celebrity now.

Gabby (*challenging*) Or because she's our friend.

Mac You are controlling, Danny. Well, you are. In the most subversive way. By seeming not to be. It's very seductive.

I'm not saying it's a tactic.

Danny So, I'm a pretender.

Mac No. You're the real thing. That's how you manipulate us.

Gabby In a *good* way.

Danny (*lets loose*) The hell with all of you. Women don't get anywhere in this world without working it. And the only thing I want, which I'm apparently trying so ruthlessly to get, is permission to show your photographs. So people can see what actual women look like over four decades in their lives.

Sil It was ours. This time we had. It was ours. It's not about us anymore.

Danny It's still about you. *And* something bigger. It's about what happened to each of us. Personally. And what happened to all of us, in the world. You can read that on someone's face. We carry it.

Sil So, you can tell which lines I got when someone bullied my child and where the meltdown at Three Mile Island left its mark? Maybe I don't want people to read me like that.

Gabby Danny wants us to be the subject of her life's work, and we can't think of enough ways *not* to thank her.

Mac "I grow old, I grow old, I wear the bottoms of my trousers rolled."

Gabby "The Love Song of J. Alfred Prufrock." Are we doing first lines again?

Mac I used to think the rolled trousers were the style of how you dressed when you got old. I seriously didn't understand the implication. That we get fucking *shorter*. This guy's pants were too damn long because his fucking bones demineralized and he got shorter. How depressing is that?

Beat.

My problem with the whole thing isn't—it's—that people might take away from how I look in a certain photograph as completely out of touch with the moral size of things. I'm not a young girl who's been raped on her way to fill the family water bucket. I'm not a refugee. But maybe in one of those pictures I look like I'm about to lose everything. When, really, what's in my face is just every day pain.

Danny You can't be personally sad? You can't have a day where you feel empty and bottomless.

Mac I don't want anyone to look at me and think I've appropriated real suffering.

Danny Ah, Mac. Is there anything you can't find the lie behind? You're always looking for something to politicize or invalidate.

Mac The standing institutions invalidate *us*.

Danny But, you have to extricate the flaw in every argument, look for the way something is really not what it seems to be.

Mac Because to me, being fed the glossy version is unbearable.

Gabby Isn't that the same thing Danny's trying to do with us? In the photographs. In the photographs. Expose what's true?

Danny Mac, you shine a light on things we'd never see if it weren't for your unrelenting itch to find them. You're my hero for that. You don't want us to turn the page on a difficult story. I don't want people to turn away from what's difficult to look at in you.

Beat.

Letting people see you. It's generous.

Sil But why us? Why the photographs of us?

Danny (*a building passion and frustration, bringing her to the brink*) Because—you're my—timetables of history. You're—rock and roll. The space launch. Civil rights. The decades that chronicle the most sweeping changes in *everything*. Style. Music. Literature. You're my—sundial, my—alphabet. My guide to better living. You're my memorial to all that.

Beat.

Bitches.

Spent, **Danny** *walks away.*

Sil *is torn.* **Gabby**'s *upset at everyone for getting in the way of* **Danny**'s *project.* **Mac**'s *exhausted from her own rants. A quiet comes over them.*

Mac *sits at the table.* **Gabby** *walks over and sits next to* **Sil**, *now sitting on the couch.*

Gabby (*to* **Sil**) What's going on with you?

Sil You don't know what it's like. To juggle so much.

Gabby No. I didn't have to complete six years of veterinary school with a baby and a professor husband who made next to nothing. (*Finding this hard to say:*) Sometimes I think you only like me to stay with you because you can play the sophisticated, worldly one.

Sil Maybe it's because I want to protect you. (*Opening up about something in their past.*) That time I let you down. When I didn't look. You asked me if I wanted to see your scar. And I didn't look.

Gabby It's—

Sil (*cutting her off*) No. It's not forgivable.

Gabby You sat Shiva with me when my father died. You don't have to keep trying to make up for it.

Sil I sat with you. I didn't have to do anything but be there.

Gabby You didn't have to be there.

Sil I don't know why it was so hard to look.

Gabby It doesn't matter now.

Sil It's always going to matter.

Gabby All right. I was thrown. I was. But then I understood why you couldn't. I was 38. You were almost that. If it happened to me, it could happen to you. I lost a breast. You didn't know how you'd react. You didn't want me to see your face if it turned out you couldn't handle it.

Sil Don't. Do that. Don't give me a break.

Gabby Why is everyone so invested in my being angry? I don't like what happens when I get angry. I can't breathe. I practically run a fever. It's very unattractive.

Sil I so want to piss you off right now.

Gabby You know, I still have the charm bracelet everyone made for each round of chemo. Yours was such a cute little doll house.

Sil Actually it was a condo.

Gabby Of course, it was.

Danny *walks back through the studio.*

She has thrown on her old, artfully worn, work tee shirt and is setting up, lightening the mood as she deliberately disregards everyone.

Danny Don't mind me.

Mac This is serious. She's wearing the tee shirt.

Sil If you're wearing that shirt to tug at our collective heartstrings, it's a fail.

Gabby I love that old shirt. I want to be buried in it.

Beat, off others' looks.

Someday.

Danny I'll put it in my will.

Gabby You're my witnesses.

Mac (*out of the blue*) I'm old.

Gabby Er. Old-*er*.

Mac When did it happen exactly? One day I'm dancing all over the house in my little bikini underpants and socks. And then, sometime in the middle of the afternoon, it happens. Just like that. I'm old.

Gabby I like thinking of you that way. Dancing in your underwear. Oh, maybe I like you more than I should.

Mac I'm cancelling my 65th year.

Gabby I'll take it.

Mac I don't know how to be an old woman.

Danny Do you think a twenty-year-old knows how to be twenty?

Danny So, I was reading a letter to the doctor who answers questions in the AARP magazine.

Mac Why were you reading a magazine from the AARP?

Danny It comes in the mail. I'm in the population.

Danny *gets her purse and takes out her wallet, from which she removes a card and holds it up as proof.*

Danny And proud of it.

Mac You laminated your Medicare card? That is so seriously upsetting.

Danny I have laminated every card bearing my name since women were first allowed to possess their own credit cards. Which, by the way, did not happen until the year *nineteen seventy fucking four.*

She puts the card back in her bag, as something falls out. A wrapped condom. She retrieves it, aware of everyone staring.

Danny What?

Sil Nothing.

Gabby Nothing.

Danny It's a condom.

Beat.

Can I continue, or do I have to explain?

Mac You have to explain.

Danny They're sometimes used in the act of having sex. I like to carry one in my purse where it fits nicely with my lipstick and flashlight.

She puts it back in her purse.

Mac So, you have actual sex with another person.

Danny When I have it, that's my preferred way.

Mac Because a lot of people now don't even bother to show up. When they can text their orgasms over the phone.

Danny Anyhow, this man writes in that his wife won't get naked in front of him. She undresses in the dark and won't let him see her. She has this terrible shame or bashfulness regarding her body in the nude.

Mac See, and I don't care who sees me naked as long as I don't have to see myself.

Danny So, the doctor writes back and says maybe it's her past that enslaves her. Or society and it's judgments of the female form. Then he goes on to list some drugs that might make it easier for this man's wife to take off her clothes in front of him.

Beat.

Zoloft, zip, down come her jeans. Prozac, she slips out of her bra. Effexor, off with the panties. Wellbutrin, socks to the floor. Lexipro, she's bare naked nude. I mean, what's the message here? Is it the AARP and its ties to pharmaceutical companies?

Mac My work here is done.

Danny Or, is the message that people over fifty should start pumping those antidepressants as fast as we can? Because we are surely going to need help with what's to come.

Sil *Or.* We could get stoned.

Sil *gets a joint out of her bag.*

Mac When are you going to grow up and start drinking?

Sil When are you going to grow up and *stop*?

A silence at the mention of this thorny topic. Then, **Sil** *lights up a joint.* **Mac** *pours herself a drink. A standoff. As they duel with their "weapons" of choice.*

Mac It's in the works.

She takes a drink.

I plan to take my last drink after I file my last story and clear out my desk.

Sil Well, that was a smooth intervention.

Sil *passes the joint to* **Danny**. *Who takes a hit. And passes it to* **Gabby**.

Mac Have you been planning an intervention?

Gabby I knew nothing of this.

Sil We've rehearsed it.

Danny Over the years. It never turned out well.

Sil In our little scenario.

Danny We had scripts.

Gabby (*as she inhales*)   Why you need to drink, Mac? You have so much.

Mac Where to start. To be in the world. To loosen the grip. To stop the noise. Every reason and no reason at all.

Sil I hope you're serious about stopping.

Mac You know how I get when something loses its charm.

Sil I've seen it. I hope never to be on the receiving end of it, myself.

Mac Sadly my love affair with vodka is not what it used to be. The thrill is gone. (*Takes a drink.*) Well, going.

Danny So, is no one interested in why Mac is cleaning out her desk? (*To* **Mac**.) You buried the lede, my friend.

Gabby You're retiring?

Sil They're letting you go?

Mac I'm on deadline for the last piece I'll probably ever write for an honest to god newspaper you can actually hold in your hands. I mean, how can you revel in getting your name above the fold? There is no fold.

Gabby This just doesn't happen. You don't get fired.

Mac Bought out. When they started talking about adjusting journalists' salaries based on views, like on YouTube, I knew it was the end of days.

Danny You're a senior editor. There had to be an option to stay.

Mac Actually, I don't have a choice.

Gabby (*on a stoned crusade*)   If this is ageism, we're going to D.C.

Mac It's the aging of the kind of journalism I was brought up on. I mean, it's been coming. Every week there are the exit cupcakes. At least no one's asked us to go door to door and deliver the paper ourselves. Yet. (*Opening up.*) I don't know how to leave. I grew up there. (*Allowing the memories.*) My first days at the paper, the men weren't having any of it. They had all these little tests I had to pass. I only made it through the day by taking frequent trips to the ladies room to cry.

Gabby Do you think men ever go into the men's room to cry?

Danny Not once in the history of the world, do I think that's ever happened.

Mac This one day, though, I couldn't hold back the tears of humiliation. And, maybe everyone was just shocked to see me like that, or that's all they ever wanted, proof I was still a girl. So snot is pouring down my face and at some point the sports editor, who was not exactly gentleman of the year, hands me his neatly pressed linen handkerchief. It was monogrammed. I remember.

Beat.

Something changed. We did our jobs. We went out for drinks. We were colleagues.

Sil I don't get it. How does a paper survive without people like you?

Mac How do I survive without a paper?

Gabby I'm canceling my subscription.

Mac (*changing mood*) Oh, god. Pity Jane.

Danny Yeah. Poor Jane.

Mac You do not want to be around me while I'm trying to figure out how to be a person in all of this.

Sil Jane is going to need back up.

Mac I'm not seeing what comes next.

Danny Just write your last piece. Call everyone out. Like you do.

Beat.

Unless. Jesus, unless it's the fucking *Best Of the Year Review*.

Mac Once! One time. A pregnant colleague was having contractions. I took it over. It had to get done. You were a very poor sport about it.

Gabby You really were.

Danny (*a rant*) Those articles always make me want to get the hell out of town and go someplace where it isn't a competition. Some place where trees and mountains and trails don't suffer if they aren't chosen the top ten trees and mountains and trails of their generation. Or feel like they've failed as trees or mountains and trails because they haven't made the *list*.

Mac Just to remind you. You have a retrospective coming up. You're on the list.

Danny (*serious*) You're right. So, sign those releases. And let me get to work.

Sil (*dreading having to confront this*) I don't know if I can.

Stopping **Danny** *in her tracks.*

Danny Well, I'm not going to Photoshop you out of forty years, Sil. This is a group series, you know that. I need everyone or I've got nothing.

Gabby Just let her take our pictures.

Sil So she can share them with the world?

Danny You have no idea how you'll appear to the world. You've never even seen the photographs.

Gabby Well, that was always part of the plan, wasn't it? We don't get to see them until it's all over. After the last shoot.

Danny Which. Is. Today.

A silence. Everyone is taken by surprise.

Gabby Why would you end this now?

A beat.

Danny Because we're all here.

The women are quiet as the meaning of this sinks in. **Danny** *goes to her workplace, retrieves an archival box which holds the photographs and places it near them.*

Danny If you don't want to see yourselves, don't look.

But you don't know what you're missing.

Danny *walks away. Gradually the lights focus in on the box of photos. Everyone is tentative. Finally,* **Gabby** *moves toward the box, opens the lid and slowly pulls out a photograph, which only they can see.*

Gabby Look at us!

The lights change, becoming dimmer, to be expressive of this moment when the women are seeing themselves for the first time in **Danny***'s* work. Their movements as they approach the photographs in silence are contemplative. After looking at a few of the photos, **Sil** puts them down and leaves by the front door. Then, **Mac** walks slowly off stage to another room. Until only **Gabby** remains. The lights come up on **Gabby**, alone. After a beat, she looks up from the photographs and turns around to realizes no on else is there with her.

Gabby Hello!

Beat.

Anybody?

Danny *walks in, from another room.*

Danny I couldn't look at everyone looking.

Mac *walks in.*

Gabby Where were *you?*

Mac Contemplating my life in the bathroom mirror. Who am I?

Gabby (*referring to photos*)   I know. What happened to those other people?

Mac (*looking at the photo* **Gabby**'s *holding*)   And the hair!

Gabby My flip! (*Looking at another.*) Your fro.

Mac It's making a comeback.

Gabby Sil's bob.

Mac An almanac of hair.

Danny That time—Mac—that woman. Who came over to us and wanted to touch your locs. You went totally off on her.

Mac I was just laying down the rules so she wouldn't make the same mistake with someone else who might not be as . . . understanding. I was protecting her, really.

Gabby (*re: another picture*)   What were we all laughing about in this one?

Danny *moves close to see.*

Danny The newsletter of my divorce.

Mac That was some of my finest writing.

Danny   The everything about Richard papers. Richard goes to a restaurant. Richard crosses 79th Street. The breaking Richard News Of The Day.

Mac (*beat, looking at photos*)   We're all so. Completely yours, Danny. It's like you own us here.

Gabby   You can see the romance we were having with the future.

Mac (*intellectually stimulated*)   Somewhere that changes, though. There's something Danny caught here. You start to see between one year to the next. (*Looking at another photo.*) What year was this one? I love it.

Danny   The glam shot. 1992.

Mac   We were. Weren't we? Glamorous. Why didn't I feel that way then?

That's what's going to happen, isn't it? I'll look back at myself today and think, *you fool*.

Gabby (*to* **Mac**)   What were you writing in that little notebook? That first day. In jail.

Mac   It's better not to know. Sacred territory. Those little notebooks.

Gabby   Oh, come on! Give me something.

Danny   She was trying to intimidate our captors. Letting them think she was taking names.

Mac   Which of course they completely ignored. And the scent of patchouli kept drowning out my ability to form a sentence.

Danny   The things we did. Well, needed to do if we ever hoped to stop being good girls.

Gabby   It's like we had permission.

Danny   We didn't ask. We just took it.

Mac   There were manuals and manifestos. We practically had instructions on how to take it.

Danny   Well, I for one am happy never to hold a mirror up to my vagina again.

Beat.

I never really understood what I was looking for.

Gabby It was such a—time. To be a woman.

Mac Only if you're talking about women here. In this country. And even here, in the smallest of realms.

Gabby Well, we didn't have the whole story.

Mac No. We had the *Can We Have it All* story. And next to what's really perpetrated on women and girls, it was the wrong story.

Gabby (*a real question*) So, now we have the information. What do we do with it?

Mac Be decent. Expose people who aren't.

Beat.

I think, exclusive of merely behaving badly, we've been decent. I'm going to assume we've all behaved badly.

Danny I've been an accessory to your behaving badly, and it wasn't pretty.

Mac But, you've never had so much fun.

Gabby Can we still? Have fun.

Danny Isn't that what we're having?

Gabby You know what I mean. Stop and think for a minute. The millenials. Do you think they're having fun? They seem exhausted.

Mac The other night Jane and I read a book aloud to each other. That was fun.

Danny *Elder* fun.

Mac Well, what happened afterwards was fun for all ages.

Gabby The photographs, Danny. I can't stop looking at them.

Beat.

I used to feel relieved. When the shoot was over. I used to think that when I got home, I wouldn't have to weigh everything against what I was or how I thought I'd be. So, I was relieved to return to people who didn't know me *when*.

Beat.

And all that matters to me now is to be with people who know me *still*.

The front door opens. **Sil** *walks in. Everyone waits for her to say something. She moves nervously. Then, pent up, about to quietly explode.*

Sil   I needed to separate.

Gabby   Are you back?

Sil   I saw the photographs. Before I left. I saw them. They're devastating.

Beat.

I feel used.

Danny (*blindsided*)   How am I using you? I didn't build a career on your backs. You didn't get me to this place. No one would give me a show of women aging if it weren't for the reputation I already have for my other work. Which had nothing to do with you.

Sil   The photo you took of us in 2008. I had an exclusive on a brownstone. Which I worked my ass off to land. The developer lived in Japan, so after we signed the deal, he went back and was hands off.

Beat.

Every day, I'd show the place. And after the last appointment, I'd walk out with the clients, close up, and when they were out of sight, I'd unlock the door and go back in. I never went home.

I couldn't go home. I had to rent out my own place just to have an income. I lived there, for Christ's sake. Like a squatter.

Overlapping one another:

Danny   That is so. Completely. (*Struggling to find words.*) Wrong. I'm so sorry, Sil.

Gabby   Why didn't you tell us?

Mac   How long?

Sil   It doesn't matter.

Danny   Who are we then? If it comes to something so basic and you don't—what do we mean to you?

Gabby   We could've helped.

Mac Jane would've been happy if you stayed with us. You play Scrabble without incident.

Gabby I blame your husband, your *then* husband, for putting you in that position.

Mac At least he's being punished for it.

Sil I should have seen it coming. But, I wasn't in charge of my own future. I let Patrick take it all on.

Mac That's why it was so hard to talk with you then.

Sil I'd be sleeping on top of these gorgeous reclaimed wood floors. Breathing in the history of a neighborhood. You were writing these scathing articles about privilege and gentrification, and I was contributing to it. Working with one of those opportunistic investors who put people out of their homes. I felt guilty and angry that I felt guilty. And sick over how I was living.

Mac You should've come to me, Sil.

Sil I was trying to keep you out of it. You would've gone after Patrick. And why shouldn't you? What happened to the idealistic law student I married is a good story. One more sad American tale of wrong. But, he's paying for it. And my kids don't need to be reminded of their parents' failures.

Beat.

You got what you were after, Danny. Which is a testament to you. Just seeing the photograph from that year puts me back there. Only it's not a place I want to be.

Danny What should I do? Airbrush the mistakes, the disappointments? It's a life. Why would you want to erase any of it?

Sil There are so many things to say about that.

Beat.

At least, you don't have to look at yourself.

Danny I have to live with myself.

A long pause. Then:

I'm going to make French toast.

She walks into the kitchen. She has prepped the French toast earlier, so now she finishes it and starts getting things to take to the table. **Sil** *and* **Gabby** *remain where they are. After a moment,* **Mac** *walks over to* **Danny**.

Mac   I love that you still have Simon's little grade school drawings up on the fridge.

Danny (*coldly*)   Can you hand me the butter?

Mac (*seeing* **Danny**'*s upset*)   Look, everyone is just—It's not that I'm not on your side.

Danny   Really?

Mac   It's just that I'm seeing all points of view.

Danny   Nothing ever gets accomplished with that level of fairness.

Mac   Then maybe it's not supposed to.

Beat.

I'm not saying it won't.

Danny   I should have fed everyone. How could I forget to feed everyone?

Sil *takes a peace offering out of her bag.*

Sil   I brought that special fig jam everyone likes.

Sil *tries to open it, but can't.*

Gabby   Here, let me try.

She can't open it either.

All (*almost in synch*)   Arthritis.

Gabby   Remember when we all had our periods at the same time?

Danny *checks on the French toast. It's ready. Her friends help bring food, dishes to the table. A few overlapping words and sounds of pleasure. Trying to put a hold on the dissension.*

Gabby   I didn't know I was this hungry.

Mac   Heaven.

Gabby   I love that smell.

Danny   Sil, I used that vanilla you brought last year.

Sil   Are you ever going to reveal your secret French toast ingredient?

Danny (*beat*) Love.

They all sit. Some silent eating. Then:

Mac Everything is all so—(*can't think of the word*)

Sil What?

Mac It's all so—

Sil What?

Mac When you don't know what's coming next. It's all so—(*trying to remember the word*)

Gabby Mysterious?

Mac No.

Gabby Iffy.

Mac Like that. But not that.

Gabby Tentative.

Sil Up in the air.

Gabby Random.

Danny (*pantomiming*) Sounds like—

Mac Stop! No. Really. (*Seriously worried.*) I'm losing it.

Gabby There's a new test for dementia where you have to recognize famous people and then be able to say what they're famous *for*.

Sil So, if you don't read *People* magazine you could be diagnosed as having lost your faculties.

Mac I want to know exactly what the situation is. You will not try to placate me with the disturbing and frankly uncomforting anecdotes about people my age all having the same trouble. You don't know if it's the same. And if it is, then my god we're utterly incapable of helping each other.

Danny You know what would be a relief *not* to remember? Where I was on *the day of*. You know how everyone started cataloging things that way. By what you were doing on the day of the terrible thing.

Gabby Which terrible thing?

Danny Well. Let's review.

Beat.

I was in science class. For the first terrible thing. Our teacher was telling us how to escape from quicksand and tidal waves and other inescapable situations. And the loudspeaker came on. They were sending us home.

Sil The Kennedy assassination.

Danny It wasn't ever personal to me. I mean it didn't go deep, the way it did later with other things. Just that it was the President, you know. It was a shock to how you saw the world afterwards.

Mac Fire hoses and attack dogs. I was staying with my grandmother in Birmingham that summer. She wouldn't let me out of her sight. Four little girls, she kept saying.

Danny The things that happened before we were even sentient. Auschwitz. The atom fucking bomb.

Sil (*unleashing a litany of iconic words*) I am the destroyer of worlds.

Mac Have you no sense of decency, sir!

Gabby The whole world is watching!

Sil Anita Hill. I know exactly where I was. On the phone with all of you, watching the hearings together. Screaming at the television.

Danny The names. The names on the Quilt. The names on those little post-its all over the city. Have you seen my friend. He worked on the 56th floor.

Mac Say their names!

Gabby Doesn't it seem like there used to be more space between the terribleness?

Danny Well, because despite what someone—I forget his name—said about history being over—

Gabby Francis Fukuyama. He wrote that essay. "The End of History." (*In response to her friends' nonverbal expressions.*) What? I didn't only study the anatomy of a cat.

Danny Anyhow, if what he meant was that we've figured it all out, humanity is progressing and there's no chance we'll ever go backwards—that we're, post racial, post feminist and goodness prevails—isn't that just the renaming of things to disguise what's really going on? We aren't post anything. Except truth.

A beat.

Mac November 8th, 2016.

A pause. As this lands. Then:

Sil My son-in-law is teaching the kids how to escape from the trunk of a car.

Gabby (*pointed*) Does this mean we can talk about them now?

Mac Gabby, how's your granddaughter? She's been on my mind.

Gabby She still wants to be called Michael. She won't answer to her real name at all. And she won't look at you if you use the wrong pronoun. It's hard to know the right thing.

Sil She's so young. Can't she just be a tomboy?

Gabby Not if she thinks she's a *real* boy.

Beat.

I'm so scared for her.

The thought of what happens to trans kids hangs in the air for a moment.

Danny So, what do you call her?

Gabby Sweetie, cookie, mouse. But just last week she said—(*correcting herself*) *He* said, "Why don't you ever say my name, Gab-ma."

A pause.

Mac I'm glad I don't have children. Not that I don't worry enough about yours. But I don't know how parents of black children ever take an easy breath.

Beat.

And who can understand what young people are saying? They don't open their mouths when they talk. Although they seem to understand *each other*. Sometimes I think we may be missing the brilliance of their contributions.

Gabby Except for Simon. Your son never mumbled.

Danny If anything, he spoke too clearly.

Mac And still does.

Danny After Simon was born and I got the call that I was going to be a mother, I all of a sudden had this terrible guilt for whatever I did as a child to hurt another child.

Gabby   I can't imagine you were ever cruel.

Danny   You've never been to summer camp.

Sil   Cruelty runs rampant in summer camp.

Danny (*pained that she participated in this*)   The girl in our bunk with broken glasses and acne. One day we told her that she had a bad case of ear lobes. And when it was painfully clear she had no idea what that meant, she was told the only cure was taping paper cups over her ears. She wore them all day.

Gabby, *especially, feels this in the pit of her stomach.*

Sil   Well, if we're talking about the worst things we've ever done. When we first met. At the *thing*. I wasn't there for the reasons you were all there. I was there to meet men.

Mac   It's not like we were in the Polish Resistance. We were testing the waters. You're forgiven. Though I don't remember any cute men. (*Off Sil's look.*) What? I like men.

Sil   I have to say—don't take this—but, I admit I was surprised when you finally told us you were gay. I mean. You were kind of a slut.

Mac   What makes you think that changed?

Gabby   Did you have a hard time, Mac? You never talk about it. Coming out.

Mac   Well, there isn't just one moment. It's a kind of a rolling admission. Which is annoying. Because being gay is not the first thing that comes into my mind when I get up in the morning. Sometimes having to stop and *remember* I'm gay in the middle of a conversation takes up a lot of space in my head which I'd rather keep available for other things.

Sil   Can you *be* a slut with other women?

Gabby   And there was at least one cute man.

Mac (*dawns on her*)   I completely forgot that's where you and David met. Well, he wasn't cute. He was beautiful.

Gabby   He was. (*A brief flash of what losing him would mean.*)

He is. (*Putting it out of her mind.*) So. Are you and Jane going to get married? Now that you can?

Mac   It doesn't mean we must.

Gabby   How will you protect yourself, though? If something happens to one of you. That's the whole point.

Mac It shouldn't be. The whole point. It's got to be a romantic decision, too. And, I already feel married.

The first time a gay couple appeared in the paper's Vows column, I cut it out and put it up on the refrigerator. I started to collect them like baseball cards. I'm a wreck at every ceremony. But, what if I turned out to be a bad example? What if I make a terrible spouse? Then it's not just my relationship that's failed, it'll be a strike against the cause.

Gabby You put a lot on yourself.

Mac When you're an African American and a woman and gay, it can be a little tricky as to which cause you're most afraid of not living up to at any given time.

Beat.

And—I don't want to get divorced.

Danny Wow.

Gabby That's a shame. A gay wedding would definitely move us all up a rung on the ladder of cool.

Danny Not everyone lasts. Some marriages turn into something else.

Mac As in, just friends?

Danny As in family. Richard and I were too young in the beginning. Then being apart for so many years gave us a lot of time to work things out in the middle. So we can be together in the end.

Mac (*dawning on her*) Oh my god. You still have the cemetery plots.

Gabby I liked Richard. He was smart and funny.

Danny And difficult. But then I'm drawn to difficult men. (*Pointed at* **Mac**.) And *woman.*

Gabby What happened, really? I never understood why you two get divorced?

Danny I blame Sil.

Sil How is it my fault?

Danny You were having an affair.

Sil I was not having an affair with your husband.

Danny But you were having an affair with somebody's husband which led me and my husband to a moral and theoretical impasse. Which led to the break up of our marriage.

Beat.

Well, it wasn't the only thing. But, it was a thing.

Sil   How does this make any sense?

Danny   I had to keep your secret. Which is a strain. On everything. I still have a file of letters you asked me to keep. The letters from Sil's affair file.

Sil   I didn't mean forever. Throw them away.

Danny   I'll give them back to you. You throw them away.

Gabby   We don't see each other enough. Why don't we?

Beat.

Well, we should.

Beat.

We could go somewhere. Together.

Danny   You say that every year.

Gabby *goes to her bag, takes out pamphlets.*

Mac   You've got brochures. I get shpilkas when I see you with brochures.

Gabby   There's a barge trip in France. You stop and ride bikes, eat cheese. And it's private. Unlike those bacteria swarming cruise ships.

This is on me. My gift. My party.

Gabby*'s cell rings.*

Gabby   Say yes.

She answers her phone, moving slightly away.

This is Dr. Lyon. (*Listening.*) Uh huh. Well, what did the x-ray show? (*Listening.*) That's not good. I was afraid of that. No. No, I'll call him. Thanks. I'll let you know. (*Ends her call.*)

Danny   Everything all right?

Gabby   I have to deliver bad news. A twelve-year-old Lab I treated since he was a puppy. It's like I'm a pediatrician and a gerontologist all in one. They aren't with us long enough.

Mac   I wonder if they know what's happening to them. When they start getting old and can't jump up on the bed anymore.

Sil Is that something *you're* worried about?

Gabby Sometimes you can almost see a flash of surprise in their eyes. Like: *How did I not see the humans come through the door?* Or, *I can't climb the stairs. What's that about?* And then they just accept how it is and adjust. It gives me such a tenderness for old animals.

Gabby *starts to get emotional.*

Sil Hey! Hey. It's okay.

Mac I guess you never get used to it.

Gabby This whole thing. Maybe it'll be me. I'd rather it be me.

Mac What are we talking about?

Sil I think she means David.

Gabby I can't do this without him.

Danny You don't have to. Don't lose him before he's even gone.

Mac (*trying to lighten things*) What's his name? The dog.

Gabby Mr. Tuffy.

A moment. Then hearing herself saying "Mr. Tuffy" out loud makes **Gabby** *laugh.*

A pause of relief. Then, making an announcement:

Danny It's *that* time.

Danny *moves with singular purpose to her iPad and turns on the music which is already cued up to the same song they dance to every year before each shoot. With the first beat of "You're All I Need To Get By" they're goners.*

Danny I *will* break you.

Under the music, a few protestations.

Sil Not fair.

One by one they give themselves up to the music and dance. No matter what they've been through, once they let themselves go, they're the same women who met long ago. They dance until **Danny** *turns the music off at a certain logical place in the song. And then they all collapse.*

Gabby (*breathless*)   And we're all still almost breathing!

Danny   Water? Who needs water? Besides me.

Danny *moves off to get water.*

Mac (*hatching a plan*)   Do you have your cell phones handy?

Sil   Why?

Gabby   I can't move. It's in my bag.

Mac *retrieves it, hands it to* **Gabby**.

Sil   Again, why?

Mac *holds up her cell phone and starts taking* **Danny**'*s picture.* **Gabby** *and* **Sil** *follow her lead and join in, snapping away, turning the tables on* **Danny**.

Danny   No, no, no. There is no taking photographs of the photographer. On penalty of extreme displeasure.

They pay her no heed.

I'm serious. (*Giving over.*)

Fine. Have at me.

Danny *lets herself have fun with it, even striking poses. Then, out of the blue:*

Mac   *Precarious!*

She has remembered her forgotten word!

Gabby   What?

Mac   *Prefuckingcarious*. Thank god.

Danny   See, you didn't lose it. It was always there. Just not available to you in the usual location.

Mac   Too many things feel unavailable to me. It's not just a word. It's like I'm in the wrong body. I don't know this body. It feels almost as unreliable as when I was a teenager. I'm molting as we speak.

Gabby   I know. I used to be so *wet*.

Sil   Can we not—

Danny   There are products. You can be juicy again.

Gabby But, if I'm not actually, you know, lubricating on my own, isn't that like I'm faking it?

Mac Accept the gift.

A pause. Then, a shift. **Danny** *becomes quietly serious.*

Danny The light's perfect. You're perfect. We're done with this part. So, go take off your makeup. While I get some things ready.

Mac I'd rather take off my clothes.

A long moment as everyone assesses what **Danny** *has just said, thinking how to respond. Is this* **Danny***'s final stand? No one moves until* **Gabby** *finally makes a move toward offstage area.* **Mac** *follows her, but* **Sil** *remains in place.*

Gabby Sil? Are you coming?

Sil In a minute.

Sil *waves her off.* **Mac** *and* **Gabby** *move off stage.* **Sil** *remains behind and moves to* **Danny***. After a moment, with difficulty:*

Sil Danny—

With a small physical movement or slight shake of her head **Sil** *lets* **Danny** *know that she is not going to do the shoot.* **Danny** *responds with a pained expression, a subtle movement. Shocked. Let down.*

Danny You're telling me this?

Sil I'm sorry.

Danny (*a mix of deep disappointment and anger*)   That's it then.

Danny *moves off stage.*

Sil (*calling after her*)   Are we going to recover from this?

The door buzzer. **Sil** *doesn't have it in her to answer.* **Gabby** *comes back in and opens the door. To* **Simon** *and* **Bess***. Taking* **Gabby** *aback for an instant.*

Gabby Bess, it's so nice to see you! Simon! Sweetie. Your mom said you'd be out of town.

Simon That was the plan. But I stopped to see this lady. I thought she needed a change of scenery, so we're here. Right, Nan?

Bess Oh, sure. (*To* **Gabby**.) Do you know my grandson?

Gabby I do.

Simon Nan, do you want to sit down?

Bess That'll be good.

Simon (*leading her to a chair*) I think this has your name on it.

Mac *enters, with fleeting surprise.*

Mac My favorite people! (*To* **Bess**.) Can I give you a hug?

She hugs **Bess**.

Sil (*to* **Bess**) Stylish as ever.

Mac (*quietly, privately to* **Simon**) Are you okay?

Simon Is Mom?

Bess You're the—friends.

Mac That's right. That's us.

This lands almost imperceptibly with **Sil**, *who registers a pang of guilt.*

Bess That's wonderful.

Simon Nani, do you want to take off your coat?

Bess Am I staying?

Danny *walks back into the room, not expecting to see her son or her mother.*

Bess Danny's here, too! When did you get here?

Danny Just now, Mom. I just got here.

Simon Nani wanted to see everyone.

Bess He's doing good things. He's on the right track.

Danny *and* **Simon** *silently acknowledge how much they're both carrying.*

Danny Ma, you know Gabby, and Sil, and Mac?

Bess I think *so*. They want to—find—they want—(*Struggling to express her thought.*) They do it for you.

Danny And *you*.

Bess I'm okay. I get in the mood of things.

Danny (*to* **Simon**)   I didn't expect to see you.

Simon (*holding back til they get a chance to talk*)   Change of plans.

Bess (*looking at* **Simon**)   He's my heart. His voice does everything for me.

Mac   Bess, can I get you some cocoa? I know you like cocoa.

Bess   Oh, no thank you. I'm not hungry. I don't have meals anymore.

Gabby   Well, we need to fix that.

Bess (*looking at* **Gabby***'s shoes*)   You have pretty—walkers.

Gabby   I like yours too.

Bess   Can I take you girls out to dinner?

Danny   I just fed them, Ma.

Maybe later.

Bess (*studying* **Mac**)   I think I know your childhood. (*To* **Danny**.) Do you have my pajamas?

Danny   Are you tired, Mom?

Mac (*sensing* **Simon** *and* **Danny** *need to talk out of* **Bess***'s presence*)   Why don't we go to Danny's bedroom and we can look for them?

Gabby   Come. Keep us company.

Bess   Oh, that'll be good. You can fill me in.

They move off. **Danny** *and* **Simon** *are quiet for a moment.*

Danny   Well, you still look like yourself.

Simon   You, too.

Danny   Simon.

Simon   Everything's. I'm okay. It's all—

Danny   Talk to me.

Simon   I saw her. She was sitting in the back of the restaurant. In a booth by a window.

Danny   That must've been—

Simon   I didn't go over.

Danny   Did she see you?

Simon   I don't know. I left.

Danny   You left? I hope she didn't see you.

Simon   I wrote a note. I gave it to the waitress. I said I'd be back. Just not today. It wasn't possible today.

Danny   What stopped you?

Simon   I couldn't see the next thing. I didn't see how to fit everyone in it.

Beat.

I went to see Nani on my way out of town. When I got there, she was packing up her clothes. In a garbage bag.

Danny *is visibly struck by this, as her heart sinks.*

Simon   I tried to distract her. I took her on a mental tour of the house on Taft Street.

Danny (*lifted*)   That's brilliant. What a lovely, brilliant thing to do.

Simon   We walked through the whole house. I told her Zayda was playing the violin in the garage. Then we went into the family room. She seemed happy to be there. I named every book on the shelves practically. Will and Ariel Durant. *The History of the Jews.* Watercolor painting. Arthur Miller's *Collected Plays*. We opened the big dictionary to look up words. Words she taught me. And then, the kitchen. Where we played Parchesi. The kitchen brought up the time she wouldn't make me macaroni and cheese and I took the pot in protest and left the house. She always tells that story. When we got to her bedroom, she looked like she could actually picture it. It seemed like she was sinking into the bed. Like she was finally home. I asked her what she remembered? And she just looked at me and said, *I remember everything.*

Beat.

But, after I left her and got to Pennsylvania, I just wanted to turn around. Nan knows me. She still knows who I am. As long as that's true, how can I go on this—self indulgent odyssey to find everything that makes me someone else. How can I do that to you?

Danny   You are someone else. Every time you walk through the door. But, you still walk through the door. Not a different person. Just, more of a person. My five-year-old. My teenager. They're all still here. And, I get to have you.

She didn't.

Beat.

You need to go back.

Simon   Will you be all right?

Danny   You mean, will *we* be all right? Don't you know?

Simon (*wanting to say something which, if he does, will make them both too emotional*)   Mom—

Danny (*lightening the moment*)   Dude.

The other women re-enter.

Mac   Bess nodded off.

Simon   There's a lot of that where she lives now.

Mac   Something to look forward to.

Gabby (*always the savior*)   I'm sure they have activities.

Danny   Lots of sing alongs.

Simon   And political discussions. There was a heated argument about one of them backing the other to run for chairman. Of what, it was never clear. But, it got intense. He didn't want to run. Nani actually rolled her eyes.

Danny   That was probably Harry. He taught history. And Louise. She was a librarian. And did you meet Bob? I've gotten very fond of Bob. I found out he'd been a barber. Last time I was there, he came over to me and brushed a strand of hair off my face.

Simon (*to everyone*)   So, how did the shoot go?

Danny (*covering*)   Late start. We've been having too much fun.

Simon   Do you still have fun? Because my friends don't. We don't have fun. We're too busy aspiring.

Gabby (*harkening back*)   See!

Hey, Mac. I'm doing a new segment for the Young Turks. About the tradition of family owned newspapers coming apart? Can I get a quote from you?

Mac (*taking credit for his political voice*)   I raised him well.

Simon   Considering my bedtime stories came from *The People's History of the United States*. It was my Doctor Seuss.

Sil   Mac gave a copy to you, too?

Danny   The day he was born.

Gabby   All my kids.

Mac   You were expecting "Pat the Bunny"?

Simon   Is it true your paper's downsizing, Mac?

Mac   Sadly. And I'm one of the downsized.

Simon (*struck by this*)   You know there are other ways to deliver your opinions. I could help you.

Mac   How, other than writing my last column, can you help me?

Simon   Watch.

Simon *opens his iPhone to a video. This is his jam and he's psyched to share it.*

Mac   I like paper.

Simon   You'll save trees.

Mac   I like ink.

Simon   We have paper. We have ink. We have desks. We just don't *cling* to them. It's not how the message goes out anymore. It's a different delivery system, that's all. (*Jokingly reassuring.*) Don't worry, I still have a poster of *All The President's Men* on my wall.

Beat.

You know, if you wanted to do something for us, Mac, it would be insane. It would be really excellent.

Mac   Work for the Young Turks?

Simon   We need your people.

Mac   Which people? I have many people.

Simon   The Boomer people. The Turks lack perspective. We don't have representation from a generation like yours that made it possible to do a show like ours.

Gabby   Take him up on it, Mac.

Simon   You could still teach a journalism class at Columbia and work with us.

Sil   What class?

Mac I don't teach a class. I've been asked to teach a class. I always say I don't have time.

Gabby Well, now you do.

Simon And, I'm looking at your website, Gabby. I think your practice would benefit from a redesign.

Gabby I have a website?

Simon And you really should be on Instagram.

Danny He really wants everyone to be on Instagram.

Simon (*with humor*) Everyone *is* on Instagram. Except the people in this room.

Beat.

Just trying to bring you all into the *now*.

Mac I have an issue with some of the *now* on your last show.

Simon Fine. Good. Argue the point. Be our public watchdog.

Mac (*the idea growing on her*) I'd need complete editorial ownership of whatever I wrote.

Simon Mac, you're pretty much the reason I'm doing what I do. And why I want to be good at it. So, anything you want.

Mac *takes this in. Then suddenly,* **Bess** *calls out, "DANNY?" and walks out of the bedroom.*

Danny I'm here, Mom.

Bess *has pulled out one of her hearing aids and is holding it in her hands.*

Bess What is this thing?

Simon It's your hearing aid, Nan.

Bess Oh. What should I do with it?

Simon Here. Let me fix it.

He puts it back in his grandmother's ear.

Bess I've been going through strange ideas and situations that haven't come to fruition for me. I don't know who to call who might be on top of things to know what I'm talking about.

Danny   You can talk to me.

Bess   I know, honey. That's the way with us. It's automatic. It's a diamond.

Danny   That's what it is. (*To everyone.*) Did you know my mother had her own show on the radio? Right, Mom? And she sang with one of the big bands. Tony Candellori and the True Tones.

Bess (*sings*)   "It's very clear—our love is here to stay. Not for a year but ever and a day..." (*She can't continue.*) Oh, well.

Simon   Awesome.

Sil *starts to clap.* **Gabby** *joins.*

Bess (*to* **Simon**)   Are you doing well in school, honey?

Simon (*sensitively*)   I'm done with school, Nan. I graduated.

Bess   I didn't know that. Well, you're old enough to vote now. (*A new concern, to* **Danny**:) Did I vote?

Danny   Of course. I would never let you *not* vote.

Bess   Is she doing a good job? The President.

A stunned silence. **Danny** *temporarily at a loss. Then:*

Danny   Everything you could have hoped for.

Then **Simon** *takes charge.*

Simon   So, Nan, let me show you the work I'm doing. And we'll let Mom finish hers.

Bess (*to* **Simon**)   Then you can tell me everything. (*They start to walk off. To* **Danny** *and her friends.*) You girls have each other. That's as it should be.

Bess *and* **Simon** *walk off to the bedroom. A moment after they leave*:

Gabby   I love seeing Bess and Simon together. The way he is with her.

Sil (*to* **Danny**)   You brought up a good man.

Danny   Didn't we figure out that was the only way to change the world?

Mac   I can't believe she's 91.

Danny   Don't tell her that. She has no idea.

Gabby   She's still trying to be in it with us. Asking us out to dinner. Still asking.

Sil (*moved and in some way affected personally*)   And still herself, really. It's. I mean, a lot of people—you know, you've seen how it is—they get angry. But, she hasn't changed that way.

Mac   I love that woman.

Danny   I think I'll keep her. (*Then, serious.*) I mean, I'm keeping her. With me. Here. I've decided.

Beat.

I'm not taking her back to the place.

Mac (*realizing she's serious*)   You can't take care of her by yourself.

Danny   I can hire someone.

Sil   It will eat up everything you have.

Gabby   And Danny, do you think another move at this point is a good idea? She's safe there.

Mac   I'll visit her.

Gabby   We'll all visit her.

Danny   She's my mother. And, I don't know long I'll get to be a daughter.

Beat.

Or a parent. Or a friend. (*Long beat, a new determination.*) Let me have those releases. I'm tearing them up.

The women are unmoored.

Gabby   What does this mean?

Danny   When I look at the photographs of you, I don't see the retrospective as the prize. You are.

Beat.

And that's how I want to leave it. The people I love are all around me right now. Present and accounted for. How often does that happen?

Beat.

The Museum will probably be *happy*. I had to fight a little too hard to convince them of the direction I was taking, anyway. So, don't worry.

Gabby   This isn't right.

Danny (*especially for* **Gabby**)   I have a lot of other pictures I'm proud to put up. Including *Council Meeting with Donuts*.

Mac What about today?

Danny (*full*) We spent it.

Beat.

I'm going to go check on my Mom.

Danny *walks away. After a moment, She walks back into their view.*

Danny One more thing.

Gabby There's always one more thing with us.

Danny Just what I was going to say. Only *Gabby* said it better.

Beat.

Now I'm done.

Danny *walks off. Leaving her friends alone.*

Mac Don't. Anybody. Talk.

Gabby I just have to say—

Mac No, you don't.

Gabby That maybe this is all going to—

Sil Work out. You think? Really. You hope? Or you think?

Mac She *wants*.

Gabby (*after a moment*) I'm going back to my hotel. Does anybody want to come?

Mac Those were words. I heard words.

Gabby *quietly gathers her things, then moves toward the front door.*

Gabby Okay, last ones. Room service. Massages. And a nap.

She opens the door. A light pours in.

And a nap.

She closes the door behind her. As the main lights on the studio dim.

The wall/screen goes down as lights go up on the TED Talk. The present.
Danny *resumes her talk.*

Danny The actress comes on the screen. Her face fills the frame. Someone in the audience gasps, "She got so old!" The horror! Like it was a crime. Like she went out in her underwear or had food in her teeth.

Like she did it purposely to affront us. She completely let herself get old. I mean, she didn't have to if she didn't want to. If she really tried, she could have saved us the suffering and indignity of having to gaze upon the hideous and unforgivable countenance of someone un-young. It's a betrayal. And we blame her for it. Our loyalties crumble. What a shame. She got so old.

Beat.

I used to think old people came into the world that way. There were babies. Children. Adults. And old people. It didn't sink in for a long time that one person, including me, would actually change, inexorably, from one to the other. That one person could embody all those opposing forms. And for a while I thought my friends were staging a mutiny against that very idea. That by showing the stages of their lives in the photographs, I'd be ratting them out somehow. And consigning them to some kind of blacklist.

But, doesn't our acquiescence to this collective shame about being a certain age have a diminishing effect on our ideas and culture? Are we willing to let that happen? Are we really willing to sacrifice a generation each time it grows old?

Beat.

I've never felt abandoned by mother's dementia. I don't think of her as not being the same person anymore. She's everyone she's ever been. Every sentence she's ever spoken and is no longer able to. Her words are everywhere. Suspended and held forever by all the gorgeous articulations she's already put out into the world. My mother still says I love you in every shared moment. That's her enduring vocabulary.

Beat.

The same way it is with my friends, who carry every version of themselves into this uncertain time in our lives. Their faces say *we continue.*

Beat.

And the photographs documenting those faces are cued up. I came prepared. Permission from the subjects granted. Well, not so much granted, as the only thing it felt right to do under the circumstances. So I'm prepared. I just don't know if I'm ready. When everything is so—(*Can't find the word.*) The thing when you—dammit. Oh, come on! You know this. It's all so—

Mac *walks on to the stage from the wings. It is not a surprise to* **Danny** *that* **Mac** *is here, but the timing of her entrance is.*

Mac *Precarious.*

Danny Saved. Thank you.

Sil *walks on and stands next to* **Mac**.

Sil I was going to say terrible.

Danny (*to audience*) I told them not to come. All I wanted was their approval to use the photographs. I told them it wouldn't help if they showed up. But of course they came anyway.

Beat.

Except the one person who never gave me any trouble. And always gave me permission. She's not coming. I want to say she'll be here any minute. That we're just waiting for her. Like we do. We're waiting for Gabby to find her way. Because she's always getting lost. But, this time, we lost her. She wasn't sick. The cancer didn't come back. She was out for a walk with her dogs. And she fell. She just fucking fell.

Gabby died. And here we fucking are. (*Collecting herself, then adjusting her camera.*) My old Leica. The one I used to take the first photograph of everyone. That day forty years ago.

Beat.

I never got to do the last shoot the way things happened. And I didn't want to show you something incomplete. But, it's always going to be that way. Like Gabby said, there's always one more thing with us.

So, as long as these impossible women showed up, we might as well do one more thing.

Danny *turns towards* **Mac** *and* **Sil**.

Sil Where do you want us?

Danny (*suddenly lost*) I don't know.

Mac (*saving her again*) Does that take selfies?

Mac *walks over to her. When* **Danny** *realizes what* **Mac** *is doing, she almost resists, but doesn't, finally. She adjusts the camera's timer.* **Mac** *escorts* **Danny** *into a position next to her and* **Sil**. *After a few seconds, the timer goes off. The picture is taken.*

The new and final photograph of the series— **Sil**, **Danny**, *and* **Mac**—*is projected next to the* first *one taken of the women in jail. The absent* presence *of* **Gabby**, *and the inclusion of* **Danny**, *reflecting a new reality.* **Mac** *and* **Sil** *turn toward the screen.*

Mac   Look at us.

A beat.

Danny (*stepping out slightly and to the audience*)   Look at us!

A collage of the photographs taken of them over the years fills the screen.

At last, the picture of them in jail returns and fills the space, as the lights go down.

End of play.

Susan Miller is a two-time Obie Award winner and Guggenheim Playwriting Fellow, whose play *20th Century Blues*, after its premiere at CATF, went on to a successful Off Broadway run in the 2017/18 season at the Signature Theatre in NYC, directed by Emily Mann. Susan is also known for her critically acclaimed solo play, *My Left Breast*, which premiered in Louisville's Humana Festival and has been performed across the United States, Canada, and France. She received the coveted Susan Smith Blackburn Prize, as well as The Pinter Prize for her play, *A Map of Doubt and Rescue*. Miller's work has been recognized with a Rockefeller Grant and two NEAs. She has been a Core Writer at The Playwrights Center in Minneapolis and her plays, which include *Nasty Rumors and Final Remarks, Flux, Confessions Of A Female Disorder, Cross Country, The Grand Design* (finalist, Heideman Award), *Arts And Leisure, For Dear Life, It's Our Town, Too,* and *Reading List* have been performed at The Joseph Papp Public Theatre, Second Stage, Naked Angels, New York Stage & Film, The Mark Taper Forum, Theatre J, Trinity Rep, Walnut St. Theatre, City Theatre of Miami, the O'Neill National Playwrights Conference, and Ojai Playwrights Conference, among others. Miller was a Consulting Producer/Writer on Showtime's *The L Word* and ABC's *Thirtysomething*. She won the Writers Guild of America Award for her hit indie web series, *Anyone But Me*, which has over 50 million views worldwide. Miller served for seven years as co-director of the Dramatists Guild of America's prestigious DGA Fellows program. For more about Susan Miller's work go to: www.susanmillerplaywright.com

Interview with Playwright Susan Miller

Researched, interviewed and edited by Sharon J. Anderson, CATF Trustee

After reading 20th Century Blues, *I wondered if you planted a tape recorder in my living room the day before I had three friends over, and surreptitiously recorded our conversation?*

I have tape recorders planted in every living room of every woman and every person. Actually, I wasn't there, but I'm so glad you think I was.

Did the idea for this play come from a conversation you had with friends?

No. While my friends can certainly relate to it, it's not based on any specific conversation or people that I know. I really wanted to create characters that were very specific who, at the same time, spoke to many, many people.

I wanted to write about women, time, and age. What I first needed to do was find a world in which those things would be just part of it, but they wouldn't be the story.

20th Century Blues *is a comedy about the blues. How does that work?*

The characters in this play have spent most of their lives in the twentieth century. It was also a time in which so many major things happened—history was made—and in the play, the characters are wondering: *Does history now ever get made?*

In an essay on comedy and tragedy, Samuel Taylor Coleridge wrote that comedy was "more useable and more relevant to the human condition than tragedy." What do you think of that?

Comedy in the sense I'm reading it and in the history of theater is more telling about the human condition. It is more revealing because tragedy is inescapable. I look at it in the larger picture of the world. I opened the paper today and I see an earthquake—a natural tragedy. Then read on . . . the tragedy of people who live in poverty, the tragedy of families who've lost loved ones in a war. Within that, are the individual human stories which have to balance against that—and there you can find some humor. I'm not sure that makes comedy more "useable," though.

Let me put it the way Joni Mitchell might say it: in her song "People's Parties" from her album, Court and Spark, *she sings, "Laughin', cryin'/ you know it's the same release." Is it?*

I think it comes from the same place . . . an absolutely natural unforced true emotion that provokes either. It's honest and you can't avoid it. When you go to that place, it is really authentic. Humor, first of all, is accessible . . . Now, from instinct, I want people to enter my work—this play in particular, but all of my work—in a way that allows them to live within it and take the ups and downs that the play provides. Once they are able to laugh, once they are able to think, "Oh, I recognize *that* in that person" . . . if laughter and tears both come from this absolutely distinctive place where you fabricate them . . . and if I provide something to laugh about at first, then I feel like we have a genuine trip that we're going to take together.

When people saw the title and description of my play, *My Left Breast*, they probably thought, "Oh my god, this is about breast cancer" (of course, it's about more than that). The first thing I do in that play (or whoever is performing it) is to come out dancing to rock-and-roll music. Then I stop, the music stops, and I say, "That's what I did on the night before I went to the hospital—I danced."

As the author and performer, I want everyone to know that whatever happens in this play—or whatever happens in *20th Century Blues*—you can laugh. And after all the laughing, if I've done it right, if I've set the tone, then when I dip down into something or stop the action, you will know that it's okay to cry or be moved. Stop. Take a breath.

Mac, a character in the play, says: "I don't know how to be an old woman." Does anyone know how to be an old woman?

Aside from problems related to specific situations, these characters, these women are getting older. How do you do that? Because suddenly you're in a category. I think we do that all of our lives. Danny (another character in the play) responds to Mac, "Do you think a twenty-year-old knows how to be twenty?" Older people have been to the younger place already. Younger people haven't been to the older place. It's a conversation.

At the end of the play, Danny asks: "Are we really willing to sacrifice a generation each time it grows old?"

When people get older and reach a certain point in life, they can be dismissed, neglected, or diminished because of pre-conceived notions. I do think that society is addressing this more now because boomers are very outspoken and will not gently into that dark night.

The "forgotten word" in your play is the word precarious. *Why?*

I wanted the forgotten word to open a window. When the characters were younger self-starters or artists—they were in a precarious position because artists always are. Your work may or may not be recognized. If you go to veterinarian school (as the character Gabby does) and become a vet, you can work until you can't work anymore. You have that skill. Then there's the character, Mac, who rises up the ranks of the newspaper world. Who would have ever predicted this current, wild, wild media world would run into so much difficulty? That makes those characters very different.

Age plays a part for these characters, but not for all of them. They each have their own individual struggles and their own individual way of being in the world that may have nothing to do with age except that big question, "How long *will* I be in the world?"

In an exchange between Mac and Danny, Mac says, "I don't want anyone to look at me and think I've appropriated real suffering." Danny responds with this challenging statement: "Because the only valid representation of the human condition is in the cruelest of situations." How can we nurture more patience and empathy for everyday brokenness?

Danny has dealt with issues such as, "Is it worthy of me to take pictures of people in a community theater green room as opposed to being a war photographer?" She's come to a point of thinking that depicting human beings in any situation is valid and eye-opening. If you let people look at your face and see what's really there, that's generous. That's a gift.

What about this line from the play, "Don't spend your life trying to forgive yourself. That's the biggest load of crap ever disguised as spiritual healing." Isn't forgiving yourself Therapy 101?

I love these characters. I get to be able to say things through them. In other plays, I haven't had quite the fun with characters that I've had with the characters in *20th Century Blues*. We can look at ourselves over a period of time and think, "Oh my god, we were so hot! We were so pretty! I was so thin!" But we can also think, "Oh my god, the mistakes I made, the things I did!" Someone might respond, "You have to get over that." These movements toward forgiving yourself, loving yourself—you just get to a point where you don't want to go there anymore. You make mistakes. You don't have to see them that way. It can be spiritually healing to say, "That's a load of crap."

One of the things you advised young playwrights was "to find your voice and be true to that voice." How do you do that?

For a writer it's asking, "How do I distinguish myself?" Sometimes people don't find their voice. In an art form like the theater you actually rely on that other character in the play—the audience—to let you know if you have your voice. There's no formula. It's a very cool thing when people say, "Of course, that's a Susan Miller line," even though my plays are all different and populated by different characters.

If you write something and you feel satisfied yourself—not because it's perfect—but because you simply like it, say that: "I like it." That's pretty cool.

Do you have any twenty-first-century blues?

I now have a grown son, so I'd say that I have twenty-first-century worries. The blues are now more personal, the worries are more global. I don't really know. I think the century is too new. My biggest blues are a deep, deep sorrow that my parents are gone, that certain people have passed, that friends, mentors, family members—there's a navigation that has to happen in the world without them.

This is a play written by a woman with all women characters with the exception of Simon. Why is a man [Ed Herendeen] directing it for the first time?

My first instinct was for a woman to produce the play. Then I met Ed. The questions he asked about it, what he saw in it, what he felt from it were very exciting to me. I felt a real connection and understanding from him. He didn't try to sell me on his directing it. He just asked questions, and based on this I decided the play needed to be in the hands of this great person.

Is there a question you wish an interviewer would ask you?

Why, in the world of Snapchat, Twitter, the ability to make art on an iPhone, celebrity-driven casting on and off Broadway, the restrictive amount of new work a theater can actually produce in one season, reviews that can close you down in a heartbeat—*why* do you write plays? Or are you just a crazy person?

Is there a question you would refuse to answer?

Yes. Joe Papp, who was producing one of my plays for the Public Theater, taught me (or tried to teach me) not to do interviews before an opening . . . I don't know if I've ever been in a situation where I would refuse to answer a question, but I probably would refuse to answer any question that might impinge upon someone else.

Maria Irene Fornes said, "We can only do what is possible for us to do. But still it is good to know what the impossible is." What's the impossible for you?

For most of the plays that I have written—some more than others—I am most interested in writing the play I don't think I can pull off.

www.ingramcontent.com/pod-product-compliance
Lightning Source LLC
Chambersburg PA
CBHW050333230426
43663CB00010B/1846